The New Shape of Old Island Cultures

About the Author

Francis X. Hezel is a Jesuit priest who has lived and worked in Micronesia since 1963. Although he has made his home on Pohnpei since 1992, he formerly resided for over twenty-five years in Chuuk. At different times he has served as high school teacher, school administrator, fill-in pastor, and regional superior to the Jesuits in Micronesia. For close to thirty years he has also been director of the Micronesian Seminar, a church-sponsored research-pastoral institute known for promoting open discussion of contemporary issues in island Micronesia. Besides conducting political education programs, workshops, and conferences on a range of concerns, he has conducted ongoing research on suicide, trance and spirit possession, mental illness, and alcohol and drug use over the years. One of his latest research interests is the emigration from the Freely Associated States that has grown so rapidly since their independence. The author has written and spoken widely about social change and its impact on island societies. He has also written several books on Micronesian history, including *The First Taint of Civilization* and *Strangers in Their Own Land*.

The New Shape of Old Island Cultures

A Half Century of Social Change in Micronesia

Francis X. Hezel, S.J.

UNIVERSITY OF HAWAI'I PRESS
Honolulu

Printed in the United States of America
10 09 08 07 06   7 6 5 4 3

Library of Congress Cataloging-in-Publication Data

Hezel, Francis X.
    The new shape of old island cultures : a half century of social change in Micronesia /
Francis X. Hezel.
    p.   cm.
    Includes bibliographical references and index.
    ISBN-13: 978-0-8248-2380-1 (cloth : alk. paper) —
    ISBN-10: 0-8248-2380-X (cloth : alk. paper)
    ISBN-13: 978-0-8248-2393-1 (pbk : alk. paper) —
    ISBN-10: 0-8248-2393-1 (pbk : alk. paper)
    1. Social change—Micronesia.   2. Micronesia—Social conditions.   3. Micronesia—Social
life and customs.   I. Title.

HM831.H49   2001
303.4'09965—dc21   00-064898

Designed by Ivan Holmes

Printed by Integrated Book Technology, Inc.

Contents

Preface

While I would hope that this book is more than simply a personal view of change in Micronesia, it is at least that. The observations and stories with which it is peppered are drawn from my thirty-five years of life and work in the islands. If these seem to depend too heavily at times on examples from Chuuk, it is only because I lived there for twenty-five years before moving to Pohnpei in 1992. My relationship with Micronesia began in 1963, when I arrived in Chuuk as a young Jesuit scholastic to begin a three-year teaching stint at Xavier High School, and, except for three years of theological studies in the United States, I have spent my entire adult life in Micronesia. During that time, in the course of my work with Micronesian Seminar, the research-pastoral institute that I direct, I have had the opportunity to make regular visits to all the major islands in the area. Throughout this period I have come to know and count as personal friends many of the people who have survived the changes described in this book as well as dozens of the anthropologists and other researchers who have written of them.

Social change has always been my consuming interest. The first books I wrote were high school social studies textbooks that aimed to help young Micronesians understand the extent of change that had engulfed their islands. Micronesian history, on which I have also done some writing, was fascinating to me only insofar as it reflected social change rather than merely political upheavals. The succession of kings and chiefs held no special interest for me; it is the transformation of the lives of the men and women in the village that has never ceased to beguile me.

Perhaps the most enthralling of the classical Latin works that I studied during my own high school and seminary years was Juvenal's *Satires,* a glimpse of first-century life in imperial Rome from the curbstone. This wasn't the stuff of which epics are made—accounts of glorious military deeds or grand views of dynasties being made or unmade. It was a sneak look at what went on in the public baths, the nastiness of small merchants, the ruckus caused when chamber pots were dumped out of second floor windows and splashed passersby. It was an early and formative encounter with the tale of how human beings lived and what made them change.

For a few years early in my life I naively set off on a journey to find the philosopher's stone, the secret of the alchemy of human societies. Surely there must be some set of formulas to explain the mystery of social change, I thought. The search was futile, as more experienced social scientists could have told me; we may know something about the how and why of social change, but the outcomes always seem to be beyond prediction. Even so, I found that I couldn't resist the challenge, years later, to try to make some sense of the forces of social change as they have affected island Micronesia over the past several decades. Even if changes cannot be foretold, I imagined there must be patterns discernible in retrospect and at least hints of some of the links in the causal chain of social forces. The result is this small book. I would be happy if this work offered Micronesians and those studying their evolving societies a helpful filter through which to view much of the change that has occurred in these islands over the last half century.

To look at the broad patterns of change over the last half century, I have had to blur the very real differences from one culture to another within the broad area that is known as Micronesia. Islanders and social scientists alike, although for different reasons, may object to the kind of generalizations that are presented here. Micronesians could easily feel that the distinctiveness of their own culture, that which differentiates it from its neighbors, has been lost. Social scientists might see this presentation as an attempt to force societies with a wealth of singular features into a Procrustean bed, one that may appear to suggest an evolutionary framework and common origins that are far from proven. While I recognize the dangers of the approach I have taken in this book, the time has come to move beyond the ethnographic particularism that has marked most of the postwar period and attempt bolder syntheses of the main cultural features of these island societies. The commonalities of these islands have received far less attention at the hands of American anthropologists than the distinctiveness of each.

Although "Micronesia" is an equivocal term and one that some feel is meaningless, it has always been a very real concept to me. My work has put me into close contact with people from just about every island group from the Marshalls to Palau, and lately my range has come to extend to the Marianas. If the differences in cultural features between island groups within Micronesia have been obvious, the similarities are no less so. They include, for instance, such cultural features as general strategies for conflict resolution, broad norms for division of labor by gender and age, and safeguards against the monopoly of political authority. In this book I have stretched my generalizations as far as I think they will go, but I've also tried to be fair in indicating wherever possible the boundary line for these common traits or generalizations. Not all the changes have equally affected all island groups, as I hope I have made clear.

I will have to ask the reader's indulgence for some of the generalizations that are made in this book. The adjectives "most" and "all," when used of island cultures that exhibit a certain trait, can raise red flags. These words should be understood to mean that the trait or practice in question is very widespread throughout the area, even though such generalizations admit exceptions. Even if such statements do not always stand literally, please bear in mind that the key point is the way in which the common cultural feature, whether universal or not, has changed in the last half century.

In documenting these changes, I have drawn both on my lived experience in the islands and on the wealth of anthropological literature that has been produced on Micronesia since World War II. My hope was to offer a stimulating and helpful perspective for viewing these changes without either slavishly adhering to the ethnographic sources or turning this volume into merely impressionistic personal reminiscences. This book, while indebted to the insights of anthropology and the work of its practitioners, is not intended as a strict anthropological treatment of the topics it treats. To make the book more accessible to readers, I have deliberately tried to keep social science terminology to a minimum.

This small book is for the people of Micronesia. Not just dedicated to them but written for them. It is a modest thank you for letting me peek and probe into the workings of their societies for all these years. If the book is in any way useful for others as well, all the better. They are more than welcome to read over the shoulder of the people about whom this book is written, people who are not just faceless subjects of study but dear friends.

Acknowledgments

I would like to offer special thanks to Bill McGarry, Bob Kiste, Eugenia Samuel, Don Rubinstein, Craig Severance, and Glenn Petersen for their careful and critical reading of my manuscript. Their comments helped greatly. Thanks also to Jay Dobbin for his general advice and for his insistence that I add footnotes and provide citations for all references.

I am indebted to all those who offered assistance in helping me illustrate this volume. Len Mason, Kim Kihleng, Karen Peacock, Jack Fritz, Larry Cunningham, and Julie Tellei were all helpful in finding photographs. I also acknowledge the help of the Pacific Collection at the University of Hawai'i Library, the Micronesian Area Research Center at the University of Guam, the Lidorkini Museum on Pohnpei, and the Congress of FSM Library on Pohnpei. Catherine Wiehe spent many hours designing the illustration that was meant to grace the cover of this volume.

My gratitude to the Jesuit communities that housed, fed and supported me while I was writing this book. Special thanks goes to my own community on Pohnpei, but I am also indebted to the Jesuits of Loyola-Marymount in Los Angeles, Canisius in Buffalo, and St. Ignatius Loyola in New York. The staff of the Jesuit Seminary and Mission Bureau in New York deserve special mention for their kind support.

My colleagues in the Micronesian Seminar helped in hundreds of ways, big and small, and offered camaraderie throughout. I thank Elsa Veloso, Jason Aubuchon, Augustine Kohler, Blanca Amado, Marcus Samo, Melba Veloso, Deborah Crippen, and Judy Caldwell.

My thanks, as well, to the people who inspired the stories at the beginning of each section, for it was they and people like them who first made me aware of the need for a book like this.

Introduction

M icronesia—"the tiny islands," as they were labeled in the first half of the nineteenth century—is a geographic designation, based on the belief that this part of the Pacific shared many broad cultural features. Over the years, depending on the need, this term has been adjusted this way or that. Here, Micronesia will be understood to include the four states of the Federated States of Micronesia (Pohnpei, Chuuk, Yap, and Kosrae), the Republic of Palau, and the Republic of the Marshall Islands.

The History

Social change was not unknown in the islands, even before the United States took possession at the end of World War II. While there had always been some change as one island group came into contact with another in the course of canoe voyages, this process accelerated with the islands' first contact with the West during the so-called European Age of Discovery in the early sixteenth century. During the nineteenth century, after a two-hundred-year lull in European voyages to the area, contact with the West intensified greatly owing to commercial voyages of China traders, whaleships, and copra vessels, all of which had interests in the area. Often these were not just fleeting contacts; the ships brought bêche-de-mer parties, deserters, freebooters, and resident traders who would take up residence on the islands, sometimes for the rest of their lives. Protestant missionaries first arrived in the middle of that century, and the first Catholic priests followed them thirty years later. Meanwhile, islanders acquired not only a pair of religious creeds, but also iron cooking utensils, steel axes, cloth and apparel, firearms, liquor, rice and other select imported foods, and trade stations at which they might exchange local produce, especially copra, for a variety of foreign goods. They also picked up some familiarity with foreign ways and a smattering of some of their visitors' languages. The basic island cultural institutions, however, remained intact by and large.

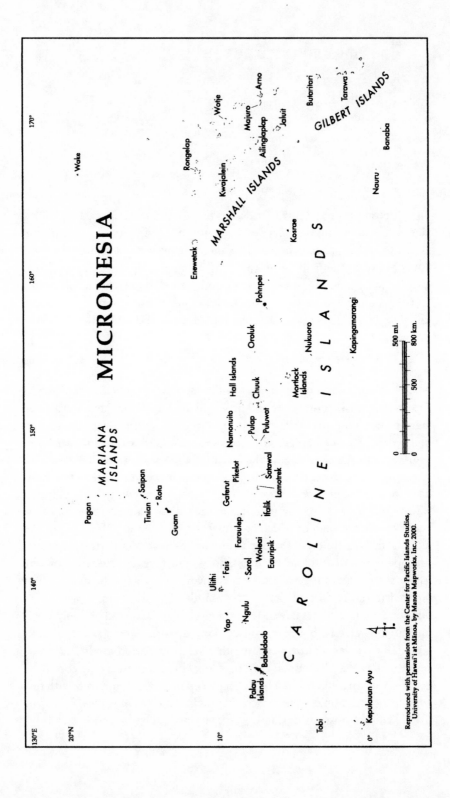

MICRONESIA

130°E   140°   150°   160°   170°

20°N

· Wake

MARIANA
ISLANDS

Pagan ·

Tinian ·· Saipan
·· Rota
Guam ··

Yap ·
Ngulu
Ulithi
·· Fais
Faraulep
Sorol
Woleai
Eauripik
Ifalik
Lamotrek
Satowal
Faferut
Pikelot

Namonuito

Hall Islands

Pulap
Puluwat
Chuuk

Oroluk

Mortlock
Islands
Nukuoro

10°

C A R O L I N E   I S L A N D S

Kapingamarangi ·

Pohnpei
·

Kosrae
·

Enewetak ·

Rongelap

Kwajalein

Wotje

Majuro
Atinglaplap
Jaluit
Arno

MARSHALL ISLANDS

Butaritari
Tarawa

GILBERT ISLANDS

Nauru ·

Banaba ·

Palau
Islands / Babeldaob

Tobi ·

Kapulauan Ayu

0°

Scale:
0   500   500 mi.
0   500   800 km.

Traditional village scene in the outer islands of Yap. (Micronesian Seminar Collection)

Following the inevitable parade of gunboats and naval ships through-out the century to defend the national interests of Western stakeholders, the Marshalls was annexed by Germany in 1885, and the rest of the area came under Spanish colonial rule a year later. By the turn of the century, Germany had acquired the former Spanish possessions in Micronesia, and it ruled throughout the area until the start of World War I. At the onset of the Great War in 1914, Japan seized the islands and occupied them at once, later legitimizing its rule when it gained a League of Nations mandate over the area at the Treaty of Versailles. The Japanese, who established the first public education system in the islands, attempted to instill in local people a passion for production. They offered an even richer assortment of entice-ments than others before them—bicycles, wooden frame housing, exotic clothing, and various delicacies for purchase—but in the end they gave up on the local people and brought in their own émigrés to operate the high-powered economy they had developed. Even before Japanese troops arrived in great numbers a year or two before the outbreak of World War II, the number of Japanese in the islands exceeded the size of the local population.

Although designated a trusteeship under the newly formed United Nations in 1947, Micronesia really passed into American hands as a war prize. The United States had "bought" the islands, its military leaders insisted, with the blood of the 32,000 Americans killed and maimed in the Allied campaign across the western Pacific. For a few years, the U.S. Navy administered the former Japanese possessions, providing emergency rations for the people, managing the rehabilitation of the war-torn islands, and setting up an administrative system that would be taken over by the U.S. Department of Interior in 1951. Almost immediately after the war, the trappings of Western democracy were introduced to the islands: popular elections, the chartering of municipalities, and district councils (later to become legislative bodies) for each island group. An education system was fashioned from local teachers working in thatched huts to replace the one started by the Japanese. A corps of medical officers and nurses were trained to introduce basic health care to the main islands. In addition to their legacy of quonset huts and surplus military fatigues, the Navy reestablished a network of island trade stores throughout the islands. But the infrastructure that the Japanese had built up before the war could not be restored with the very small annual budgets, and so the island economy remained a shadow of what it had been during the height of Japanese productivity.

Micronesians, in the first decade after the war, lived off a subsistence economy that was not much different from the way their ancestors had lived a century or two earlier. The U.S. administration, which in principle was opposed to any forced change, allowed islanders to set their own developmental pace—and that was very slow. Only in the early 1960s under the Kennedy administration did this go-slow philosophy change. As the contest between the United States and the Soviet Union for the allegiance of the Third World heated up, America reversed its position and adopted an altogether new policy in its Trust Territory. During that decade, as its budgets doubled and redoubled almost yearly, it invested heavily in education and health services, while adding thousands of Micronesians to the government payroll. By the mid-1970s, as the U.S. subsidy continued to increase, the groundwork was laid for a dual economy: a cash economy in some of the towns superimposed on the traditional subsistence economy in more rural areas.

Other changes followed rapidly. The increased U.S. aid led to the buildup of a commercial sector with modern department stores, restaurants, bars, and movie theaters. With public high schools now operating in each island group, opportunities for a secondary education were expanded. Later hundreds of these graduates began leaving the islands to attend U.S. colleges, nearly all of them returning home afterwards in search of jobs. At the same time, the thrust toward self-government had gathered momentum with the creation of the Congress of Micronesia in the mid-1960s. Soon political status negotiations with the United States were initiated, and a constitutional convention was convoked in 1975. With the status issue resolved but not yet signed into effect, the United States granted the islands self-rule in 1978. By that time the former Trust Territory was forever dissolved, for the islands had split into several political units. The Northern Marianas alone remained closely attached to the United States as a commonwealth; the remainder of the trust territory broke up into the Federated States of Micronesia (FSM), the Republic of Palau, and the Republic of the Marshall Islands.

The recent half century, from about 1950 to the present, has been a critical era in the history of island Micronesia. It has also been an era of unprecedented change, marking as it has both economic and political revolutions. It has been an era of rapidly expanding self-awareness for Micronesians, who formed their own governments and began to look with unblinking eye at the new shapes that their ancient societies were taking. It is this era that is the subject of this book.

The Islands and Their Cultures

Marshalls (population 51,000). The Marshalls is an independent nation today. This easternmost part of Micronesia is composed of two chains of coral atolls running north and south. Crops and plant life are fewer and rainfall lighter on these coral atolls than in other parts of Micronesia. Despite its limited resources, the Marshalls had a Polynesian-like authority system headed by paramount chiefs, or *iroij,* that distinguished it from other coral atolls in the region. Chiefly authority in the Marshalls today is far stronger than in any other part of Micronesia. It is the only island group in Micronesia where chiefs have retained their share in landownership up to the present day. Marshallese are matrilineal in that they derive their membership in a clan and lineage from their mother. At one time they may have tended to live in lineage groups on pieces of land inherited from their mothers, but residence groups are more mixed today.

Kosrae (population 8,000). Kosrae, now a state in the Federated States of Micronesia, is a single high island with a cultural tradition that was probably very similar to that of Pohnpei. During the nineteenth century, however, Kosrae suffered a drastic loss of population over a forty-year period that left the island with only 300 people by the end of the century. This depopulation, brought on by Western diseases, was far more severe than that suffered by other islands in the region. As a consequence, many of the traditional institutions collapsed. They were replaced by social and political structures introduced by the American Protestant missionaries then working on the island. Today rank and prestige are acquired through church office or a high position in the government. Married couples usually live on the husband's land as part of a larger kin group. Many Kosraeans still support themselves by cultivating breadfruit and taro and by fishing.

Pohnpei (population 37,000). Pohnpei is the capital of the Federated States of Micronesia and its largest state. The high island of Pohnpei, with an area of about one hundred square miles, is one of the largest in Micronesia. Scattered throughout the state are seven atolls, each with its own linguistic and cultural differences. In contrast to Chuuk and the coral atolls in the central Carolines with their relatively simple political systems, Pohnpei has the political stratification of a Polynesian island. There are five kingdoms on the main island, each headed by its own high chief (Nahnmwarki) and underchief (Nahnken) as well as parallel lines of titled nobles. Offerings of traditional prestige foods at feasts and funerals—pigs, yams, and kava (called *"sakau"*)—have always been a major avenue of social advancement. Although the society is organized into matrilineages, children inherit their land from their father, and married couples usually reside on the husband's family estate. Pohnpeians generally live in homesteads scattered over the countryside rather than in more compact villages. While the social organization in the outer islands resembles that in Pohnpei to some extent, these atolls are without much of the formality of Pohnpei's feasting rituals and prestige economy.

Chuuk (population 56,000). The heart of the state of Chuuk is a barrier reef embracing a number of rather small volcanic islands. This center, Chuuk Lagoon, is surrounded by several coral atolls to the north, west, and south, on some of which the traditional dress of loincloths and sarongs have been retained even to the present. Authority was traditionally so fragmented that individual islands were seldom unified under a single chief. The main social unit has always been the lineage group, descended from a single living woman. In the past this group usually resided together on one or more parcels of land. In contrast to most other parts of Micronesia, women in Chuuk do offshore fishing while men work in the taro patches and pick breadfruit. Although food is commonly exchanged with other relatives, there are few of the competitive food exchanges that are still commonly found on Pohnpei and on some of the other islands of Micronesia.

Central Carolines (population 5,000). The coral atolls known as the central Carolines, although politically joined to Yap State, are populated by a people who bear very little cultural affinity to Yapese. These Outer Islanders, as they are called, speak a language and practice customs that are much more similar to those of Chuuk than to those of Yap. Their way of life is simple; they subsist on fish and taro or breadfruit, wear their traditional dress (loincloth and lavalava), and carry on the long-distance canoe voyages for which their islands were famous. Like Chuuk, these islands are strongly matrilineal and have a political system that is much weaker than those of most parts of Micronesia.

Yap (population 7,000). Yap is a cluster of high islands comprising the administrative center of the westernmost state in the Federated States of Micronesia. Yap has a reputation for being the most traditional of all the island groups in Micronesia. Until the early 1970s men walked around town wearing loincloths, while women dressed in grass skirts. Although most have now adopted Western clothing, Yapese retain a deep respect for their cultural ways. Women work in the taro patches to produce the staple item in the diet, while men fish. The villages of Yap are tightly organized and ranked according to a caste system, with each village having its own chief and council. Within the village, parcels of land are named and ranked. A married couple will usually take up residence on the man's estate along with the man's father and possibly some of his brothers. Although the patrilineal kin group dominates, Yapese still maintain a strong interest in their matrilineage, which is the refuge for those who are unwelcome in their father's kin group.

Palau (population 17,000). The high islands of Palau, the largest land mass of all Micronesia, share many of Yap's social and political features. Palau is divided into villages, or districts, each under the authority of a chief and a council. Traditionally, however, each village was divided into competing halves at every level to encourage a rivalry for production that was rewarded with local "money" and the prestige that it carried. As in Yap, the women traditionally worked in the taro patches while the men gathered the fruits of the sea. Palau, too, is a matrilineal society, but married couples generally resided on the husband's family's estate. In one major respect, however, Yap and Palau differ greatly. Palau has always had the reputation of being the first and fastest island group to modernize. Long before the other islands, it sent hundreds of young people to school and sent young adults to find work outside Palau. Today it is considered the most economically advanced group in Micronesia and forms a separate nation.

1 Family

The Emergence of the Household

A man looks furtively around to see whether anyone is watching before slipping off his zoris and entering the safety of his concrete-block house. He slides a large paper bag full of groceries onto the kitchen table. Packages of ramen, a jar of instant coffee, a five-pound bag of flour, cans of corned beef and mackerel spill out onto the table. His wife is squatting over a double-burner kerosene stove on the floor cooking the rice for dinner. Suddenly a pair of eyes appears at the kitchen window. They belong to a ten-year-old boy, the son of his wife's sister, who lives in the wooden frame house next door. The man, surprised at first to see his nephew, breaks into an embarrassed smile. "Come and take this to your mother," he tells the child as he holds out a few cans of meat and mackerel.

The man then enters one of the rooms to change his shirt. As he emerges, he glances at his young son and daughter lying on the floor of the living room watching television. "Don't forget to clean up your room before you eat," he says to them.

The definition and social geography of the Micronesian family has been altered almost beyond recognition during the past few decades. In many places the family residence has evolved from a compound, with several simple dwellings housing an extended family, to a single self-contained unit. As the family's membership has shrunk, it has become identified with a single residential dwelling, often housing not much more than a nuclear family. A few decades ago, the Micronesian family might have consisted of many more members, distributed in several residential buildings scattered on a single estate.[1]

In Chuuk during the years following World War II, a "family" was usually composed of the core of a lineage—the women and their children

A family compound in Chuuk (1966), with men's house *(left background)* and cookhouse *(right fore-ground)*. (Library of Congress of FSM)

—along with in-marrying men, numbering perhaps two or three dozen people in all.[2] Nuclear families might have had their own residences, but these were thatch huts, or later simple plywood houses, that served as little more than places to sleep. These dwellings, clustered together on a single piece of land, were almost incidental in the life of the extended family.[3] At the core of the family unit was the cookhouse, or *fanang*, a simple roofed fireplace that replaced the earlier earth oven, where the food was prepared and cooked in large iron pots before it was distributed to the members of the family.[4] Breadfruit was boiled and pounded, wrapped in banana leaves, and then turned over to the members of the households for consumption. The same was done when a catch of fish was brought home. Members of the different households took their turns preparing food for the whole extended family. Whether the entire lineage chose to eat together or take their portions to their own residences was inconsequential; food was prepared in sufficient quantity for the entire extended family and distributed to all its members.[5]

The Chuukese lineage group usually also had an *uut*, or meeting-house.[6] This important social structure evolved from the canoe house, which was a key institution throughout the central Carolines.[7] The *uut*

Chuukese boys standing alongside an iron pot.
(TT Archives, University of Hawai'i Library)

once served as a workplace for males and a dormitory for unmarried men in the lineage as well as a meetinghouse for the lineage group. There the men of the lineage congregated to pass the time, sometimes repairing fishing lines or other gear, often relating the old stories so important to the history of the family or swapping gossip on recent romances. More than any other place, the *uut* was seen as the locus of a young man's education during his formative years.

Chuuk was not very different from other island groups in Micronesia. It was distinctive only in that it was the epitome of female-centered social organization; Chuuk represented in its purest form the tight organization of matrilineal groups into residential units. Matrilocal residence, or the residence of the newly married couple on the estate of the wife's family, was the normal practice in Chuuk at the end of World War II.[8] Many anthropologists think that this pattern, which they claim is widespread throughout the Pacific and Southeast Asia, was characteristic of the early Austronesian peoples who first settled the Pacific.[9] Certainly, there is strong evidence to suggest that at one time matrilocal residence patterns extended throughout the closely related culture-language area that makes up the entire eastern part of Micronesia.[10]

The Marshalls seems to have been predominantly matrilocal at one time, with the strip of land known as a *wato* being assigned to a matrilineal group, the head of which was called the *alab*.[11] Pohnpei, too, would appear to have once had matrilineal residential groupings similar to those of Chuuk, but the residence shifted to patrilocal before or perhaps under the impact of intensive contact with the West in the nineteenth century. A vestige of the older residential system survives in the districts, or *kousapw,* which were probably once matrilineal estates managed by a lineage head who today bears the title of *soumas en kousapw*.[12] Kosrae's early residence patterns, like Pohnpei's, may have shifted from matrilocal to patrilocal even before the enormous cultural upheaval brought about by the missionization and depopulation of the island in the nineteenth century. There is a strong likelihood that its residential groups were also originally matrilineal.

Western Micronesia was less strongly female-centered than the east. Residential groups in Yap and Palau were patrilocal since before early contact, it seems, even though both places shared the matrilineal organization of eastern Micronesia. Moreover, Yap's matrilineage was balanced by a patrilineal system, producing what some anthropologists would term double descent.[13] The outer islands near Yap, especially Ulithi and Fais, appear to have absorbed some of this tendency to patrilocal residence, for women there have followed their husbands to live on their estates for as long as the people can reach back into their past.[14]

Whether matrilocal or not, most island groups in Micronesia exhibited features of social geography similar to Chuuk's in the early postwar years. In the outer islands of Yap, the extended family was housed in several residential units, with all its members eating together, as in Chuuk. On Pohnpei, where married brothers and their families often lived with their father on a single estate, there was once a single *uhmw*, or earth oven, that served as the symbol of family solidarity in much the same way a hearth did for earlier Europeans. Food was prepared for all major family gatherings in this earth oven. Even in later years, as the *uhmw* was abandoned and each of the households set up its own cooking area as a matter of convenience, food was shared regularly between the households. Large family gatherings were held in the *nahs*, or feast house, where guests were also entertained.

In the Marshalls, the lineage head supervised the family estate on which several nuclear families lived. Each of the nuclear families had its own dwelling, but all the houses were clustered around a central cookhouse, or *upaj*, where food was prepared for all the residents of the estate. The Marshallese extended family, like its counterpart on other islands, functioned as a single productive and social unit.[15]

In Palau, a single house was once identified as the seat of each lineage. Not everyone belonging to the lineage slept in this house, but food was prepared and distributed to other houses in which members of the lineage lived. The people who "ate from the same plate" once included all those in the foundation house that served as the seat of the lineage as well as its satellite households.[16] Hence, Palauans could justifiably speak of the lineage group as "one house." Yap, where groups who ate together were small, may have been the only significant exception, for residence

A Marshallese house compound on Likiep (1946), with cookhouse to the right. (Leonard Mason)

patterns and household size there were as close to that of the West as any place in Micronesia.[17]

For most Micronesians in the early postwar years, home was still a large building or a group of smaller buildings housing an extended family, with the focal point of the family identity located in a cookhouse or earth oven. It is not unusual that group identity should be focused on the "kitchen," for the sharing of food has always been an expression of solidarity among members of a family everywhere in Micronesia.[18] Where a person slept at night has never been as clear a marker of identity as where he or she ate. On the homestead there was sometimes also a feast house or meetinghouse where the entire family could gather and entertain.

Only in recent decades has this changed. The households of the extended family that once ate together, worked together, and formed a single economic unit began to operate more and more as independent entities. The lineage head no longer presides over the distribution of food prepared from the land; it is now up to the master of each household to provide for those residing in his house. As the availability of money increased, households no longer depended on the lineage head for resources, as they once did. With the surrender of his responsibility to feed the households, the lineage head has also lost the authority over them he once enjoyed. Hence, for example, the main burden of supervising youth now rests with the father of the family in each house rather than with the entire lineage unit under its leader.

In short, the new Micronesian family has gradually retreated into the nuclear household. The communal cookhouse, like the earth oven before it, is on the way to becoming obsolete. In most households the cooking space has moved into the kitchen, where the nuclear family can discreetly prepare food for its own members, sharing food with other relatives as the family budget permits. More modern houses are equipped with refrigerators, allowing the families to store food for their future use and thus discouraging some of the lavish sharing that has always been so distinctive of Micronesian households.

The new family household often has partitions, divisions into rooms, where formerly there was simply shared communal space. Parents often have a master bedroom, and even the children sometimes have their own rooms. It is a measure of the depth of the change that has overtaken the Micronesian family today that a people who once shunned solitude to the point of willingly sleeping in packed rooms just for the company have begun to value privacy in their homes.[19] New lines have been drawn within households as well as between them.

How did this happen? The shape of the Micronesian family, which had been evolving for years, began to undergo momentous changes during the 1960s as the family's resource base swung away from local produce from land and sea to cash. The 3,000 Micronesians with full-time wage employment in 1962 had doubled to 6,000 by 1965; by 1974 the figure had doubled again to 12,000. As of 1977, when self-government was granted, over 18,000 Micronesians were working for a living in Palau, the Marshalls, and what would soon become the Federated States of Micronesia. Annual wages, which totaled $2.3 million in 1962, skyrocketed to $42 million by 1977.[20] The yearly per capita income of $60 in 1962 soared to over $400 fifteen years later—a threefold increase, even after correction for inflation.[21] With the enormous increase in job opportunities during this period of rapid government expansion, average income had grown enough to make cash a major resource in island life and to permit money to supplant land as the source of livelihood for many. Thanks to the rapid expansion of salary employment, the traditional resource base was challenged by a new one: the cash economy.

These changes created fissures in the traditional extended family that widened in time until the single household, with the nuclear family at its core, overshadowed the extended family and became the basic social unit. If formerly one's livelihood depended on maintaining solidarity with the kin group that held rights to the land they farmed and the shoals they fished, a cash salary brought a certain amount of independence from that kin group. For the first time ever, Micronesians began to envision the possibility of supporting themselves apart from the extended family and its landholdings. Thanks to the growing dominance of the cash economy, the household was being emancipated from the larger kin group.

Other forces conspired to deepen the rift and to provide an ideological underpinning for the supremacy of the smaller household. One was the church, which had long taught that in marriage a man and woman leave behind their father and mother and other blood relatives to become "one flesh" in an inseparable union. Although this scriptural passage, with emphasis on a definitive break with blood relatives, did not concur with the vision of marriage in a traditional Micronesian society, it became more frequently invoked to support the marriage that was in fact rapidly evolving in the islands. The Western education system and media, especially in the form of movies, also tended to support the primacy of the marriage bond and the nuclearization of the family. Yet, without the structural change that was effected by the cash economy, it is doubtful that these other forces would have had any significant impact on the organization of the family.

The transformation in the Micronesian family constitutes a major social upheaval. With the nuclearization of the family, there have been enormous changes in the roles of family members, resulting in a great deal of confusion. As the lineage has withdrawn from its traditionally heavy child-rearing responsibilities, the burden has fallen to the parents to pick up much of the slack. Fathers are often expected to exercise various roles, many of which seem to clash with one another and with their image of what a traditional father is and how he acts toward his sons. The confusion of roles can bring about heightened tension between parents and their children, yet the broad circle of older relatives who once stood ready to intervene to relieve the occasional flare-up and inevitable friction are no longer prepared to do so. Consequently, the tension often festers and intensifies in time.

The emergence of the nuclear family brings new blessings, which have been enjoyed by many households who have made a successful transition. But it also brings serious challenges, among them the breakdown of the systems that have served for so long to protect the most vulnerable persons in society. Children and wives are easier targets for abuse today than they were in the past when the social controls operated so much more effectively. The traditional family system also provided multiple sets of parents for the young so that there was always someone to fill the breech in the event of an absent or ineffective parent. In a two-parent family, child rearing is not only more arduous but also more perilous, since the safety net that the extended family once provided is gone.

The emergence of the modern household, usually clustered around a nuclear family as the primary social unit, does not mean that the extended family is extinct. The lineage or larger family group still functions and is recognized as such everywhere in Micronesia. On certain important occasions—funerals and weddings, special holidays, and those times when the larger family is called on to contribute to a large community event—it gathers as a unit and works together as it would have in former years. The lineage plays a role in establishing personal identity and remains an anchor for individuals in the group. Nonetheless, it no longer provides the food or basic nurturing for the young on a day-to-day basis as it once did. In this change lies the real social revolution.

The Absent Father

It is early evening, about 7:30, a time when people in the villages of Chuuk are most relaxed. Families have eaten, a cool breeze is beginning to come in off the sea, and everywhere in the village people are engaged in gentle conversation. In one of the houses, a family group sits on the floor with their coffee cups in hand talking idly about the day's happenings, occasionally teasing one another. The mother of the family, a woman in her late forties, chats with her thirteen-year-old daughter, another girl a few years younger, and a boy with a ponytail who may be about eighteen. There is banter and easy laughter in the small group, an intimate family circle at its warmest, until the father walks in. Fiftyish and heavyset, with a ready smile, the father seems open and friendly, but his appearance has an electrifying effect on the small circle. As soon as he senses his father's presence, the teenage son undergoes a sudden transformation; the conversation that flowed from him so easily a moment before has come to a halt, and he now stares mutely at the floor. He remains frozen in this state for a short time before slipping wordlessly toward the door. Within

a minute or two of his father's entrance into the house, the teenage son is
already out the door; he is halfway down the village road before the
father has even had time to fill his coffee cup.[22]

The teenage Chuukese boy is not a child abuse victim with a long history
of beatings at his father's hands. There has been no recent flare-up between the boy and his father; he is probably not even annoyed at his parent.
What has happened this evening is not at all singular in the normal pattern
of life in this family or most other Chuukese families. Sons seldom go
fishing with their fathers today or work with them on the land. This young
man is merely acting in the way that conscientious sons in many households throughout Chuuk and other island groups in Micronesia act toward
their fathers today. He is studiously avoiding the presence of his father,
thus practicing what anthropologists might call classic respect avoidance,
a strategy employed everywhere in the Pacific. Respect is shown today, as
it always has been, by acknowledging the social distance separating the
authority figure and the subject. This is often done by avoiding familiarity with the person in authority.[23]

   One might expect a stiff and formal relationship to have existed between parents and their children, but this was not the case. The relationship between father and son in earlier times was defined by authority but
tempered by some warmth, according to the writings of anthropologists
and the recollections of older island men.[24] In the remembered past, fathers
seem to have spent considerable time with their sons, often working on
projects for the lineage or the extended family. Chuukese men would often
bring their sons with them to pick breadfruit, which they would then
pound and wrap in banana leaves before turning it over to the head of the
lineage for distribution to the different households on their family estate.
Father and son could afford to be companionable in such situations despite
the generation gap, for in Chuuk they were working together under the
authority of senior members of the lineage. It was the lineage chief, one
of the older male relatives of the son's mother, who gave the orders on
most important matters, including food preparation. The father, who
was something of an outsider in his wife's lineage, was in much the same
subordinate position as his son. Despite the obvious age difference and
the authority that the father held over his son, the two were allies in this
respect, answerable to the head of the lineage.[25]

   Even in island groups where the father was living among his own
blood relatives, as in Pohnpei, Palau, and Kosrae, he was often subject to

seniors in his family. Rarely was he the ruler of the roost, particularly if his own father or an older brother was living with him. Hence, the situation described for Chuuk was often enough the case on these other islands also. In Pohnpei, fathers were said to have once had a casual relationship with their sons, even to the point of letting them as children romp on the sacred platform of the *nahs,* or meetinghouse.[26]

The relationship between fathers and sons, while containing an element of authority, could not be defined merely in those terms. The father would call on his son to help gather and prepare breadfruit or to fish. In an earlier day, they might work together for hours to prepare the earth oven for a feast. Even after the earth oven was abandoned, fathers and sons would spend time together in the cookhouse and even longer periods of time in the men's house, to which most males in the family would retreat to tell stories, engage in the repair of fishing equipment, and relax with their kin. Avoidance pure and simple was out of the question. Fathers and sons worked together, ran afoul of one another at times, but learned to respect one another despite the authority lines that have always been etched so strongly onto Chuukese and other Micronesian cultures.

Fathers could afford to be tolerant of their sons, even after the latter reached adolescence, because the maternal uncle was expected to correct the young man when this became necessary and to play the lead role in guiding him through the labyrinths of proper customary behavior. The relationship between a young person and his maternal uncle (the mother's brother) was once a key one everywhere in Micronesia, important enough to warrant a special kinship term.[27] In a matrilineal society the young person belonged to his mother's lineage and received his social identity from it. The maternal uncle represented the dominant claims of the lineage on him. As the opposite number of the father, he played a complementary role to the father in guiding his nephew through youth and young manhood.

In Palau, the maternal uncle assumed the role of guardian and disciplinarian over the young man, underscoring the point that the mother's lineage bore a major part of the responsibility in socializing the young. A Palauan father could discipline his son if need arose, but only the boy's maternal uncle had the right to punish him severely or to beat him.[28] The young man, after all, belonged in a deeper and truer sense to his mother's kin than he did to his father. Marshallese referred to the father as the "outrigger" of the family, implying that while he was a steadying influence, the father was just an appendage to the "hull," representing the mother's lineage.[29] In view of this distribution of responsibility in the extended family, it is easy to understand how the father could have such an easy relationship with his son.

Only in Yap were the roles of father and maternal uncle reversed. Fathers were expected to be disciplinarians, while maternal uncles took a more kindly, supportive role that entailed offering advice and guidance rather than punishment.[30] Even so, Yapese men, middle-aged today, fondly recall accompanying their fathers on fishing trips when they were teenagers and sometimes even drinking their first beer with them. Their stories suggest that older Yapese had a strong affectionate bond with their fathers.

What has happened to change the relationship between father and sons today? In the first place, the role of the maternal uncle has all but vanished on many islands as the extended family unit has broken up. Very few of my students at Xavier High School twenty years ago were even able to recall the kinship term in their own language, so much has the maternal uncle faded as a significant figure in their lives. Meanwhile, the authority once held by the maternal uncle has been transferred to the father as the smaller nuclear family has replaced the larger extended family. As authority is increasingly concentrated in the father, his role has shifted from that of outrigger, or stabilizing figure in a balanced extended family system, to the load-bearing hull. This shift alone could explain why sons are inclined to avoid their fathers far more today than in the past.

In the meantime, fathers and sons stopped working together as frequently as they had in the past. Using Chuuk as an illustration, one finds that the intergenerational male work force stopped functioning, by and large, when the lineage food production unit broke down. When the lineage chief was no longer in a position to preside over the distribution of pounded breadfruit and fish to all the households in the lineage, the father-son team suffered a serious blow. In the wake of this change, the father provided for his own household or, alternatively, his son did; but they no longer labored side by side to provide for their family. In some cases, the father may have taken advantage of his release from customary work obligations to try to find cash work. In other families, the son may have looked for a paying job. Even when neither had recourse to cash earnings, tension seems to have mounted between fathers and sons, just as when two persons who have managed to relate to one another well enough in a group are suddenly left to themselves and find they cannot converse easily with one another. Father and son were no longer allies in the service of another power. Their relationship was gradually redefined, with its focus narrowing on authority. The much fuller and more complex relationship that they once enjoyed became a thing of the past.[31]

Daughters and mothers, by contrast, have continued to interact with one another on a regular basis even up to the present. Girls' day-to-day ties with their matrilineage are anchored in their relationship with their mother rather than their mother's brother, since such ties are usually formed with lineage elders of the same sex. Since the mother's role, unlike the maternal uncle's, has been undiminished by the breakdown of the lineage, life can carry on for girls much as it always did. There were no jarring authority changes in their relations with their mother. Moreover, girls and their mothers cannot escape one another's company as easily as boys and their fathers, for they work together daily doing household chores. From early childhood on, girls are expected to help their mother clean the house, tend to the younger children, prepare food, and perform the countless other tasks that are part of their daily routine. As a girl reaches adolescence, even greater demands are imposed on her by her family. From the moment she returns home from school, she is given jobs by her mother one after another so that she becomes the extension of the mother—an extra pair of hands. However prickly her personal relationship with her mother may be, a teenage girl cannot avoid spending several hours a day with her as they work together on their domestic chores. Mothers and daughters might get cross and peevish with one another, but they generally learn to live with this and to accommodate one another regardless of their occasional outbursts of temper.[32]

Even in the face of the contrast it presents with the relatively warm and secure mother-daughter ties, many Micronesian adults seem to regard the troubled father-son relationship that has evolved over recent years as the "traditional" one. Unaware of the more casual, multifaceted nature of this relationship in the past, fathers believe that men have always had minimal interaction with their postadolescent sons. This is the island way, they profess. Meanwhile, fathers all too often leave their sons without the parenting they so badly need, shorn as the family is of the rich childcare assistance that relatives would have provided in an earlier day.

For the past twenty-five years I have been studying and writing about the phenomenon of Micronesian suicide, which has been growing alarmingly since the late 1960s. The rates for the general population are now among the highest in the world. Suicide rates among young males are especially high, with the rate for males aged fifteen to twenty-four exceeding 200 per hundred thousand on some islands.[33] The patterns everywhere in Micronesia are very much alike: suicides are almost always brought on by a disruption in a close family relationship, usually when the young man is angry at the way he is treated by a parent or older brother.[34] The growing suicide problem might suggest that the level of family conflict has escalated over the years for some reason or perhaps that young men are more sensitive than they once were to the jostle and abrasiveness of life within the family.

But there is still another explanation, one that I find more convincing: the structural changes that have reshaped the family have also rendered it less equipped to resolve the tensions that arise in the family. The father's role has expanded so that he has become the primary caretaker and disciplinarian of his postadolescent sons. At the same time the modern family must get along without the support roles that other extended family members once played in disciplining the young, in assuaging their hurt feelings, and in serving as intermediaries between parties involved in clashes. To put it another way, the relationship of the father to his sons has become more charged and potentially explosive, while the resources available to defuse the tension are fewer. Employing the common strategy of suppressing the direct expression of anger against persons owed respect, but acting out these feelings against oneself while withdrawing from the source of the problem, young men have increasingly resolved these problems by taking their own lives.[35]

Fathers today may be less accessible to their sons for guidance and support, if only because they must bear the weight of increased authority over them. In that sense one can speak of fathers being absent to their sons. It appears that, owing to the sweeping changes in the structure of the family that have caused a breech between fathers and sons today, a whole generation may be suffering from the "absent father" syndrome.

When Brothers Have a Falling Out

One Sunday afternoon while driving back from the beach on Weno, Chuuk, I was startled by the echoes of what sounded like a sledgehammer coming down on corrugated steel. I looked off to the side of the road, where a man was furiously battering the tin wall of a house with a large crowbar. When I asked my Chuukese companion what was going on, he told me not to worry. This was just part of a longstanding feud between two brothers. It all began a few years earlier when one of the brothers corrected the other's teenage son for public misbehavior that he claimed reflected on the whole family. The parent of the young man who received the scolding had never forgiven his brother for this impertinence, so from time to time, when his anger peaked under the influence of alcohol, the offended brother would take his crowbar to the wall of his despised brother's house.

This incident, which I witnessed some years ago, raises two different issues: the care of children within the extended family and settlement of conflicts between brothers. The former touches on child rearing, an intergenerational issue in the family, while the latter deals with the resolution of tensions that threaten to rip apart the family.

An increasing number of parents in Micronesia today jealously guard what they believe is their exclusive right to correct their own children. They regard themselves as not merely the main caretakers of their children, but often the only ones. This is especially true in those cases where the family has moved away from the broader lineage group to establish their own home somewhere else. A few years ago, when a Pohnpeian man scolded his nephew for his bad manners, the boy scornfully asked his uncle who he was to reprimand him. The boy's insolence was rewarded with a slap in the face on the spot. When the boy's parents heard of the incident, they were outraged that the uncle took it upon himself to correct the boy. They demanded that the uncle apologize. In support of their position, the parents declared that since they had raised their children themselves, with no help from the wider circle of relatives, their children were their own responsibility and no one else's.[36]

Although it is true that in the past the mother and father usually bore primary responsibility for supervising their own children when the latter were young, parents had a great deal of help. Older members of the extended family, who interacted with the children on a daily basis, freely helped in their rearing. When children reached adolescence, the large circle of relatives who shared in supervising and disciplining them often became the main custodians of the young men and women. This circle included not just maternal uncles with their special role, but older relatives on both their mother's and father's side of the family. Indeed, the very fact that parents could surrender much of their role of guardianship over their adolescent children to others in the family made it possible for them to develop a warmer and more relaxed relationship with their children in the past.

Such a broad-based child-rearing system offered other advantages.

Within the larger family group there would be older relatives with whom the young man or woman could establish a more informal relationship. There was also a wider range for selection to allow for better personal compatibility and an effective back-up system. If the young person experienced harsh treatment at the hands of one senior relative, he or she could usually find another to plead his or her cause. If one should find oneself in conflict with some "parent," the system provided several potential intermediaries who could help resolve the conflict. The partition and distribution of authority was a good check against the possible abuse of authority by adults, something that could lead to festering resentment in the young person, especially during the difficult years of adolescence.[37]

The assistance that the extended family once rendered parents in child rearing is a casualty of the nuclearization of the family over the postwar decades. Grandparents, aunts, and others who shared in the child-rearing task in island societies—where it took a village to raise a child—often no longer live on the same estate. Even when they do, they are rendered impotent by the redefinition of the family according to Western standards. Nowadays the family has commonly come to mean the parents and their children together with the one or two other relatives who may fill out the typical Micronesian household.

A person who attempts to exercise what might have been traditional prerogatives in looking after a close relative's children is liable to run afoul of their parents. Although the old kinship terminology in most Micronesian languages extended the terms "mother" and "father" to many senior relatives on both sides, distinctions based on new terms such as "uncle" and "aunt" have grown ever more popular. The change in terminology is not merely verbal; it reflects the transformation in the roles of close kin in today's island society.

A second issue raised in the scenario of the quarreling brothers is why the conflict between them wasn't settled long before. The two men who fought over their different notions of who has the right to discipline children were surely not the first pair of brothers to develop a serious rift between them. The bond between siblings, although a privileged one in the eyes of all Micronesians, is open to tension and can be strained to the point of near rupture for many reasons. Traditionally, the relationship between brothers was bound by a strict respect code based on age, with an older brother exercising authority over those younger than him. Younger brothers, even in childhood, would try to avoid situations in which they would be obliged to socialize with elder siblings. For this reason, it is unusual for brothers, at least in Chuuk, to join one another during a weekend drinking party. Ordinarily, in Micronesia, there is no easy familiarity between brothers.[38]

Younger brothers at times have challenged the authority of their older siblings in family matters, particularly when they have felt that the judgment of their older brothers was bringing harm to the extended family or undercutting their own rights. A younger brother in a family I know refused to speak to his older brother for some months because of a disagreement over the type of medical care that should be given their father during an illness that proved fatal. Conflicts over land are especially common. On Pohnpei in the 1950s an argument broke out between two brothers over land rights and became so severe it almost resulted in a fight. In such cases, the family would almost always turn to a senior member who possessed enough authority to settle the matter. Thus, the family of the feuding Pohnpeian brothers asked the maternal uncle of the two combatants to step in and settle the matter. He did so decisively. He summoned the two brothers, administered them a tongue-lashing, and resolved the dispute by dividing the land equally between the two of them.[39]

The difference between this conflict and the one described at the beginning of this section does not lie in the cultural contrast between Chuuk and Pohnpei; both island groups once employed very similar forms of conflict resolution. Forty or fifty years ago, it was expected that one could find within the family circle someone who commanded sufficient respect to settle sensitive rifts between siblings, whereas today the circle has contracted so much that such figures are no longer available. The maternal uncle today does not play the same significant role that he did years ago and so is unable to heal the quarrels that he might have in an earlier day. To resolve a dispute between brothers today, the family might well have to resort to the modern legal system, calling in the police to protect property and persons, and taking the issue to the land court for a decision. The family today, in Chuuk and Pohnpei as on other islands, lacks the resources to do much of what the traditional extended family was able to do in the past.

Overall, the lines of authority seem to be narrowing today. As the vignette opening this section illustrated, the authority over children, which was formerly distributed throughout a wider family circle, rests increasingly with the father and mother alone. Another authority gap results from the absence of a figure with sufficient stature to make peace between the two feuding brothers. As authority becomes more concentrated today, it is often more difficult to resolve conflicts between adult members of a family.

Where Do Women Turn?

The young woman came into the parish office in tears. Her husband, who had a weakness for beer that he often indulged during two- or three-day binges, had beaten her again. He had resolved never to do this again after their last reconciliation, but now, less than three months later, he had given her a nasty purple welt on the neck and a black eye. She wore sunglasses to hide the black eye, but she could not conceal the welt on her neck. She said that she had decided to leave him, but she could not stand the thought of living apart from her two young children, who were staying with their father. Besides, when she turned up at her parents' doorstep and asked if she could stay with them through the crisis, her parents were embarrassed by the position in which they were put. Each day her husband called her, begging her to return to him and the children. After a week, her parents pleaded with her to heed her husband's calls and to rejoin her family, where they felt she belonged. A few days later, less than ten days after she moved in with them, she yielded to her family's supplications and, against her better judgment, returned to her husband.

Wife beating arouses great indignation in this day of heightened sensitivity to the rights of women. When trying to account for the seeming increase in domestic violence today, most look to the rise of alcohol abuse among men for the explanation. Since the liberalization of the liquor laws in 1959 allowing islanders to purchase and consume alcohol, drinking has come to occupy a major place in the life of very many Micronesian males. Two-thirds of the adult males in Palau, well over half the adult males in the Federated States of Micronesia, and one-third of the adult males in the Marshalls drink at least occasionally.[40] Besides serving as a means of relaxation while bonding with friends, alcohol often provides an occasion for venting pent-up anger and frustration. In the past the expression of these emotions often led to bar fights and other forms of violence, and occasionally it does even now. Increasingly, however, the anger that surfaces in drinking seems to be vented within the family, with wives absorbing the brunt of it.

While most look to alcohol abuse as the principal cause of wife beating, others blame what they generally regard as a growing permissiveness in today's island societies. Still others focus on the psychological demons that they feel haunt males nowadays, especially an explosive rage stemming from other frustrations. Few seem to seek the explanation in the weakening of social controls that once effectively checked the propensity of males to take out their anger, whatever its source, on those closest to them.

In Chuuk, Pohnpei, Yap, and the Marshalls at least—and possibly on some of the other islands of Micronesia as well—there has always been a certain degree of tolerance of what is today called wife beating. Indeed, women in Chuuk were said to welcome an occasional display of anger by their husbands as an indication of interest: the husband cared enough for his wife to scold her or even raise his hand to her from time to time.[41] Tales of men's physical display of impatience toward their wives are legion. A woman who burned the rice or was negligent in caring for the children, for example, might be cuffed for her oversight.

Yet, there were limits to what was regarded as acceptable in this respect. A woman who was seriously hurt, who showed marks on her body from the blows she received, or who was subjected to repeated beatings by her husband was judged to be mistreated, even in the more permissive days of the past. In such cases, her own blood relatives, particularly her brothers, would intervene to protect her against further abuse at the hands of her husband. They might retaliate directly against the offending husband and give him a taste of his own medicine. More often, however, they would bring their kinswoman back to her own home, where they could protect her against any further mistreatment. When this happened, the offending husband had to submit to the embarrassing ritual of a formal apology to his wife's family. He was obliged to find some spokesman in his own family who would approach his wife's family to plead on his behalf for the return of his wife. In doing this he was subjecting his own blood relatives to the indignity of having to apologize for his personal faults, with the implicit promise that these abuses would not happen again. In Palau, the man's family was also expected to offer a piece of traditional money to his wife's family as a form of reparation.[42] With or without any formal restitution, the process was humiliating enough to motivate the husband's family to do all in their power to check his angry outbreaks in the future.

The power wielded by the woman's family in the Marshalls was even more decisive. When the abuse reached a level that was unacceptable to the woman, she had only to complain to her eldest brother, who would take her back under his protection and inform her husband that the marriage was terminated. A husband was beholden to his brother-in-law in the Marshalls and so was reluctant to offend him in any way.[43]

In all Micronesian societies without exception, the bond between brothers and sisters has always been sacrosanct. This relationship, which anthropologists have come to regard as the keystone of island social organization, demands mutual assistance.[44] Brothers and sisters, although they were prohibited from spending much time in each other's company, were expected to look out for one another's interests. Brothers were quick to step in when the well-being of their sisters was threatened.[45] They protected their sisters from unwanted young men with amorous intentions or from those who were foolhardy enough to use crude language in their sisters' presence. They were even more ready to guard their female siblings from physical danger. For their part, sisters were also supposed to defend their brothers from harm when the occasion presented itself. When a drunken Chuukese youth was in danger of provoking a fight that might endanger him, his sisters would hurry out of the house to drag him out of harm's way, even though they might receive the brunt of his abuse and sometimes his blows. On one such occasion some years ago when I tackled a very drunken young man in a taro patch and held him until our school truck arrived to carry him off to jail, I found myself smothered by a band of young women who were tugging at my legs and arms in an effort to force me to release him.

The strong cultural bond between brother and sister has traditionally been grounded in their joint stewardship of lineage property. Their roles may have differed, but together they were overseers of the land and guardians of the lineage interests. The blood ties that joined brothers and sisters were reinforced by the responsibility they shared in caring for the resources their lineage needed for its survival.[46]

In view of the strong bond between siblings, the failure of brothers to protect their married sisters from the drunken abuse of their husbands today might seem surprising at first. Yet, the balance today has tilted away from the extended family toward the nuclear family, consisting of husband, wife, and children. In today's Micronesia, where a woman is more likely to be supported by her husband's income than by the fruits of her own lineage land, her brother's legitimacy as her guardian has declined. Brothers, although still linked to their sisters by strong cultural ties, often have marginal economic interests in common with them. This fact almost certainly diminishes brothers' sense of responsibility toward their married sisters even as it accentuates the importance of the marital bond. It is as if the new, smaller family unit is cordoned off from the intrusion of those who formerly were expected to maintain vigilance over their female

Women preparing food in the outer islands of Yap. (Micronesian Seminar Collection)

relatives. The husband has replaced the brother as the protector of his married sister, even though he—the husband—may constitute the main threat to her well-being.

Moreover, the brother is often enough in no position to see to his married sister's welfare even if he wanted to, for many more married couples today are setting up their homes in places that lie well beyond the reach of the woman's blood relatives. A move to town or an even more distant location like Guam or Saipan offers the abusive husband freedom from the social controls that once made him very hesitant to display the full force of his anger toward his wife.

The force of this widening gap between brothers and sisters was brought home to me not long ago when a middle-aged man from Chuuk died in the Hawaiian hospital to which he had been referred. Even before the man drew his last breath, his sister and his wife began arguing about where the body should be buried. His wife, a woman from another island group, prevailed, and so the body was sent off to be buried in the place where the man and his nuclear family had lived and worked since his marriage. Forty years earlier there would have been no question about the burial site. It would have been taken for granted that the deceased would be interred on his own land with his blood relatives. It was from this land and this blood that he sprang, and to it he would return. However, that was before the nuclear family became a force that could compete with lineage ties, especially those sacred bonds between brother and sister.

Sharing Children with Others

When the eighteen-year-old Palauan girl first explained to her parents that she intended to leave her infant in their care, she was met with a cold stare. Their daughter was unmarried, but she knew her parents had no desire to see her marry the boy who had fathered her child. She told her parents that she hoped to move into town to find a job but could not care for her infant at the same time. Her parents glanced quickly at one another. Would she take advantage of her freedom in town to find new boyfriends and perhaps have other children? Would she help support the child, or would they have to take on the entire burden by themselves even though they had no regular cash income? Could they provide everything that the child would need as it grew older?

The old adage is that children, legitimate or illegitimate, will never lack for a home in the Pacific. Everyone wants children. They are a valuable resource that ought to be shared with others in the community. Nonetheless, the scene described above is one that is enacted ever more frequently on many of the more modernized islands of Micronesia today. Relatives who once would have been honored to accept a child to raise now seem to have serious hesitations.

Not long ago, adoption was the rule rather than the exception in many parts of Micronesia. A majority of the children in a typical community in Palau, the atolls of the western Carolines, and parts of Chuuk and Pohnpei were given out in adoption to others. A survey of Melekeok in Palau, done in 1973, showed that 58 percent of the population had been adopted, with the average household containing five adopted members.[47] A similar survey made of school children on Pulap, a distant atoll reputed to be one of the most traditional in Chuuk, showed comparable results in 1980: 53 percent of the children had been adopted.[48] Adoption was especially common on the atolls between Yap and Chuuk, with Alkire reporting that half of the children on Lamotrek and over three-fourths on Satawal were adopted.[49] In other parts of Micronesia, too, adoption was common, even if not as widely practiced as in Palau and Pulap.[50]

In most Micronesian societies adoption was distinguished from fosterage. On the one hand, children who were handed over to others in the lineage—maternal grandparents or a maternal aunt, for instance—were thought of as remaining within the "family" or lineage. For this reason, they were not regarded as adopted out; they were merely being cared for, or fostered, by other family members. Fosterage frequently occurred when the biological parents died or were otherwise unable to care for their children. Adoption, on the other hand, meant affiliation of the child with people outside its own lineage. In most cases, as a matter of fact, the adopting parents were closely related to the natural parents, even if they were members of other lineages.

Adoption was by no means exclusive. Rather than implying the loss of one set of parents in favor of another, it meant the addition of a new set of parents and by implication new kin ties with them. In the recent past children were easily passed this way and that through their kin circle so that some children might have two or three sets of parents. Not all of those adopted in childhood necessarily moved out of their homes to live with their adoptive parents, but many did. Others shuttled back and forth between the homes of their natural and adoptive parents, living for a period with one family before changing residence to stay with the other.

A biological mother and father were expected to be ready to entrust their children to others, whether in name or actually to be raised by them. Adoption in the past was not so much a way of providing for neglected or abandoned children as a favor for couples that had no or few children of their own. It was an act of generosity to childless adults, an offer to share the wealth that children represented with families not as lavishly endowed in this resource. Adoption was a way of insuring that married couples without children would be cared for in their old age, since the boys and girls that a couple raises can be expected to return the favor and provide for their parents in later years. Children, whatever else they were, embodied a valued form of social security. Adopted children would be rewarded for the services that they rendered their adoptive parents. In due time, they could be expected to inherit property and carry on the name of the family.

But adoption was not simply or primarily an act of benevolence. It offered real benefits to the couple that gave their child to another family. The kind of adoption that occurred between close relatives would serve to strengthen the bond between the two lineages and link them even more closely than before.[51] Adoption by a close relative could also protect land and other valuable resources from alienation. A brother's child, for instance, might be adopted by his sister and her husband, thus incorporating the child as a member of the sister and brother's own lineage. In such cases, the land the child received from his or her adoptive parents would remain within a tight family circle, even if it passed from one lineage to another. These were strong considerations in adoption as it was formerly practiced in Chuuk, Pohnpei, the outer islands of Yap, the Marshalls, and Palau.[52]

There were other benefits of adoption, too. On some of the atolls of the central Carolines like Fais, it was unusual for a child not to have adoptive parents. Sometimes one child was adopted by several sets of parents in succession. In these small atoll communities, adoption was a strategy for exposing the young person to an ever broadening circle of adults on the island. It was a way of teaching the child that he or she belonged to the entire community, not simply to a single set of parents.[53] Since adoption was traditionally inclusive rather than exclusive, adopted children always retained their membership rights and duties in their family of birth as well as in any other families into which they were adopted.

Generally, adopted children were well treated by their new parents; indeed, they were often better treated than the adoptive parents' biological children. In Chuuk, such children were often given a breadfruit or coconut tree of their own, and sometimes even a parcel of land, at the time they were adopted into the family.[54] Understandably, adopting families would have been ashamed to show their adopted children anything less than the same consideration that they showed to their biological children.

Although childless couples still seek to adopt children, the practice has declined enormously in the present day. A Pohnpeian woman who gave out seven of her own fourteen biological children for adoption reported that of all her grandchildren, who number about sixty, only one has been adopted out. She says that no one has been adopted into her family in the past twenty years.[55] Other Pohnpeians tell of some adoptions in recent years, but all agree that the practice has become much rarer. This seems to be the trend in all the more modernized islands of Micronesia, although figures to support this statement are difficult to come by. In Yap, however, there are data that document this trend; a 1947 survey shows that 24 percent of the population was adopted, while the 1972 figure indicates a rate of only 15 percent.[56]

The reasons sometimes given for the decline in adoption are that parents are too busy taking care of their own children, there are fewer childless couples because the survival rate of infants today is greater than in the past, and people are more reluctant to accept the financial burden of raising children. In addition, as the sense of lineage solidarity weakens, members may be less concerned than in the past about strengthening kin bonds.

Many families no longer see adoption as a distribution of wealth, but as a strategy that enables others to rid themselves of inconvenient children. Children who would have been cherished in an earlier day may be regarded as a burden to the adopting family and treated as such. One boy who was adopted into a family in Palau was so poorly treated in comparison with the other children in the family that he ran off and became a drifter. A ten-year-old Yapese boy was sent to live with his paternal grandfather, as custom dictated, when his father died and his mother remarried. His grandfather neglected the boy so badly that he moved out to live with his mother and step-father, but his life was so miserable with them that he moved out of that household also and became a wanderer.[57]

In recent years adoption has commonly become associated with child abuse or neglect, as surveys of the region in the mid-1980s show.[58] It is a measure of the social change that has beset families that adoption, an institution that once bound families together, should be increasingly viewed as a shackle rather than a benefit.

Yet, this is not the whole story. Throughout Micronesia young children are still "shared" with others today, even if not through adoption as it was once practiced. Children from villages are often sent to live with relatives in town while they are attending school. Today as in the past, they often circulate among relatives as they move from one household to another for short periods of time. Meanwhile, adoption itself, although less common than it was, has taken some new turns. In the Marshalls and Pohnpei, and perhaps even more widely, the rules that once governed adoption are being discarded for other norms. Rather than adopting the offspring of a closely related family member, women sometimes adopt needy children who lack strong family support. Often these are either children of young single mothers without the means to feed their children or young people from the outer islands without a family to care for them.[59]

The Marshalls has recently witnessed a revival of adoption but of a very different sort than was practiced in the past. Foreign couples, mostly American, have been coming to the Marshalls in ever greater numbers to adopt island children.[60] Many parents are willing to surrender their children to be raised abroad in the hope that their children will have access to benefits, such as quality education and health care, that they would probably not receive on their own islands. Although they may not receive payment for the children they offer for adoption, Marshallese parents expect that their children will eventually return to the Marshalls to take care of them during their old age. In traditional adoption, where parents did not replace but supplemented one another, this could easily happen. In foreign adoption, with the geographical distance and cultural gap that it opens, such hopes may be doomed to frustration.

2 Land

Land as Life or as Livelihood?

Peliciano, a middle-aged man, hesitated for a few seconds before entering the store. He had been there hundreds of times before to buy rice, canned meat, and other groceries, mostly on credit. A few months before, as he began serious work on the construction of his new house, he had started picking up lumber and building supplies from the store. The store owner, an old friend of his from high school days, had told him that he could add the cost to his tab. When he returned three weeks ago to pick up some electrical wiring and plumbing fixtures, the manager invited him to his office. There he explained that because the store was experiencing cash flow problems, they would have to begin collecting from the people who owed them money. His own debt was now close to $10,000, and they would have to ask for payment. Now Peliciano was standing outside the store with a long shopping list in his pocket and a land transfer form in his briefcase. Since he had no savings and no steady income, he had no recourse but to offer the store manager a piece of land to pay off his debt. He had been hoping to give this land to his sons, but it would have to go to the store owner instead.

This scenario is common today. Land is parlayed into cash, which is used to pay for imported food and other merchandise. Land has come to be regarded as a salable commodity like bags of cement, lumber, and the fruits and vegetables that the land itself produces. During the past twenty or thirty years, land offices everywhere in Micronesia have been recording numerous land sales. A partial survey of land transactions recorded in Chuuk during the early 1980s showed between sixty and eighty land sales yearly, with the total value of land sold exceeding $200,000.[1] The recipients of the land in most of these exchanges were store owners or well-to-do businessmen. Those who sold their land usually did so in order to settle a debt with a store owner or to obtain ready cash for a purchase. As the circumferential road was being built around Pohnpei during the 1970s, landowners in each village it reached would sell pieces of land to buy themselves pickup trucks. During the early 1980s, as the video craze hit the islands, many people purchased television sets and VCRs with the proceeds of their land sales.

Pohnpei, which recorded forty-three land sales during the period from 1981 to 1984, showed very few land sales during the 1950s and 1960s.[2] Pohnpeians, like other Micronesians, disliked selling their land and even considered it shameful, as an anthropologist working on the island in the early 1950s notes.[3] The anthropological literature attests that the sale of land was very rare before the 1970s.[4] The readiness to parlay land into cash these days represents a big change in the attitudes of Micronesians, since land was once such a cherished part of a group's and an individual's identity. Nearly as much as one's kin ties, land determined who one was and where one belonged.

Throughout the centuries land has been the source of life for Micronesians. If this was true of all agrarian societies, it was all the more true for the population of a group of small, land-scarce islands. To have rights to land—understood as including the offshore flats and reef or fishing areas—was to be able to provide for all one's basic needs: food, housing, transportation, and medicine. Land was as much a basic element of life as the food that was grown on it, and the two terms were used interchangeably on many islands. People spoke of eating from their piece of land. It is difficult to exaggerate the importance that land has always had in the eyes of Micronesians. "Land is our strength, our life, our hope for the future," a Chuukese proverb declares.

Land is not only life, but it is also a way of life, Alkire once wrote.[5] By this he did not simply mean that the patterns of life in Micronesia, as in all subsistence societies, must be in tune with the rhythms of nature and respond to the availability of resources. In any land-based economy, people exhibit a cluster of attitudes that are associated with a traditional society and that distinguish them from a more modernized people. Alkire was claiming more than this, that "throughout Micronesia the basic social institutions have been molded by adaptation to the concept and reality of limited land."[6] Adoption practices, for instance, were designed not only to strengthen the ties between two families but to keep land parcels within a tight kin circle, as seen in the last chapter. The same could be said of the way marriage partners were typically chosen in the past. Kinship itself was molded to fit landownership patterns. "Land creates the concept of 'blood,' " is the way one author expresses this idea with regard to Palau.[7] This close relationship between land and blood is reflected in the local languages: the term *"bwogat"* on the central Caroline atolls can mean either a cluster of land parcels or the people who reside on this land. The word is used interchangeably of both, according to Alkire.[8]

The belief in the primacy of land is expressed in various ways in different island groups. In Yap people are named after parcels of land. Titles to chiefly powers there derive from ownership of estates rather than the other way around. Hence, the Yapese say, "The man is not chief, the land is chief."[9] In the Marshalls, people in the not so distant past would usually identify themselves as belonging to a certain named piece of land, for the land was a better means of identification than one's own name.[10] Until recently in Palau the head of a household would take his title from the name of the estate that he held, so he might be known as "Master of a certain piece of land."[11] Palauan attitudes on the subject were captured in a phrase that an anthropologist on Palau heard again and again: "People come and go, but the land and the name of the land stays and never, never changes."[12] Such practices and beliefs express the almost mystical relationship that Micronesian people seem to have developed to their land. The dead were buried on the land, the dying sought its refuge, and new generations were nurtured from its soil. The history of the land was an integral part of the family history and an extension of the kin group.

People parted from their land about as willingly as they would lop off one of their own arms or legs. If land was life for traditional Micronesians, then loss of land was a form of death; in Chuuk, according to one author, it was lamented with the cry "I am no longer alive."[13] A Yapese who had lost his land, usually as punishment for some serious offense, lost his voice and, in great measure, his identity. As one writer baldly puts it, "A landless individual was effectively a nonperson."[14]

Land was sometimes given up in traditional times, of course. It could be lost by conquest, when a family took possession of land by force of arms; it could be surrendered to compensate another family for injury done to one of its members; or it might be offered to another in exchange for services such as healing or the care of an old or infirm lineage member. Land was also commonly passed from the husband's lineage to his wife's, either at the time of betrothal or marriage, as in Chuuk, or later in recognition of a wife's services, as in Palau.[15] Finally, on some islands, land was customarily given by a father to his children, who always belonged to another lineage—that of his wife. Hence, the father's lineage understood this practice as "giving away" land. In these last cases, however, the gifts could be seen as circular, for the man's lineage could expect to benefit by reciprocal gifts—if not of land, then of traditional valuables (in Palau and Yap) or services.

Although land stood at the center of the traditional resource base and was once sacred, its position is being redefined today. The cash economy, in providing an alternative resource base, has undercut the centrality of land and eroded the mystique surrounding it. No longer the marker of identity that it once was, land is coming more and more to be seen as alienable. In the eyes of some, it has already become just another marketable commodity. As a Marshallese government official succinctly put it, "Once people said that they belonged to the land; now they say the land belongs to them."[16]

The Rise of the Individual Landowner

The deacon explained to me that he and his family had lived in their house next to the parish church for many years. Now, just two days ago, the family of the woman who had donated the land to the church over sixty years ago told him that they wanted to repossess some of the land. Eugenio, a man of about seventy and the appointed spokesman for the family, addressed the deacon hesitantly and apologetically at first, then a little more forcefully as the conversation continued. His mother had made a gift of the land to the church sixty years ago, he reminded the deacon, so that a church could be built and parish activities carried on. Some years ago, however, the deacon and his family had moved onto the land, and they were living in a house alongside the church. It was not his mother's intention, he said, to provide land for a Micronesian family. After all, the deacon had land of his own on which his family could live if they wished.

"But didn't Eugenio's mother give the land to the church as a gift many years ago?" I protested. "How can her descendants take back now what they already gave?"

The deacon smiled sadly and replied: "Land gifts rarely last forever. Eugenio's mother was giving the church the right to use the land for a time, not to own it forever."

Downtown Majuro in 1946. (Leonard Mason)

. . . and fifty years later. (Leonard Mason)

Who owns this piece of land? Anyone familiar with land issues in the Pacific knows that such a question can never be answered directly. It has no simple answer. Better to ask who has what rights to a piece of land, as anthropologist Jack Fischer once suggested.[17] Ownership is not a helpful term when applied to land, for various groups might have claims of different sorts to a single land parcel. Asking to whom a piece of land belongs is like asking that question about a child. The child's mother and father have a large claim on him or her, but not the only claim. Others have a stake in the child: the grandparents and other relatives, even brothers and sisters. The comparison between a land parcel and a person is not as far-fetched as it may at first seem, for people in Micronesia ascribe personal attributes to the land. Both are named, have their own histories, and are spoken of with a genuine affection that might seem out of place when referring to inanimate things.

At one time virtually no land was individually owned; land rights always lay with the lineage or other kin group.[18] In the more stratified, Polynesian-like societies in eastern Micronesia—Pohnpei, Kosrae, and the Marshalls—ultimate ownership rested with the paramount chief, with land rights granted out to families. Yet, one author, writing of the Marshalls, prefers to use the term "joint ownership" of the land, for he sees some rights vested in the chiefs and others in the people using the land.[19] In Chuuk and on the coral atolls of the central Carolines, the land that people lived on was recognized as originally stemming from the senior clan on the island. The other people could be seen as more or less permanent tenants of the land they occupied. To acknowledge the prior land rights of paramount chiefs or senior clans, they periodically offered first fruits, or a gift of food from the land, to the "owners."

The corporate rather than individual ownership of land and the shared rights to pieces of land by different groups underscored an important tenet of life in Micronesia—that land was a communal resource to be overseen by chiefs and used for the benefit of the community. This tenet was clearly illustrated in Palau by the village chief and council's control over the use of interior lands.[20] In Pohnpei the paramount chief exercised the same authority over interior lands and mangroves.[21]

The traditional forms of land tenure began to change with the beginning of intense foreign contact in Micronesia from the middle of the nineteenth century. The paramount chiefs' hold over land began loosening almost immediately. In Pohnpei, this process began with the arrival of the first missionaries, long before the imposition of the new land laws by the Germans in 1912. In Kosrae the powers of the paramount chief diminished quickly, owing to the rapid population decline in the late 1800s. Only in the Marshalls has chiefly "ownership" of the land been maintained up to the present day.

Meanwhile, the patterns of landownership on larger islands, under the influence of colonial regimes, began shifting from the kin group to the individual. Beginning with German rule in the early twentieth century, foreign administrations, intent on encouraging the productive use of land by people, sought to wrest it out of the control of kin groups. The latter were regarded as a drag on modernization, whereas highly motivated individuals with land to invest could transform the economy.[22] It is not easy to determine just how far this new trend went. By the end of World War II, over 80 percent of the land parcels in Melekeok, a district of Palau, were registered in the name of individuals rather than kin groups.[23] This figure could misrepresent the move toward individually held landholdings, however, for many of those who registered the land at the great Japanese land survey of 1938 might simply have bowed to Japanese preferences and registered the land in their own names as a matter of convenience.

Even if the figures from such surveys do not provide an accurate measure of the change in landownership patterns, they may be significant in other ways. They reveal that individual landownership was becoming more widely accepted, especially among the new elites. Moreover, the descendants of the persons who had registered lineage land in their own names at the time of the Japanese land survey would use this precedent to support their own claims to these lands. Registration of parcels as individually owned in 1938, although a fiction then, provided the buttress for what would become a reality years later.

Soon after the war, during the early years of U.S. administration, there may have been a revival of traditional land tenure practices. Lineages were reconstituted at that time after the dispersal of families brought about by the war. Moreover, there was no pressure on people anywhere in Micronesia to convert their land into commercial ventures, since the drive toward economic development was absent. In some places, family land was let out or "leased" to others, but ordinarily no rental fees were collected.[24] On Majuro in the 1950s, a landowning group would expect nothing more than food gifts for residential buildings put up on its land by another person or group. Only for bakeries, stores, and other commercial enterprises were cash rentals exacted.[25]

The 1960s, with increased government budgets and greater cash opportunities, saw the beginning of a huge swing toward individual landownership. As more people were freed from the need for land as a source of food and livelihood, thanks to their cash incomes, they could look on land with an increasingly cold eye for its monetary value. Moreover, land investment opportunities increased as the government expanded and new businesses in the private sector opened to offer a variety of services—restaurants, gas stations, pool halls, and grocery stores. There were new opportunities to sell and mortgage land and so acquire a cash income. On the other side of the widening divide between ordinary villagers and the new elite, the purchase of land with an eye to leasing it later was becoming more attractive. People understood, as they never had before, that land could be parlayed into a cash equivalent.[26]

Public lands, as government-held land was called, represented a special problem. These public lands, once held by traditional chiefs in trust for the community, were confiscated by the German or Japanese government and passed on to succeeding administrations. By claiming all land that was not registered under an individual title, the Japanese administration enormously increased the area of public land.[27] Even before the U.S. administration returned these lands to the local authorities in the late 1970s, some of them had already been homesteaded out to individuals.

Today the land situation in Micronesia defies simple description; it is a mixture of the traditional and the new. While the outer islands of Yap continue to observe the traditional group ownership, individual landownership has made great inroads in more modernized areas. In Palau, individual ownership is now the prevalent form of land tenure.[28] Between these extremes lie a wide range of mixed land practices.

The effects of what appears to be an evolution of landownership from group-owned to individually owned land are observable. On the one hand, there is a greater concentration of land in the hands of a few wealthy people. This is not an entirely new phenomenon, for Henry Nanpei in his heyday at the end of the nineteenth century was said to have owned almost a third of the registered land on Pohnpei.[29] On the other hand, the sale of land has led to the creation of a small class of landless people, some of whom can be found on every major island in Micronesia. These people, who gambled away or sold their land, must throw themselves on the charity of their relatives. Just as foreign administrators had once en-

Main Street in Kolonia, Pohnpei (1965). (Francis X. Hezel)

The same scene today. (Anelisa Garfunkle)

visioned, many individuals are today free to invest as they choose without feeling the necessity to honor the desires of their lineage mates. Indeed, the lineage and other extended family groups are being further weakened as they lose control over what was once their most valuable resource—land.

Yet, there appears to be still another swing back to collective ownership of land. One writer refers to the resurgence in Palau, where individual landownership has progressed most, of tenancy in common. Tenancy in common means that related persons register as a common group of tenants rather than as individuals, preferring to resolve conflicting claims among themselves rather than submit such matters to a law court.[30] Other authors point out that on homesteaded land plots, which were originally awarded to individuals, customary landownership patterns have been reestablished. Hence, many of these plots have gradually shifted from individually owned parcels to group-owned parcels.[31] Custom dies hard, especially with respect to land.

Breaking the Unbreakable Lineage Bond

The two middle-aged Chuukese women stood in the middle of the school-yard hurling insults at one another, while a crowd gathered to watch the quarrel. This had happened before; the bystanders all knew there was a good chance that the argument would heat up and evolve into a full-fledged fight between the feuding women. Tosiko, the heavier of the two women, was the wife of Seremiah, the owner of two parcels of land that had been under dispute ever since Seremiah's father died. The other woman was married to Seremiah's first cousin, Leo. Seremiah's father, a strong and respected member of the community, was the head of his lineage. When he died, it was assumed that the land he held in the name of his lineage would go to his sisters' children, of whom Leo was the oldest. Yet, to the surprise of his relatives, he left the land to his own sons, the eldest of whom was Seremiah. Leo and his brothers were deeply upset at the decision. From this time on, the relations between Seremiah and his cousins had been strained. At first they simply avoided one another and would not speak to each other, but in time things worsened. Seremiah's and Leo's families were drawn into the conflict. Soon the children in the two households would get into scraps and stone each other's houses, and eventually the wives started to lash out at one another in public. Where would it all end, the community wondered.

Land tenure in small island societies is too important to leave to chance. In most of the islands of Micronesia, land was customarily passed on to the children through their mother's lineage. The link between land rights and lineage membership is hardly surprising in view of the close relationship between kinship and property that existed in traditional island societies. Even today, people everywhere in Micronesia still regard their own lineage as a fallback in time of desperate need. It offers a secure home when all else fails. Even if the father's family rejects a young man or woman for failures or incorrigibility, he or she can be certain of a place in the matrilineal estate.

This is not to say that islanders could not inherit land from their fathers at times. They did so (and still do) routinely in Chuuk and at least occasionally in Palau, while in the Marshalls and on the outer atolls of Yap they might do so under certain circumstances. Even so, land inheritance from the father's lineage usually tended to be more risky and was more likely to be contested than inheritance from the mother's lineage. On the Western Islands of Chuuk, for instance, land received from one's father could be taken away if the one to whom the land was given did not properly meet his obligations to the father's lineage.[32] The same was true of land inherited from the father in Palau. In the Marshalls land was only passed from a father to his children in extreme circumstances. The land inheritance systems probably reflected the relative fragility of the father-child bond compared with the matrilineal bond, which a Palauan saying describes as the "tie that can never be broken."[33]

This pattern of land inheritance, on some islands at least, began changing during the nineteenth century under the influence of foreign contact. Kosrae and Pohnpei have both adopted father-to-son land inheritance systems similar to the traditional inheritance system in Yap as well as in most Western countries.[34] American missionary influence on Kosrae and German land policy on Pohnpei resulted in greater changes in land inheritance in those two places than anywhere else in Micronesia. In Yap the switch to a patrilineal inheritance system occurred long before, most likely in precontact times. In all these places, a person may sometimes inherit land from the mother, but this practice is far less common than inheritance from the father.

The shift away from land inheritance through the mother continues today. Chuuk and Palau provide the clearest examples of this shift. The episode recounted at the beginning of this section indicates what may happen when the change in land inheritance takes the family by surprise.

Seremiah's father was expected to show the traditional regard for the interests of his lineage by returning the land to his lineage so that his sister's children could use the land and build up the fortunes of his kin group. Instead, he passed what his family regarded as lineage land on to his sons. In doing so, he shocked his lineage mates and threw the family into consternation. While it was a betrayal of traditional values, his decision was perfectly understandable in the light of the breakup of the extended family that is occurring today. In the nuclear family that is becoming more and more the norm, a father must invest in his children rather than in his sister's children, even though the latter are members of his own lineage. The important role of the maternal uncle is falling into disuse everywhere in Micronesia, as the father's direct authority over his children grows stronger with time.

The same trend is evident in Palau. One anthropologist, writing of the late 1970s, observed that wives were urging their husbands to purchase land in the names of their children so that the wife and children might be guaranteed land after the man's death.[35] The same anthropologist went on to state that sons were laying claim to their father's land "by right of inheritance," while the blood relatives of the father challenged these claims on the grounds of "traditional rules of inheritance."[36] Which inheritance rules should apply: those based on the old family form or those based on the new?

This ambiguity is a common cause of land disputes today. Lineage land that individuals registered under their own names in Palau during Japanese times is now being claimed by their descendants as individually owned land. The rules for land inheritance have changed, they argue, from the traditional matrilineal ones to father-son descent. In former times the matrilineage sometimes selected one of its members who would be represented on official documents as the owner of the lineage land, even though it was understood that the land would belong to the entire kin group. Now, however, Palauans worry that this person might actually claim the land for himself and his children.[37]

In Chuuk, meanwhile, the file drawers in the Clerk of Courts Office are filled with notarized papers from various lineages attesting that the signature of all senior members of the lineage is required before any land transaction is recognized as legally valid. This is a precaution born of sad experience. Often in the recent past lineage heads have sold land or transferred it to their sons without the approval of their lineage mates.

The traditional land inheritance norms are passing into oblivion on some islands. Older Chuukese complain that land tenure rules, which were once an indispensable part of life, are coming to be thought of as a kind of arcane lore retained only by a special group of elderly men: land commissioners, judges, and masters of traditional legends. Meanwhile, it is felt, the new forms of land inheritance gaining currency today are sure to work themselves into the code of land law.

An inevitable effect of the conflict between old and new patterns of land inheritance is the growing number of disputes over land that reach the courts. Land, prized as it is by Pacific peoples, has always been disputed, but very few of these disputes before the late 1960s ever came before the courts. Conflicts were settled by the head of the lineage if they involved two members of the same family or by a local authority figure when the dispute occurred between different lineages. Land cases were first brought before the courts with some regularity in the 1960s, while during the 1970s and 1980s the number of court cases grew rapidly.[38]

In turning to the court system to resolve land disputes, people are employing an adversarial system that pits one party against the other, with the winner taking all. "There are no ties in this system," remarked a Chuukese judge when describing the Western judicial system.[39] Because of its confrontational method, the court system often exacerbates the bad feelings between contesting parties, even after the final judgment is made. Recourse to the courts may result in clear judgments, but these courts do not offer the possibility of compromise solutions that might assuage rather than increase the bitterness between disputants.

3 Gender Roles

The Gender Gap

Twenty or thirty Micronesian women stood at the front of the covered stage singing to a small audience. The sign over the outdoor stage next to the ball field proclaimed "International Women's Day." The audience of about forty persons, perhaps half of them Americans or Australians, had accepted an invitation to attend the program that was to mark the beginning of a week filled with women's activities. A few Micronesian men had come to support the efforts of their wives. On the road next to the ball field cars slowed down and heads turned as drivers gawked at the spectacle, some smiling and shaking their head as they moved on. The singing, a gesture of solidarity among Micronesian women, was the last item on the agenda. Participants had just heard an American woman issue a summons to her Micronesian sisters to stand firm and demand their fair share of the political power in the nation. "Men have no right to exclude women from public office, here or anywhere else," she thundered. "The positions men occupy must be open for women as well. Justice and equality demand as much."

Many parts of the world today are witnessing a war between the sexes, with males and females contesting rights and roles and jobs. Within the last two decades women's groups have issued a call for women's involvement in the political arena and for access to key leadership positions. Men, for their part, often resent women's intrusion into what they regard as an exclusively male domain. In recent years, the Pacific has become yet another battleground in this struggle.

In all Micronesian societies there has always been a sharp distinction between the roles of males and females. Women were expected to do the weaving and plaiting, care for the small children, and perform many of the household chores, while men did the deep-sea fishing (and in most islands the offshore fishing too), built the houses and canoes, and conducted warfare. Work was divided differently from one island society to another. For instance, women did shoreline fishing in Chuuk, Pohnpei, and the Marshalls, but not in Yap; whereas, Chuukese and Marshallese men did taro cultivation, something that was strictly women's work in Yap and Palau. The line could be drawn even more finely at times; in the eastern Carolines both men and women did reef fishing but never the same kind. Men might engage in throw-net fishing and spearfishing, for instance, while women might use small hand nets or circular nets that required several women to handle. Wherever the line was drawn, there was always a sharp boundary between men's roles and women's roles.[1]

Even when working on projects involving the entire community, men and women performed different parts of the work. By way of illustration, consider the procedure for thatching the roof of a meetinghouse that is followed even today in the outer islands of Yap. In preparation for the project, the men would twist the rope from coconut fiber while the women would plait the thatch segments to be used for the roof. When the community assembled to replace the roof, the men would climb up to haul down the old roof and position the new pieces of thatch. The women, meanwhile, would prepare the food for lunch.[2]

On something as commonplace as preparation of breadfruit in Chuuk, the principle of division of labor by gender is still rigorously employed. The men pick the breadfruit and carry it to the cookhouse, where the women scrape off the skin, cut it up into pieces, and cook it. When the breadfruit is cooked, the men pound it and shape it into loaves, leaving it to the women to wrap the loaves in banana leaves and store them.[3] Women's work was clearly distinguished from men's work in every detail of joint work projects, but the completion of the project depended on both. Hence, these examples of division of labor are also illustrative of the complementary nature of the contributions of the genders.

Just as labor was divided by gender, so were other roles in Micronesian societies. Men and women enjoyed their own respective spheres of influence. On many islands women were looked upon as the caretakers of the land, and they consequently exercised a large measure of control over the allocation of land use rights within or outside the family. Men, for their part, were the spokespersons for the family and the village; they held the titles and the chieftainships. To use the distinction that Smith employs of Palau, men's power is "public," while women's is "pri-

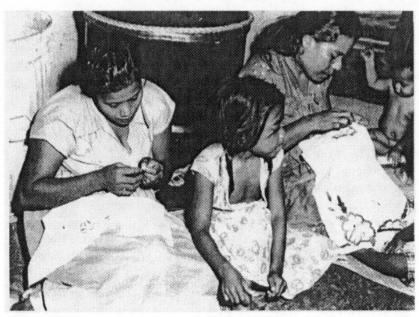

Marshallese women embroidering. (Saul Riesenberg Collection, MARC)

vate"—that is, its locus is inside the lineage rather than outside in the community.[4]

On some islands women occasionally received public recognition in the form of titles, sometimes but not always out of consideration for the high title that a woman's husband held. By way of example, a woman married to a high chief on Pohnpei was given a counterpart of her husband's title, but when her husband died she was often given a special title of her own. The senior woman in a very high matrilineage on Pohnpei might also receive a title in her own right.[5] Palauan women from chiefly families had titles corresponding to those borne by their brothers. In the Marshalls, women could attain *leroij* status, parallel to the *iroij* status of the paramount chief but without the power to exercise authority. Women there have also often held the position of leadership in the lineage, especially in the past forty years.[6]

These marks of formal recognition are generally few, however, and so one can easily be misled into believing that women were relatively impotent in island societies. Titles and access to chiefly status have never been an accurate gauge of the power of women, since their authority is indirect and often concealed from view. In any case, it would have made

Ulithian men repairing a fishing net. (TT Archives, University of Hawai'i Library)

little sense to attempt to weigh the relative power of males and females, no matter what measure was used, for they were always seen as forming opposite halves of a single system. The two sexes were the "yin and yang," the dual elements that, in dynamic relation with one another, made up the whole social world.

In gender relations, as in other aspects of island life, there was a strong element of reciprocity. Just as women were required to show certain kinds of deference to men, especially to male relatives, men were also required to practice respect behavior toward women. Men were not only prohibited from using certain kinds of language in the presence of women, but they were expected to withdraw from the presence of close female kin in keeping with the avoidance behavior that was so common in island societies. Women on the atolls of the western and central Carolines—and originally in the eastern Carolines and the Marshalls as well—were expected to keep a lower position than their male kin, crawling in front of them if they should be seated. But, by the same token, the males were supposed to avoid putting their "sisters" in a position where they would have to do so. The code of respect that governed their relations with female relatives ordained that they avoid entering the room or if entering remain standing or go off to a distant part of the room to spare their "sisters" the embarrassment of having to defer to them so obviously.

What are today called women's rights were well protected in traditional society. These rights fall considerably short of today's modern standards, for women might be slapped or hit by their husbands. Even so, the woman's family kept a close watch over her and was poised to intervene on her behalf in case of perceived excess. Women in Micronesian societies some years ago surely did not enjoy equality with men, but they were not without a large measure of security and even power in those societies.[7]

The principle of complementary but different roles that was so solidly established throughout Micronesia and the rest of the Pacific is being challenged today. Women's past roles, decried as too limited and limiting, are being scorned in favor of new and more exciting possibilities. The call has gone out for women's involvement in the political arena and access to key government positions. Women throughout the world today are demanding real equality with men. They are asserting their right to pursue not just careers preselected for women but any of their choosing for which they have the necessary talent and training. In demanding access to all fields of endeavor on an equal footing with men, they are seeking a definitive end to the system of gender differentiation that underpinned traditional Pacific societies.[8] Such changes have far-reaching implications that can affect all areas of human life.

After helping to organize a program like the one described at the beginning of this section, two women came to see me to talk over their efforts. One of them was almost in tears as she recounted the rude responses she received from many of her male fellow islanders whenever she raised the question of gender equality between men and women. Her companion added that men seem to regard any feminist gesture as a declaration of war on men and respond in kind. She admitted that she was thinking seriously of limiting the feminist agenda of her like-minded friends to discussions of women's roles in the home and the church since anything else was too explosive an issue. "How can we assure men that we want to be partners, not competitors for the same roles?" she asked. "Otherwise, we'll never be able to live in peace with one another."

Men's Changing Roles

As I stepped off the boat and onto the dock, the deacon hurried over to greet me. Fortyish and with an athletic build, he shook my hand vigorously and, telling a boy of about ten to carry my bag, led me to his house slightly uphill from the church, not far from the dock. It was just three days before Christmas. I was to stay with the deacon and his family for the next few days while helping him tend to the pastoral needs of his parish and preparing for the Christmas masses. When we reached his house, someone stashed my bag in the room that had been prepared for me while the deacon called his wife over. The woman hurried over with a child cradled in one of her arms and some half-folded sheets draped over the other. The deacon asked his wife to prepare some hot water for coffee for us while we discussed plans for handling the parish work for the next few days.

The deacon's wife, an attractive woman in her late thirties, lost the harried look on her face for a moment as she smiled graciously at us before turning away to continue her work. A minute later the look was back. After filling the thermos from the kettle of water that was boiling over the fire, she asked one of her daughters to find the cups, spoons, and sugar. She was about to bring the thermos when one of the smaller children, a girl of three or four, began howling. The deacon's wife picked her up to comfort her and, when she was satisfied that the tot had calmed down sufficiently, assigned her to the care of a slightly older child. Then she resumed gathering the freshly washed sheets and towels off the clothes-line. I could see another washbasin filled with clothes that still needed to be washed, and one of the sacristans was bringing in an armful of altar linen and surplices for laundering.

As the deacon and I chatted over our cup of coffee for the next forty minutes, his wife was in perpetual motion. She was hanging things on the clothesline, balancing toddlers in her arms, supervising the play of her children and producing snacks for them when they began whining for food, sweeping outside her kitchen and removing litter from the lawn, fielding questions from parishioners on the time of church services, and serving her husband and me with unfailing good grace.

Perhaps the situation that I have just described was atypical. Certainly it occurred at what was an exceptionally busy time for a deacon pastor and his wife. Yet, again and again I have walked into situations where the woman of the house was trying to manage several tasks at once while her husband appeared to be the very soul of amiable leisure. The impression of many outsiders like myself and the conviction of Micronesian feminist activists is that women today are doing more than their fair share of the family chores.

This was not always the case. To judge from what one reads and hears about the past, there would seem to have been a fairer distribution of household chores along gender lines. Women then, as now, would have borne the main responsibility for caring for the children, cleaning the house, and doing much of the food preparation. Women's work around the house thirty or forty years ago was probably not much different than it is today. But men's work is an entirely different matter. Men were called on to take a much heavier share of the subsistence-level work load, and so there would have been a better balance in the gender distribution. (This does not take account of men's role in the government or business workplace, but I will explore this later.)

Consider the changes in men's work in Majuro as an illustration. Adult males on Majuro, as described by the anthropologist Alexander Spoehr in the late 1940s, were expected to do all the heavy labor such as house building and canoe making.[9] In those days before the advent of local construction companies, families ordinarily built their own houses just as they would usually provide the labor for building or repairing the canoe (or increasingly, as time went on, the motorboat made from plywood). Men also did any woodworking that might be required, cared for the boats, and spun the coconut husk fiber into rope. Men were also the ones who collected the food, although it was turned over to women for preparation. Marshallese men, like males on other islands, not only did the fishing—with a few minor exceptions—but did the gardening as well. They collected breadfruit, coconuts, and bananas and tended the taro patches that provided another of the staple foods.

The male work load that Spoehr describes on Majuro has changed considerably since that time, in great measure because of urbanization and wage labor, although his description might prove fairly accurate for the outer atolls even today. Men still are expected to do the heavy work nowadays, but no canoes are being made since motorboats or fiberglass whalers are ordered from abroad and house construction is often contracted out to building companies. Rope is bought, no longer made. Males continue to do fishing, in some cases as a pastime rather than a means of feeding the family, but much of the fish consumed today is purchased in tins. Work in the taro patches has ceased, at least on Majuro and Ebeye, and little other food is grown in these places. The male domestic work load, therefore, has been greatly reduced from what it was some years before.

Kosrae, as described by Scott Wilson in the early 1960s, offers another example of the way in which male work roles have changed.[10] One of the most time-consuming male activities at that time was clearing land

and putting in drainage ditches, usually in conjunction with planting or food gathering. Men were responsible for planting crops, including yams and taro, and tending the fruit trees. They also dug the pits used for preserving breadfruit during the off-season and lined these pits with stone. In addition, they raised pigs, did line fishing and trolling, caught coconut crabs and other edible animals, and made copra.

Today Kosraean men, especially those who do not have wage labor, continue to clear their land, but they do much less planting than in the 1960s. They no longer make pits for preserved breadfruit, nor do they make copra nowadays. Like men on other islands, they still fish with a passion and sometimes collect coconut crabs and other marine creatures. They engage in no more house building or canoe building today than the men of Majuro do. Meanwhile, the women of Kosrae continue to cook, keep the household clean, do laundry, and care for the children.

In the days when food was regularly cooked in earth ovens, the male work load seems to have been even heavier than in the early postwar years. To maintain the oven, to light the fire and keep it burning, and to carry the food in and out of the oven was fatiguing work that could not easily be turned over to women. Hence, much of the labor of cooking food in addition to collecting it fell to men rather than women. The iron pots that were a standard trade item in the nineteenth century eventually revolutionized the Micronesian "kitchen" by reducing the time and labor spent in cooking food, but they also occasioned an important shift in the division of labor. As cooking became progressively lighter and easier, it was assigned almost exclusively to women.

Over the years the list of women's roles has gradually become slightly longer, even as the list of men's roles has shortened. A more contemporary illustration can be found in Chuuk as breadfruit gave way in some families to rice. Most of the work associated with the production of breadfruit has always been done by men. They picked the breadfruit, left it for the women to peel and boil, and spent hours pounding it after it was cooked. Although a great many Chuukese families continue to eat breadfruit when it is in season, fewer seem to depend on preserved breadfruit when the crop is out of season; and younger people increasingly seem to prefer rice. With the growing reliance on rice as the main starch in the diet, Chuukese men are being freed from one of their most time-consuming tasks. With rice preparation assigned to women, yet another shift in gender work roles is contributing to the increase of women's roles in food preparation and the decline in men's.[11]

Male work: Casting a throw net on Kosrae. (TT Archives, University of Hawai'i Library)

Even on the raised outer island of Fais such changes have occurred, although for slightly different reasons. Rubinstein noted that even in the early 1970s gardening, which had always been a male task, was being taken over by the women of the island. So many young men had gone off to school or to find wage labor abroad that women were compelled to start their own gardens.[12]

Women's position in the past is often portrayed as enviable. Their life on Pohnpei, as reflected in the writings of Andrew Cheyne, an English trader who lived there for a year or two in the 1840s, was far from over-burdened. "Much respect and attention is awarded to females at this island, and they are not made to do any work but what rightfully belongs to them. All the outdoor labor is chiefly performed by men, whose employment consists in building houses and canoes, planting yams, fishing and bringing home the produce of their plantations, also planting kava and cooking."[13]

Throughout the years, men may have been the main beneficiaries of the changes in diet and food production as these affected work roles, but they did not get off free in the exchange. Most of the changes in food production could have never occurred had it not been for the salaried jobs that provided the wherewithal for families to purchase store-bought food. In 1960 a mere 3,045 persons on the Caroline and Marshall islands had full-time paying jobs. Thirty years later, in 1990, those with wage employment numbered 21,884.[14] In 1960 only 9.6 percent of the labor force (all persons between the ages of fifteen and fifty-nine inclusive) had full-time employment, while in 1990 about 27 percent had jobs. The percentage of the labor force working for money in 1990, therefore, was three times what it had been thirty years before.

Most of the jobs went to men, as one might expect, 70 percent of them in the Federated States of Micronesia, and 55 percent in Palau, as recent censuses show.[15] While advocates of gender equality might see this as an indefensible bias in favor of males, the predominance of men in the salaried work force made good sense if wage labor is understood as a substitute for the "food production" role that men had always enjoyed but that had been eroding over the years as women's responsibilities increased. Even during this period of change, the male remained the "provider of food" even as the female saw an expansion in her own role of "preparer of food" —to use the terms commonly employed of the gender role division on at least one outer island.[16]

Even those men who don't work probably spend more of their time hosting visitors and attending meetings than they ever would have before. Both visitors and meetings have swelled in number, thanks to modern transportation and the demands of today's bureaucratic government at all levels. These tasks, as well as attending to other political affairs, were very much a part of men's age-old responsibility in the community. In sipping coffee with me, a visitor to his island, the deacon who welcomed me was being as faithful to his culturally defined obligations as his wife was to hers.

Notwithstanding some minor adjustments, the role division between males and females in the household remains essentially what it was thirty or forty years ago—men are the providers and women the preparers, men the collectors and women the cooks. Because the nature of the resources men draw on to provide for their families has changed so much, men are far less visible contributors to the household than women are today. Men are obliged to spend less time in the traditional food-gathering activities now that so much of their foodstuff is purchased rather than grown. Women, for their part, carry out their conventional household tasks— cleaning, washing clothes, caring for the children, and cooking—much as they always did. At bottom, the realignment of gender work roles in the household may be more apparent than real.

The Cultural Roots of Women's Power

The members of women's church groups gathered at a downtown hotel on Weno, Chuuk, to begin their demonstration. Catholic and Protestant, they arrived from all parts of the island, many carrying signs that proclaimed: "Alcohol causes harm to many people" and "Alcohol destroys marriages." Then the women began their march to the legislature building, two hundred strong, waving signs and singing hymns. A fire engine carrying more women followed, its siren emitting occasional blasts, as the vehicle lumbered along the road. On their arrival at the legislature building, the women milled around outside, lifting their signs so that the legislators inside the building could read them. The lone female member of the legislature called for a recess so that her colleagues could speak to the protestors.

The women camped outside on the lawn in front of the building every day for nearly a week before the Speaker invited a few of their leaders to present their case to the legislature. They presented petitions against alcohol that had been circulated throughout the state. Quietly but firmly they stated their opposition to any attempt that the legislature might make to rescind the ban against alcohol that was carried out by plebiscite on the island the year before. As one woman presented their position, "We were carrying out the wishes of the people and encouraging the senators to give the people peace and not destruction."[17]

These Chuukese women might be thought to be adopting a modern feminist mindset and strategies, but the women themselves would have explained it differently. They saw themselves as drawing on a rich cultural tradition of women's intervention in community affairs.[18] The Chuukese women who marched on their legislature in 1979 were not the first or the last women to demonstrate publicly. On Pohnpei in late 1971 nearly two hundred women, most of them from Kosrae and Kapingamarangi, took to the streets in an effort to keep the bars closed when the legislature considered reopening them.[19] Through most of the 1980s in Palau, a group of women waged a public campaign against changing the Palau Constitution so as to permit the transport or storage of nuclear materials there.[20] Appearances to the contrary, Micronesian women have always been a vital force in arriving at decisions in the family and community. If this long tradition often goes unrecognized, this is probably because of the inadequacy of the models brought to the analysis of women's roles in the islands.

"I was brought up to feel important as a woman," a Chuukese friend of mine once flatly stated. She was expressing a truth that usually eludes the grasp of newcomers to Micronesia, who are shocked to see island women accept what they judge to be a subservient role to men.[21] Some Micronesian women themselves, as they come to accept Western contemporary norms for gender equity, are beginning to wonder whether women in Micronesia were ever more than household drudges. Yet, women's roles in the past extended far beyond child rearing, housekeeping, laundry, and food preparation. As is true of nearly everything else women do, their authority is understated to the point where it can easily be missed. Moreover, it is almost always exercised indirectly, through a male group. Still, the authority is real. Nearly everywhere in Micronesia, women appear to have held at least four major roles, all of which were critical to the functioning of their society. They were guardians of the land, keepers of the peace, counselors on family and community matters, and producers of cultural valuables.[22]

In many places, women have always been regarded as the custodians

of the land. In Chuuk, for instance, the senior women in the lineage decided who was to have the use of what piece of lineage land. Their authority was even greater when there was question of alienating a piece of land altogether. If a male member of the lineage wished to give away a piece of the lineage land to someone—in restitution for an injury that his son inflicted on another boy in a knife fight, for example—he would be obliged to get the approval of his sisters before giving away the piece of land. This would remain so even if he held the position of lineage chief.[23] In effect, the women of the lineage held veto rights over the chief's power to dispose of family land. Women in the outer islands of Yap enjoyed similar rights over the disposition of the land. In Yap the sister of the head of an estate and her descendants retained an interest in the land for several generations. During this period she and her children continued to exercise protective rights over the land, even to the point of disinheriting the man's children if they should neglect their father.[24]

Much of this authority derives from the matrilineal nature of these island societies. Just as women had the responsibility for propagating the lineage and carrying on its name, they were also entrusted with the guardianship of the land that fed the lineage. (Land and people were closely linked.) Women were expected to pass this land on from generation to generation through their daughters.

Today we are witnessing a change in what was once the strong check women held over the disposal of the land. As land tenure practices change, women's role in protecting the land is eroding. A growing number of land parcels today are owned by individuals rather than kin groups such as lineages, so the father of the family has unrestricted power to dispose of it in any way he wishes. Even lineage-owned land today is sometimes being passed down from father to son contrary to the old land inheritance practices, while the wishes of female kin, who would normally have had a large hand in the decision, are being disregarded.

A second important role of women was as peacemakers. In the event of a dispute or even a brawl, women were expected to reestablish the peace. One Yapese woman tells of a fight that once broke out between two cousins in the men's house on one of the outer islands of Yap. Other men came running out to the men's house to break up the fight but were not able to do so. Instead, the commotion grew, with more and more men becoming involved, as the fracas moved into the heart of the village. Finally, when one of the older women from the clan appeared, the fighting stopped instantly. The men dusted themselves off, rearranged their loincloths, and when asked what had been going on, began laughing and stoutly denying that anything at all was wrong. Her presence was enough to restore peace in the community.[25]

Women in the Yap outer islands bore the responsibility for keeping good order in their communities. Whenever there was some problem, or when the men had been neglecting their duties because of long and frequent *tuba* drinking sessions, the women would gather at the men's house or the chief's home and hang up lavalavas. This was a way of signaling that they had enough and wanted good order restored. Generally, the chief would soon afterwards summon a meeting and tell his people that certain changes would thenceforth be put into effect. Usually this entailed a ban on *tuba* drinking for a period of several weeks or even a few months.[26]

It is not only in the outer islands of Yap that women assumed this role. In Chuuk women have always been peacemakers. They are expected to protect their male kinsmen from injury—to pull them out of harm's way when they are drunk and are liable to hurt someone or be hurt—even if such a woman runs the risk of receiving blows from the one she is protecting. Marshallese women, like those in the outer islands of Yap, could end a fight by simply presenting themselves and demanding that the trouble cease.[27]

Third, women were looked to for their general advice on family and community matters. In Palau, where the influence of women was as strong as anywhere in Micronesia, they chose the men who would become lineage leaders and would represent them on the village council or even serve as village chief. They also had the authority to remove someone with whom they were dissatisfied.[28] In the Marshalls, the male head of a lineage might not make a decision independently of his sisters; to do so would invite a unilateral revocation of the decision by the women.[29]

While women played a vital role in the community, their decision making was never institutionalized to the same degree that men's was, nor were women's institutions represented by visible structures as men's were. In Palau, as Alkire points out, "each village had a women's council and women's clubs organized along lines nearly identical to those of men. The women's organizations could have great influence in village affairs, but women generally lack the impressive buildings for their organizations."[30] The position of women in the community and their influence on community events might have been similar to the "shadow government" or "kitchen cabinet" that existed in many parts of Polynesia (notably Tonga and Samoa). In many villages women met as a group at times and discussed important family or community concerns, but their advice was brought to the formal decision makers outside the council house or meeting hall. Women's power blocs, lacking any real institutional form and embodied in no building, had a will-of-the-wisp quality that often seems unreal to those today who look for surer structural signs of power.

Finally, women had a special productive role in the community as weavers and makers of cultural valuables. In the outer islands of Yap, for instance, women plaited pandanus mats and wove lavalavas out of hibiscus or banana fiber. These were goods that were in demand for weddings, funerals, and ritual exchange of gifts on the island, as well as for the purchase of handcrafted canoes. Rubinstein writes of the fine-quality work that went into producing the "extraordinarily detailed, museum-quality tapestries" used as burial shrouds, the weaving of which may have required three hundred hours of labor or one year to complete.[31] In addition to these ceremonial items, women in the outer islands of Yap also manufactured ornaments—belts made of seashell or coconut shell, bracelets, and decorative beads—all of which had prestige value. On Pohnpei, women played a large role in the manufacture of embroidered handkerchiefs and skirts as well as other prestige items that were used for exchange purposes in the community.[32] Marshallese women, who never had the loom, plaited fine pandanus mats that had ceremonial functions in addition to their household use.[33]

Women provided these valuables for the family networks, which in turn conducted cultural exchanges with others in the community at appropriate times. To expect women to maintain control over their own produce was unreasonable in any traditional Pacific society, since women were simply part of a kin-based team that always included their brothers. It was to them that women's products went for distribution.[34]

These four major roles of women all extend well beyond the usual household roles that are identified as "women's work." In such ways women everywhere in Micronesia were called on to make a substantial although hidden contribution to their extended family and community. Since to a large extent women's roles—as custodians of the land, peace-keepers, and shadow government—are embedded in the lineage, there has naturally been some attrition in these roles as the extended family weakens in force. As a result of the breakup of the lineage and the emergence of the household with its nuclear family, Micronesian women will continue to lose some of their most important traditional roles. Worse still, the customary roles of women will go unrecognized today by people who would like to reduce these roles to that of the household drudge and nothing more.

Yet the change in women's roles hasn't been entirely a loss. In recent years women seem to have been asserting their traditional community roles in strikingly new ways. The Chuukese women of the Protestant church group who marched through Weno on behalf of prohibition of alcohol in the late 1970s were only fulfilling their task of intervening to keep the peace, as some of them explained their public stand.[35] The Palauan women who took the lead in the antinuclear movement in the 1980s and the Pohnpeian women who marched in protest through the streets of Kolonia in 1971 could claim the same thing.

Women today are also contributing to the community through their involvement in civic and church organizations. Indeed, women have a near monopoly on such organizations at the village level. These organizations, which are often affiliated with the local church, can trace their origin to the informal community associations that women once possessed in many parts of Micronesia. Today they are now largely engaged in entertaining visitors, keeping the village or church clean, and doing

Three early Micronesian women leaders departing in 1961 for a training program in Samoa: Anastasia Ramarui, Mary Lanwi, and Rose Makwelung. (Library of Congress of FSM)

volunteer services in the community. But they also represent a resource that could be directed toward community education and other work that better draws on their potential and is more in keeping with their vital roles of an earlier day.

The Wave of the Future?

Norlihnda turned from the stack of purchase orders on her desk to glance at the clock. It was clear that she was going to have to work late again today to finish the financial statement before the department meeting tomorrow morning at ten. She picked up the phone and called her husband at the EPA office. He would already have picked up their two children from school, dropped them at the house, and returned to his office to finish the work day. She was going to have to ask him to prepare dinner for the children and to take the trash out to the dump. The report took a little longer than Norlihnda thought. It was eight o'clock when she finally pulled the car into the driveway of their two-story stucco house just out of town. When she walked in, she found the house unusually hushed: no blare from the television, no boisterous shouting from the kids at play.

There on the sofa in the living room sat her husband Jason reading bed-
time stories to the two girls, all of them so engrossed in what they were
doing that there was barely a welcome for mom. In the kitchen, she
found an empty plate on the table and three pans simmering on the stove
with what remained of the family dinner. The trash had been taken out,
she noticed, and the dishes washed. With a sigh of gratitude she sat down
to her late meal.

This domestic vignette might be a scene from a contemporary American
television show, with its cozy family aura and its emphasis on partner-
ship in performing household chores. In truth, however, scenes like this are
being played out ever more frequently in some parts of Micronesia today.
Such families as Norlihnda's can be found in the towns and among the
enclaves of island emigrants abroad. Young couples, with both husband
and wife working for a living, are adopting new rules for dividing the
responsibilities in the household. Like the husband in the opening scene,
some of these men are beginning to take over chores that would have been
regarded as women's work in the past. They are cooking meals, washing
the dishes afterwards, cleaning the house, taking care of the children, and
even doing laundry—something that has always been regarded as quintessential female work. These young families have been guided by pragmatic rather than customary norms in distributing the work responsibilities in the household between husband and wife.

One Pohnpeian man who works at a government office nearly always
reaches home before his wife, who is a senior employee in a large private
business. By the time she arrives home, he has prepared dinner, fed the
children, thrown their clothes in the washing machine, cleaned up the
dirty dishes, and helped the children with their homework. Another man
whose wife has a full-time job does not go quite as far as this, but he often
cleans the dishes and tidies up the house when his wife is occupied with
other work. In the towns of Micronesia it is becoming more common each
year to see men carrying small children in their arms, even in those places
where this was simply not done in the past.[36]

The number of families that have adopted these new pragmatic
norms for division of labor is still quite small, but they may be modeling
changes that will eventually be commonly accepted in the islands. If so,
they can be said to represent the wave of the future. The families that are
pioneering these new arrangements are usually young, with both spouses
Western-educated and both engaged in full-time employment. In other

words, the couple has not only been exposed to the theory and observed the practice of Western gender equality, but because they are both working outside the home, there is good reason for them to attempt to apply these new norms. One other condition for such social experimentation is freedom from cultural pressure to conform to the old rules. Thus, nearly all these families live beyond the day-to-day reach of their extended families; they have a house of their own, usually in or near town, in which they live by themselves, removed from the interference of older relatives. This last condition is a crucially important one. Even in the most progressive households, the presence of an older, more traditional-minded house guest will usually shame the young family into reverting to former norms for apportioning work.

Another social phenomenon that, like the two-salary young family, reflects the changes in women's roles in Micronesia is the increase in the number of single mothers living in their own homes. Many women who were once married but whose marriages have broken up continue to live in a house of their own in town, sometimes with their children. Often there are no other relatives living with them, although some of their kin may stay for a time when they come to town.

Even in the recent past, it would have been unthinkable for women with children to attempt to raise them without a family of some kind to offer support. Normally, women whose marriages had ended owing to the death of their spouse or divorce were reabsorbed into their own lineage groups, where they could find the stability, material sustenance, and child-rearing help needed to provide for their children. (Indeed, not so long ago on some islands—like Chuuk and the outer islands of Yap—they would never have left their family in the first place.) Although a return to their own lineage remains a possibility for such women even today, more and more are choosing to strike out on their own. In doing so, they are forgoing the benefits that women would have sought in the past in order to pursue their careers and their independence. Self-reliant single mothers of this type are especially numerous in Palau and Pohnpei, although some can be found in nearly every part of Micronesia.

Single mothers living on their own support themselves, run their own households, and maintain a greater measure of independence than is usually afforded to women. Yet, even this autonomy has its limits. These women, while they are mistresses of their own households, still participate in the customary exchanges through their brothers with their own kin group. They have loosened the reins to permit themselves an unusual degree of freedom but have not by any means thrown off all traditional obligations.

These families are at the very frontier of social change. Yet, the conditions that made it possible for them to advance so far have affected the lives of a much larger group of Micronesians. Until society had opened up sufficiently to permit women to aspire to better jobs, single-mother families and two-income families with a new division of labor would have been impossible. The percentage of females in the work force of the Federated States of Micronesia has nearly doubled between 1960 and 1994, growing from 17 percent to 30 percent of the total.[37] In the Chuuk that I remember during the early 1970s, there were relatively few women teaching in the schools and almost no females in senior positions in government offices. Today the number of employed women, although still far smaller than males, is growing. There are a few women today who have attained senior positions in government departments, and there are some who own or manage businesses.

By and large the distinction between gender roles that is so deeply ingrained in Pacific cultures is honored even today, but there are many little breaches in the wall that separates male from female. The elimination of all distinctions in male and female aspirations, in the name of the gender equality that is so earnestly promoted by social reformers, is not likely to occur soon, but there have been surprising gains in unexpected quarters. There have been no political upheavals on behalf of women's rights, no great rush to elect women legislators, but a number of alternative lifestyles offer models for future directions. To assess women's progress narrowly by such measures as the positions of elected leadership women hold can obscure the substantial gains that they have made in the last thirty or forty years.

4 Birth

Returning to the Nest to Hatch

Albertina climbed the boarding ramp unsteadily, but her younger sister grasped her tightly around the waist as they reached the door of the 727 jet. Albertina sighed and asked her sister to look at the boarding passes to find out where they were sitting. Her sister, Casmira, was only fifteen but had learned enough English at the private high school she attended to speak with confidence to the flight attendants. She spoke briefly and in a low voice to one of the stewardesses. "We're sitting in row 25," she told her sister, but Albertina only half heard what she said. She was struggling with her carry-on bag as she made her way down the aisle, clutching at the seat backs to steady herself. Finally she plopped into a seat, weary from the effort she had made since leaving the departure area. She was seven and a half months pregnant and tired easily, but she was relieved at the thought that she would be delivering her baby on Guam. The hospital is clean and safe, her husband's family, who had been living on Guam for three years now, had assured her. Besides, their child would be eligible for welfare benefits because it would be born on American soil.

Her mother had objected strongly when Albertina told her that she would be going to Guam for the delivery, noting how important it used to be for women to return to their own families for help in their delivery. That was when Albertina agreed to take her younger sister with her to Guam. They would both stay with her husband's relatives until she was admitted to the hospital for the delivery. After the baby was born, she would return to their house and stay until she was strong enough to travel back home.

Albertina represents a new and growing group of Micronesian women who, late in pregnancy, are now flying off to Guam or Hawai'i to deliver their children.[1] These women are most often from Chuuk, but they might also be from Pohnpei or Yap or Palau; those from the Marshalls who choose to leave home for childbirth will usually head off to Hawai'i. Their motivation is the same as Albertina's: the superior health care that Guam and Hawai'i offer, and the bonus of American citizenship for their children along with the entitlement to welfare programs that flows from it.

Albertina's mother had good reason to be shocked at her daughter's decision to leave her own island to deliver in a distant place. Formerly, Micronesian women headed in the opposite direction when childbirth loomed near. As they advanced in pregnancy, they returned to their own nests in the confidence that they would receive the best care from their own blood relations. In Palau, Kosrae, and Pohnpei, where a woman ordinarily follows her husband to live on his estate, she would return to her mother's household several months before she was due and remain there under the care of the family for some months after she had delivered.[2] Sometimes the woman's husband might accompany her. In the event that it was impossible for them to return to their own home, young mothers would send for their own relatives to stay with them during childbirth. Women in Chuuk and the Marshalls who happened to be living on their husbands' land observed the same practice.[3]

Not so long ago, islanders followed an old custom of burying the placenta and umbilical cord of a newborn child on the land of the child's mother.[4] The umbilical cord, as the link between the mother and her child, was more than a mark of the emotional attachment between parent and offspring; it was symbolic of the enduring lineage ties that would forever bind the child to his or her matrilineal relations. The same tie bound the lineage to the land on which they dwelt. Moving to her land to deliver was an affirmation of these ties by the expectant mother.

Childbirth, although eagerly anticipated, was a fearful trial in the past. With the high mortality rate of infants, the survival of the newborn child was always in doubt, and the fate of the mother was not much more secure. Childbirth was always looked upon as an especially dangerous time for Micronesian women. Many of the illnesses and hardships that befell infants and mothers were attributed to spirits, who generally seemed to prey on weaker human beings. There were whole classes of malevolent spirits that victimized babies before and after birth as well as the mothers who bore them. The people of Chuuk, for instance, were taught to fear the class of spirits, called *chénúkken,* who frequented the shallows and reef flats. They also kept a sharp eye out for various named spirits such as

Niyang, Siemwaw, and Soumwerikes, who were thought to do special harm to infants and fetuses. Mothers on Woleai and Lamotrek lived in dread of a class of spirit-borne diseases known as *yalu* that afflicted infants.[5] Pohnpeian women feared the spirits of the sea but especially those that dwelt in the mangrove swamps. An anthropologist writes of Majuro in the late 1940s that because "pregnant women are thought to be particularly susceptible to illness caused by ghosts of the dead, they are careful to keep a lantern burning at night and a female relative usually sleeps close by in the same room."[6]

Childbirth was too harrowing an event for women to face alone. By "alone" Micronesian cultures meant without the support of their closest blood kin, especially their mothers or older sisters. Hence, Micronesian women generally left their husbands and secluded themselves in the comfortable circle of close blood relatives to endure the trials of childbirth. Their kinfolk fed them what they wanted, massaged them when appropriate, attended to their bodily needs, and provided the emotional support that the women could not have expected to receive from their husbands' kin. However close their relationship with their husbands, these women relied on their own kin at the most critical junctures of life, especially when their well-being and the survival of a child was at stake.

Even when the pregnant woman did not return to her own estate for prenatal care and delivery, her closest female relatives still provided the nursing and support she required. Although a pregnant woman from Ulithi, during Lessa's fieldwork there in 1949, normally went to the menstrual house to deliver, her own mother played the main role in caring for her before, during, and after her delivery.[7] Only in Yap, where women were also once confined to menstrual houses during delivery, did they customarily give birth without their own relatives to assist them; there they had the services of a specially designated midwife.[8] The government-trained midwives who were introduced to Micronesia during the late 1940s and early 1950s did not effect a change in this practice. Although they attended at most births taking place in the village, they did not replace the blood relatives of the pregnant woman as her chief caregivers.

Gradually over the years this custom has been weakening, although it is far from extinct today. When the Chuukese graduate of a Catholic high school married in the mid-1960s, he refused to allow his wife to return to her family on the grounds that her place, according to church teaching, was with him and their future children.[9] Other men, following his lead, presumably adopted the same position, while still others may have resisted the old practice for a variety of reasons. By the early 1970s, exceptions to the old practice had become fairly frequent, even though the great majority of women on most islands continued to return to their own households for childbirth.

The mobility and urbanization resulting from the new employment opportunities and the increased wealth of the 1970s undoubtedly weakened this practice. Micronesians who followed the jobs and moved from the outlying islands to the district centers or to Saipan, the site of the Trust Territory headquarters, may have learned not to depend so heavily on their families. In any case, they were usually in no position to send their wives back to their own households for childbirth. Furthermore, medical facilities in their new work sites were usually far superior to what would have been available to them at home. Today the great majority of all deliveries, except in the most distant villages and on the most remote atolls, take place in the hospital.

Even today, however, most Micronesian women derive comfort from having their own blood relatives with them during childbirth and try to arrange for this if they can conveniently do so. Yet, because the dangers of childbirth have diminished, they do not feel compelled to return to the nest to seek their assistance when the trip cannot be easily made. Increasingly today, women are looking for a safe medical facility to give birth in. Many are choosing Guam for this reason, to say nothing of other considerations—notably the benefits that might be gained from delivery on American soil and the guarantees of protection and future welfare benefits.[10] They may take a female relative with them, but this is often at the insistence of their mother or aunts more than because of their own felt need for such persons. Albertinas are multiplying by the year.

The growing number of Albertinas may reflect such pragmatic considerations as the quality of health care abroad and the alluring benefits of childbirth on American soil, but it also suggests how much weaker ties with lineage mates and the land have grown over the years. Unlike her mother and grandmother, Albertina will not be burying her child's umbilical cord in the plot of land from which she and her kin would once have derived their identity.

The Breast or the Bottle?

I stopped by the pediatrics ward for a few minutes on my pastoral visit to the hospital. It was the last stop on my hour-and-a-half tour. The nurse who was accompanying me pointed out a particularly wasted looking infant who must have been under two months old. The child's eyes were hollow and his belly distended in the classic sign of infant malnutrition. The mother was sitting on the floor, a towel wrapped around her head, looking dazed and mournful. I talked with her briefly, then went over and blessed her child. As we moved out of the room and headed down the corridor, I turned to the nurse and asked her what she thought of the case. She said that the child was suffering from severe kwashiorkor malnutrition. Perhaps he might recover, but more likely he wouldn't. "Bottle fed," the nurse explained, "but the folks taking care of him didn't seem to know what they were doing. They kept cutting down the amount of powdered milk to stretch the life of the can, but instead they practically killed the kid. Same story all the time. The older relatives want to help but don't know how to use that stuff, and they end up starving the kid."

Perhaps because the life of a newborn child was considered so fragile, many Micronesian societies prolonged the breast-feeding of children. In the postwar Marshalls, Spoehr reported that most infants were breast-fed for about a year, but he cites a book written by a Catholic missionary to the Marshalls forty years earlier to argue that in an earlier era breast-feeding was normally extended for as long as two or three years.[11] Yapese say that ideally a child is breast-fed for three years, although they admit that the period is much shorter today.[12] Accounts for other islands suggest that breast-feeding practices there were similar to what Spoehr describes for the Marshalls. An anthropologist studying child care in Chuuk in the late 1940s reported that "practically all children were weaned by the age of two, many when they were slightly over one."[13]

At one time, in all the island cultures of Micronesia, there was a strong taboo on sexual intercourse for a nursing mother. The prohibition on sexual relations, which began early in pregnancy, extended throughout the period of lactation. Sexual intercourse was believed to contaminate the breast milk and to place the breast-feeding infant in grave danger of contracting a serious illness. Spoehr tells of an instance occurring on Majuro in the late 1940s in which a husband resumed sex with his wife after only six months. Although the woman soon became pregnant, the infant she had been nursing died; the death was attributed to her violation of the ban on sexual intercourse while nursing.[14] Even today the fear of bringing on sickness in an infant by resuming sexual relations too soon is real to many, and older women still remind new mothers of this risk. A physician told me that within the past year he had an educated young woman tell him that she can look at an infant and tell from the state of its health whether the mother is having sex with her husband.

If one is to believe the popular sayings, the period of continence enjoined on the husband and wife was extraordinarily long. In Ulithi in the early postwar years, Lessa was told that parents were not supposed to resume sexual intercourse until their child was able to "walk on its own and duck its head under the water."[15] In other places, the end of the period of sexual abstinence was linked to other tests of maturity in the child: the ability to jump over a small fire, for instance. These adages seem to suggest that sexual relations could be safely resumed when the child reached the age of about three. Yet, Lessa observes that his study of the spacing of children in the island's birth records in Ulithi clearly show that this injunction was not observed in practice.[16] However long this period might have lasted in actual practice, the husband who was denied sexual relations with his wife had other sexual outlets. In a much earlier age, the men's house in Yap and Palau offered a selection of young women with whom he was free to take his pleasure. In other islands, the husband had sexual access to other women, notably his wife's sisters.

All this has practical importance insofar as it may have limited the birth rate in the past. The long periods of sexual abstinence enjoined after childbirth would have served to provide longer intervals between births in the family, thus resulting in a system of natural family planning. High infant mortality rates would have further helped reduce the average family size. In fact, the birth rates during the prewar years were somewhat lower than the birth rates during the 1960s and 1970s. Chuuk's birth rate for 1925–1935, for instance, was 27 births per thousand, while during the period 1958–1980 it averaged out at 36.[17] This increase, however, may be explained in other ways than by the disregard for continence after childbirth. It is quite possible that these taboos were no better observed than the society's injunctions against extramarital sexual relations. The rapid growth rate that nearly all islands showed since World War II may be more properly credited to the improvement in health care, leading to a great drop in infant mortality, and a reversal of the infertility once caused by sexually transmitted diseases.

Just as postwar change has brought about vast improvements in the survival rates and general health of children, it has had a negative effect in some respects. Breast-feeding, once highly valued by Microne-

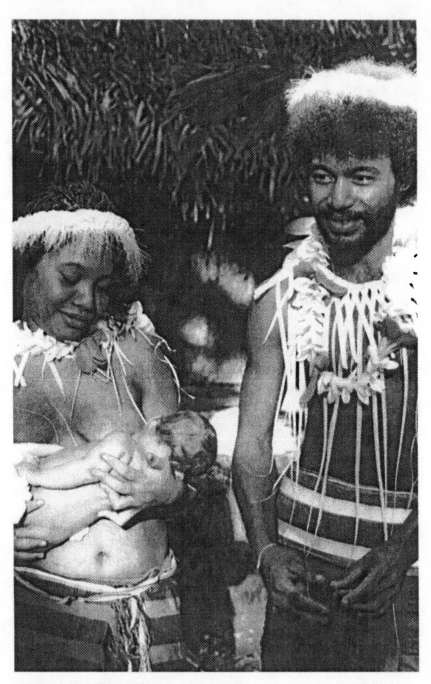

A Ulithian couple and their child. (Micronesian Seminar)

sian women, declined in many of the islands to the point that health services offices felt obliged to mount a U.S. federally funded initiative to promote the practice by advertising its relevance to good health. One study conducted in a village near the port town in Chuuk revealed that breast-feeding had steadily declined since World War II—from two-thirds of all infants after the war, to half by about 1960, to one-fourth by the early 1970s.[18] The fall-off in breast-feeding could be explained in part by the fact that bottle-feeding was looked upon as prestigious since it was introduced from the United States. It also was a badge of distinction in that it showed that the family was well-off enough to afford tinned milk. In addition, more women were busy with jobs during those days of rapid increase in government employment, and they sometimes had to turn their infants over to relatives, some of whom were unable to serve as wet nurses. Finally, bottle-feeding allowed young educated women who may have been too timid to disregard the old prohibition on sexual relations to provide for their infants while also resuming ordinary marital intimacy with their husbands.

The caretakers to whom infants were entrusted, often the child's grandparents, were usually inexperienced in bottle-feeding. Needless to say, they rarely sterilized bottles and nipples, seldom boiled the water used for the formula, and neglected other sanitary practices that modern societies take for granted. Even worse, some were found cutting down on the formula to make it last longer and inadvertently denying infants nutrition they badly needed. Sometimes, this practice only became obvious after the child suffered the onset of serious malnutrition, as in my experience in the hospital described at the beginning of this section.[19]

The switch over to bottle-feeding has been at least partially reversed since the early 1990s. "Breast is Best" signs and bumper stickers are widely displayed these days, and banners hung over the main streets of town proclaim annual breast-feeding week. Working mothers who twenty years ago would have regarded it as primitive to breast-feed their infants now do so proudly.

Yet, the problems with infant malnutrition, not all of which are attributable to bottle-feeding, persist. Health services administrators have recognized for some time now that the set of health problems that afflict infants now are changing. Infectious and respiratory diseases are less common, while malnutrition and other health problems stemming from a change in diet are increasing. During the 1980s malnutrition surfaced as a major problem in the Marshalls, where it was recorded as the number

Children on Yap. (TT Archives, University of Hawai'i Library)

one cause of death for children under five.[20] Among the deaths attributed to malnutrition was that of a child who was exclusively fed soft drinks and cheese curls by caretakers.[21] The caretakers of such children are usually older relatives, often grandparents, or young mothers, many in their middle teens, who are ignorant of the nutritional values of store-bought foods. Vitamin A deficiency is a serious problem in Chuuk, less so in Pohnpei and Kosrae, owing to the shortage of green, leafy vegetables, ripe mangoes, and other yellow, pulpy foods in the diet. One-quarter of all the deaths of children in Chuuk are due, directly or indirectly, to malnutrition.[22]

Despite the serious problem with child malnutrition that is evident on many islands today, infant mortality rates everywhere have dropped sharply from what they were forty years ago. With more children surviving, parents have begun to show an interest in limiting the size of their families. This change is reflected in the declining birth rates in nearly every island group and the drop in the number of births to the average woman during her child-bearing years.[23] Even accounting for emigration, the high birth rates that were characteristic of Micronesia up to the 1980s have fallen. With health conditions today, it no longer takes five live births to produce three mature children; three live births will suffice.

Celebrating the Survival of the Child

There was barely room to maneuver around the tables and the overflow crowd at the party. People were standing and sitting everywhere, most often in small circles with a glass or a can in their hand, but they spilled out onto the sidewalk and down the street. Some were even eating on the backs of parked pickup trucks. On the ocean side of the house lot was a string of tables about thirty feet long laden with food of every kind: huge mounds of rice and breadfruit, sweet potatoes, potato salad, fried lumpia, sushi, sashimi, three or four kinds of baked and grilled fish, Vienna sausages, hot dogs slathered with ketchup, dishes of mixed chicken and vegetables, fried chicken, cole slaw, a half dozen kinds of salad, and perhaps a six-foot length of table space covered with cakes and pies. At the very end of the tables lay the pièce de résistance—two roasted pigs, apples in their mouths, with the crisp skin cut away and lying in a pile on the corner of the table. Three more pigs were being held in reserve somewhere but would be put out as needed. Near the house was a crowded corner that looked like the bar. Cokes, soft drinks, cans of beer, glasses of something or other were all being passed out by the bartender. The conversation was loud, as it had to be to prevail over the noise of the five-man combo playing Marshallese songs. Off near the doorway of the house, at the very fringe of the crowd, was a woman holding a very young child. This was the reason for all the fuss, a little girl celebrating her first birthday.

The Marshalls was one of several Pacific societies that, while bypassing the celebration of the birth of a child, celebrated the first birthday as a major event in the community. In the past the mortality of infants was so high that it wasn't until after a year had passed that the family could be reasonably confident that the child was out of danger. Nearly one-fourth of all live-born infants on one island in Chuuk during the 1940s died before the age of one.[24]

The newborn child was at one time regarded as a nonperson in the island community. In Chuuk the child was not given a name until he or she had shown enough strength and health to give the family reason to believe the child would survive. The anthropologist who recorded this piece of information went on to conclude that "there is a feeling that until the child is strong enough to survive he does not really attain the status of an individual in the family or community."[25] By way of illustration he pointed out that if an infant died in Chuuk around 1950, the body would have been disposed of without ceremony and with no mourning.

The first birthday party for a child in the Marshalls, Kosrae, and Chuuk could be viewed as a "survival party" thrown by the family—a deferred acknowledgment that a new member, tested by the trials of infancy, has been added to its ranks. Yap had something similar through the 1950s. When a child was old enough to walk, both sides of the family gathered to celebrate his or her passage from infancy to childhood. The child was given a first haircut, with the hair from infancy shorn off to mark the departure of the spirit who was believed to have accompanied the child since its conception. The event was celebrated with a large family feast to which both the mother's and the father's relatives brought food items.[26] Palau and Pohnpei both held celebrations at the mother's first childbirth, but these celebrations, which generally were not repeated for any subsequent births, focused on the mother rather than the child, marking her emergence as a "productive" member of the lineage. She was "productive" in a double sense: she was clearly fertile, and by virtue of bearing children she could be expected to bring wealth to her lineage.[27] In recent years, however, first birthday parties have become nearly as common a feature in Pohnpei as they have always been in Chuuk and Kosrae.

The first birthday party in Kosrae, as described by anthropologist Jim Peoples in 1975, is prepared by the mother and father of the child, each working through his or her blood relatives to collect the food and gifts required for the party.[28] The celebration is not altogether obligatory; the parents can decide not to hold the event if there are good reasons for not doing so. Their wealth will also determine how large the party will be, a matter on which there is considerable latitude. The families of the mother and the father assist in the preparation of the food for the celebration, which usually consists of pigs, rice, turkey tails, and locally grown crops. The guests will often bring gifts for the child in the form of clothes items, towels, toys, and yards of fabric. First birthday parties on Kosrae, which normally are much smaller than weddings or funerals, produced an average of about $200 in gifts, aside from the food contributions, in the mid-1970s when Peoples was engaged in his fieldwork.[29]

In the Marshalls the first birthday, known as a *kemem*, is an even more important part of the life of the community than it is in Kosrae. The *kemem* has always been a key event in the individual life cycle and the island culture, and there is strong evidence that its importance has grown over recent years. Like the Kosraean first birthday party, the *kemem* is a feast sponsored by the family of the child, and it varies in size. Spoehr, writing of Majuro in the late 1940s, states that "a small party may have only 20 or 30; a *kemem* given by a prominent family with many relatives may include 200."[30] A Marshallese woman who recounted what she remembered hearing of her own *kemem*, held on Arno not long after the Second World War, said that the whole island community of perhaps one hundred or two hundred attended.[31] At some celebrations gifts of handicraft or woven pandanus mats were given away to special guests, but the essence of the celebration always lay in the feast itself. Often there was music and dancing as well. After the gifts were distributed to the most distinguished guests, the baby was paraded around and exhibited before the whole assembled crowd.

There is a significant detail in the *kemem* witnessed by Spoehr years ago that should not be overlooked. When the relatives came to the house bringing their baskets of food, those from the mother's side put their food in one place, while those from the father's side set theirs in another place. Thus, the food for the feast was separated into two piles, one representing the offerings of the man and the other, the offerings of the woman. Although this practice could have suggested a competitive aspect to the feast, some of the food from these two piles was exchanged between the family of the father and that of the mother. Spoehr writes: "A special basket of the choicest food may be given by the husband and his family to his wife's family. The wife and her kin present a similar food gift to the husband's family."[32] Whether or not reciprocal food gifts were exchanged by the two families at a *kemem*, the event was the occasion of close collaboration between them during their long preparation for the party. The celebration then not only introduced the child to the community but also strengthened the bonds between the kinfolk of the child's mother and father. As such, the *kemem* was an important "expression of family solidarity."[33]

What, then, has changed in this first birthday celebration since 1950? Certainly the expense and the size of the guest list, especially on Majuro and Ebeye. The average cost of a *kemem* today in those places might range from $3,000 to $5,000, one Marshallese thought.[34] When the party is thrown open to anyone and everyone on the island, the cost could go beyond $10,000, especially if the family provides favors for the guests that include, at the top end, such things as pillows and muumuus imported from Guam. The larger celebrations on Majuro might attract as many as two thousand guests in the course of the evening. Celebrations of this size are public displays of wealth staged by individuals to signal their membership in the elite class. In this respect first birthday parties are like lavish weddings, costly house parties, large funerals, graduation parties, baptisms, and a number of other occasions that announce and celebrate the status of the family as much as the event itself.

The cost of catering the party and feeding the guests is today often borne by the father of the family or some other close relative with considerable earning power. This practice contrasts with the celebration as it was conducted in years past, when all the relatives from both sides contributed food and labor for their party. The same change has occurred in Kosrae, although the size and cost of the party there is much smaller than it is in the Marshalls. Today the father and mother of the child usually assume the entire burden of planning and financing the event without help from their families.

The *kemem*, today as in the past, is a celebration of new life. But in many cases it is also a display of wealth and rank, as a number of other family life-cycle events have become these days. The celebration in its present form does not accentuate the reciprocity between the mother's and the father's families as it once did. Rather than strengthening the fragile bond between the two families, the *kemem* has become primarily an expression of the social position of the nuclear family that sponsors it.

5 Marriage

Selection of a Spouse

The middle-aged Micronesian priest had been in California for less than six months when a phone call came from a former student of his. Xavier, the caller, was in his early twenties. He was from the same island group as the priest, although he had been raised on a different island. Three years before, immediately after finishing high school, he had come to Texas to attend college. There he found more than just studies to engage his interest. Over the last year, he explained to the priest, he had developed a close relationship with a girl from the priest's island. Not long ago they had been married in a small civil ceremony. He was calling to ask whether the priest could inform his family and her family that the two of them had decided to get married.

Had they asked permission of their families before the marriage, the priest asked. No, the young man admitted. They had married without permission and were hoping that he could inform the families of what they had done. They were too ashamed to tell their families themselves, but maybe their families would accept the news better if they thought that the priest had given permission.

In Micronesia the formalities of entering into marriage were not much different from one island to another. Marriage had always been as much a contract between families as between individuals, and the process was very similar throughout the region.

Parents have always had a large say in whom their children could marry. At one time, long before the period treated in this book, marriages were usually arranged by parents. Infant betrothal was once quite common on some islands—Palau, Chuuk, Pohnpei, and the Marshalls—but the practice went into decline long before the 1950s.[1] In most cases, parents took the initiative when their son or daughter reached adolescence, often suggesting potential partners or even urging them on their marriageable child.[2] Matches were made in Micronesia, as in medieval Europe and many other parts of the world, for the purpose of enhancing the wealth of the family and advancing its interests. Marriage between cross-cousins—that is, children of a brother and sister—was frequently practiced in Pohnpei, parts of Chuuk and the Mortlocks, and the Marshalls to ensure that land and titles were passed back and forth between closely connected lineages. At one time it was the preferred type of marriage in these islands, even if not always statistically the most common.[3]

If parents had a say in the choice of their children's marriage partners, it was not always decisive. Arranged marriages were still found, but only "on the minority of islands" in the eastern Carolines by 1950, according to an anthropologist who traveled widely in the area.[4] Of Ulithi in the late 1940s and possibly other parts of the outer islands of Yap, Lessa writes that "parents seldom arrange marriages, the vast majority being decided by the couple themselves."[5] There was little to be gained by arranged marriages in these relatively egalitarian societies, as Lessa notes. "Wealth . . . is hardly a consideration at all, since there is little inequality in this respect. Marriage to the son or daughter of a chief is not especially sought after as it confers no extra rights or rank in a matrilineal society."[6] By contrast, in Palau, a society in which competition for rank based on accumulation of wealth was developed into a fine art form, arranged marriages were standard throughout the prewar years. "High blood," along with the willingness to work hard, was the decisive criterion in such marriages there. Even in Palau, though, arranged marriages were unlikely to last unless the feelings of the couple were taken into account.[7]

Parental involvement in the marriage of their children was not as oppressive as it is sometimes portrayed, since parents tried to consult the interests of their child in choosing his or her marriage partner. They had every reason to do so, for frustrated lovers could scotch the best laid of a family's plans. Persistent young people who were unhappy with the partners chosen for them had various options. If a young man was forced to marry against his will, he might reluctantly accept the arrangement for a time and then find an excuse to split up with his wife after a year or two. Alternatively, he could elope with his sweetheart, live in the bush or go to a distant part of their island, and hope to gain the acceptance of his family after the fact. Either way, he could bank on the fact that his parents would give greater heed to his own wishes on the choice of his marriage partner in the future.

While parents' say in their children's marriage was not always decisive, they have retained, even to the present day in most places, the power of final approval of such marriages. What the Fischers wrote of Pohnpei and Chuuk in 1950 is still true today just about everywhere: "Prior approval of a proposed marriage by the families of the boy and girl is almost universal. Where approval by one or both sides is lacking the marriage is often abandoned or if entered into may easily break up."[8] There has always been real cultural tension between individuals and their parents over who has the right to select the marriage partner. If it is obvious that individuals have a strong interest in choosing their life's partner, the decision just as clearly touches the social and economic life of their lineage group. This tension was resolved, at least in postwar years, by offering the individual freedom to choose his or her spouse while granting the parents final veto power over the choice. Thus, as Gladwin puts it, "the parents cannot force their child to marry someone he or she does not like, but they can prevent another union of which they disapprove."[9]

To finalize a marriage, whether the initiative came from the young man or his family, an older member of the young man's family would go to the girl's family to ask for her hand in marriage. Even today, when the boy is expected to choose his own marriage partner, he depends on his parents' willingness to represent him with the family of the girl he hopes to marry. If his parents strongly disapprove of the choice he has made, they have only to refuse to accompany him to the girl's house. The refusal of his parents to ratify his choice and represent him in asking for the girl can bring on a family crisis, even leading to suicide threats or attempts.

Apart from the status and wealth of the partner, there were other vital issues for the family to address in a marriage involving one of its members. Older family members kept a sharp eye out for the lineage of the marriage partner to make sure that incest prohibitions were observed. Everywhere in Micronesia marriage was strictly exogamous, so that one could not marry within one's own clan.[10] On many islands, marriage to someone of one's father's lineage was also forbidden. These rules were broken from time to time but only rarely and never without causing some scandal in the community. Parents also wanted the opportunity to look over any prospective partner to make a judgment on whether he or she was respectful, hardworking, and generous.[11] In most cases, this judgment could be easily made; there would have been few surprises in a small community whose members knew one another intimately.

For some time now, parents have been gradually relinquishing their authority over the choice of marriage partners for their children. In an earlier day, the balance often swung to the side of the parents, who were frequently able to negotiate marriages of their own choosing. By the 1950s —at least in Chuuk, Pohnpei, Palau, and the neighboring islands of Yap —parents were content to allow their children to pick their own spouses. Parents retained their veto power over the marriage, although they may have become increasingly reluctant to exercise this authority.

Since the late 1960s and early 1970s, as new high schools were built in all island groups and the opportunity to attend college was offered to hundreds of Micronesians each year, young people have been moving out of their own small island communities in unprecedented numbers. As this happened, the pool for the selection of spouses greatly widened, and it was not uncommon for a young man or woman to return to his or her community with a prospective marriage partner in tow.[12] Often enough a young person, disregarding the advice of elders to marry someone from his or her own island "so that they would have both feet on their island," would bring back a partner from some distant place. Since very few of these partners were known to the family of the young man or woman, the checks that parents would normally have employed were frequently withheld. Young people were of necessity given greater latitude than ever before in the selection of their own spouses. Even the prohibition of marriage within the clan was violated more often than formerly.[13]

Young men and women who were attending college in the United States and Guam could be expected to take even more liberty on this matter, since they were often out of direct contact with their families back home.[14] Young Micronesians began pairing off in college, often consulting their parents for permission after the fact, if at all. This delay could be quite intentional, as when they wanted to subvert marriage plans their parents might have had for them when they returned home after college.[15] Such cases represented the greatest departure from custom, for their parents lost even their power of approval over their marriage.

In the factual incident at the opening of this section, Xavier managed to circumvent his family back home while making the decision to marry and carrying it out. His nod to custom was in asking for the "permission" of a recognized authority from his island group, even if the couple had already been married and even if the priest he asked was not a family member. This gesture is a reminder of how far the wheel of change has turned in the process of selecting marriage partners today.

But the wheel continues to turn still, for parents who once would have expected to be consulted by their son or daughter about their choice of partner now leave the matter entirely in the hands of their children.

Not long ago one parent, a man who came from one of the more traditional parts of Chuuk and who had acquired a reputation for being a strict father, was approached by a small party representing the family of a boy who wanted to marry his daughter. Several of the man's own family were on hand for this meeting. When an older man from the boy's family began to make the request with the usual formalities, the father waved him off impatiently and asked the boy to speak for himself. Did he love the girl? the father asked. When the boy timidly mumbled that he did, the father turned to his daughter and asked her whether she loved the boy. When she admitted that she did, the father threw up his hands and said: "Well, that should settle everything. They love one another, so the matter is decided. They will be married." His intervention stifled the objections that the men in his own family were preparing to raise, and the decision of the young couple to wed was ratified instantly and without further discussion.

Tying the Knot

I had just exited the baggage area at the Honolulu airport when I was greeted by someone I knew, a former student of mine, now close to forty and showing all the signs of middle age. After the usual small talk, he paused for a moment, turned serious, and asked if I might be through Honolulu again soon. I told him that I expected to be back in a couple of months. "I want a church wedding, Father," he told me. "Could you arrange to do it when you return the next time? The sooner the better."

I told him that I was surprised at the urgency he felt. He and his wife had been together for almost twenty years and had four children. During all the years they had been on Yap, they had never bothered to get a church marriage. "We're married by custom," he used to tell his pastor with a wry smile. "We don't see any reason to go through a foreign ceremony." Yet, here they were in Hawai'i not even a year, and they were already banging on the church door.

He must have known what I was thinking. "It's not for me; it's for the wife and kids," he admitted. "If something should happen to me here, my wife and kids would get nothing without that piece of paper that says we're married. I need it for their sake."

In Micronesia young people have always had broad latitude to carry on sexual affairs, provided they were reasonably discreet in their conduct.

A young married couple on Chuuk.
(Micronesian Seminar)

Most young people in the past, just as at present, seem to take advantage of this freedom. As soon as a young couple decided to marry, however, they demonstrated this publicly by sleeping overnight with one another and remaining until morning. Open cohabitation was a declaration of their intent.[16]

When the preliminaries had been taken care of and permission was secured from the families of the boy and girl, an exchange of food gifts was usually arranged between the two families to seal the agreement.[17] This exchange was an important sign of the bonding of the families and their commitment to one another. The family of the young man usually supplied the fish, while the girl's side brought root crops or starch. In Ulithi the boy's family would go fishing for a day and turn the entire catch over to the girl's family, who would reciprocate with a return gift of taro at the time they received the fish.[18] What is called the *kiis* in Chuuk is another example of this food exchange, although the primary obligation to provide food formerly lay with the man's side, reflecting his subservience to his wife's family throughout his entire married life.[19]

In Yap marriages once involved a series of three exchanges between the families of the man and the woman; the first occurred as the couple began living together, the second after the woman's first pregnancy, and the third following the birth of the first male child. They signified the gradually deepening investment of both sides in the family estate. The type of food brought by the man's side and the woman's side was similar to that described above, but the size of the gift increased in each of the three exchanges. At the first exchange, as the man and woman began living together, the woman's side gave food from the gardens and stone money, while the man's side contributed fish, coconuts, bananas, and shell money.[20] Today the first exchange is the only one required, and store-bought goods are now frequently used in the exchange. Yet, the underlying mutual exchange continues even to the present.[21]

The reciprocity between the families of the man and the woman that is so basic to the Micronesian marriage celebration has been preserved even in Kosrae, notwithstanding the cultural discontinuity that the island experienced in the nineteenth century owing to the enormous depopulation there. In the Kosraean marriage ceremony as it was carried out perhaps fifty years ago, males on both the bride's side and the groom's side would work together to provide all the food that was customarily prepared by men; women from both sides would collaborate in weaving the sleeping mats and fine belts that were used as presents at the wedding feast. The woven goods that were manufactured by a joint effort of the women were then divided up so that the father of the groom could present half to the father of the bride and vice versa.[22]

In time, many of the foods traditionally raised by men ceased to be cultivated on Kosrae, and women no longer wove the fine belts that had once been prized as a commodity of exchange at island celebrations. As in other parts of Micronesia, store-bought goods became easier to procure on Kosrae and came to replace woven goods as wedding gifts. By the mid-1970s the old exchange items were replaced by new ones, highlighting even more strongly than before the reciprocal nature of the exchange. The bride's side would give the groom's family only gifts that could be used by men: pants, shirts, undershirts, briefs, and so forth. The man's side would give as its share only items of women's apparel such as dresses, panties, slips, and brassieres. The monetary value of the gifts from the woman's family was expected to be about equal to what the other side gave.[23] Despite the change in the type of goods used for exchange purposes, the mutual gift giving between the man's family and the woman's family remains as integral to the wedding celebration as ever. In this respect, Kosrae carries on a tradition that is cardinal to marriage customs almost everywhere in Micronesia despite the severe cultural disruption that occurred there.

There is good reason for this emphasis on mutual gift giving between the families of the spouses. In Micronesian cultures, kinship is created rather than assumed. Even two individuals within the same bloodline are expected to reaffirm or validate their relationship with one another continuously if the kinship between them is to be active. This is all the more true of a man and woman who are unrelated to one another. If a bond is ever to develop between the couple and between their families, a flow of gifts and return gifts must be made to signify mutual love and respect.[24]

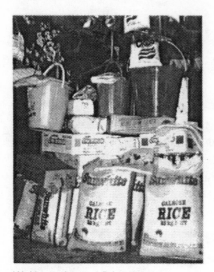
Wedding exchange on Pohnpei.
(Kimberly Kihleng)

In addition to the ritual exchange between families, which continues in most places even today, a formal marriage ceremony is sometimes carried out. Often the ceremony is conducted in church, occasionally in the court or before a magistrate. A church or civil ceremony is no new thing, of course. For years priests and ministers have been insisting upon a church wedding, often in vain, just as government officials have been suggesting that couples license their marriages in court. Couples may go through a formal church ceremony years after the pair have begun living together. Indeed, their children may be grown up by the time their parents decide to get the marriage formalized. The long postponement of a church ceremony is usually due to the reluctance of a couple to take a step that will make the union more difficult to sever if it should prove unworkable.[25]

Even though Micronesians sometimes take a strong position to the contrary, it seems that the traditional minimal procedures that have always sufficed for a marriage in the eyes of the community may be inadequate today. These practices, which have stressed the bonding of the two families, may not be public enough to meet the needs of a modern society. How does the public know when the marriage really begins and when it ends? How do people differentiate between a long affair and what might be called a genuine commitment? Such questions were of little consequence in the village life of the past, but they may be of critical importance when it comes to determining who shall receive social security benefits, life insurance payments, and inheritance rights to property. Because the modern monetized society runs on formal documents, marriage licenses that certify the formal union of a couple are becoming necessary to guarantee that benefits will flow to the rest of the family after the death of one of the partners.

Some years ago in Hawai'i, I officiated at the church wedding for the Micronesian couple whose plight I described in the vignette opening this section. They had lived together happily on their island for twenty years, but within a couple months of their arrival in Hawai'i they learned how many things they could not do unless they were able to produce a marriage certificate. Island Micronesia is steadily heading in the same direction, at least in this one respect. In the semimodernized society of today's Micronesia, marriage is taking on a formal, public dimension that it never had before. In view of the bureaucratic demands of this type of society, the legitimacy that a church or civil ceremony confers on a marriage is rapidly becoming indispensable. This is possibly the most significant change in the way marriage is contracted.

Marriage as Business

The older Palauan woman was almost in tears when she answered the question that had been posed at the conference: How do you manage the tension between obligations toward your own blood relatives and obligations toward your husband and children? We had been discussing "custom"—that generic term that is used in Palau for large community events involving contributions—and the pressures that it brings to bear on people today. Many of the participants had complained of the strain that the constant financial demands put on their nuclear families. In the past the house-building ceremonies and the first-birth ceremonies were held much less frequently, they said, and those who attended were not expected to contribute as much as they are today.

The Palauan woman rose slowly, wiped her eyes, and told everyone how she followed a strict budget in determining her contributions to the community events to which she was invited. Then she described how her own relatives teased her for being stingy at these parties. "Mrs. Fifty" is what they called her because her contributions never exceeded fifty dollars.

Marriage as practiced on many islands was a business as much as a personal relationship. Nowhere was this exemplified better than in Palau.[26] A wife was expected to use her hold over her husband to benefit her own blood family by getting financial support from him and his kin on the occasion of important life events in her family. This support, given in return for her work and sexual services to her husband, was directed to her family, not just so they could accumulate wealth but to elevate their status in the community.[27]

In other island groups, too, the husband and the wife were expected to advance the interests of their own blood relatives, even if this meant inconvenience or worse to the couple and their household. Should the wife's parents require a large sum of money for airfare for a medical referral, the couple might be obliged to provide it even if this money were earmarked for the children's tuition. In the event of conflict of interest between the families, the woman and the man were each expected to side with their respective family. If the spouse proved uncooperative, the man or woman's relatives might exert pressure to have the marriage terminated.[28] When the two relationships came into conflict, the blood tie had to be honored above the marital tie. As the Pohnpeian adage puts it: "The ties of marriage can be broken, but not blood ties."[29]

Marriage was the bonding of two families, not just two individuals, as is clear from the gift exchanges between the families that marked the event and the continuing obligations of the couple to the blood kin of each spouse. This is not to say that Micronesian marriage was nothing but a financial merger between corporations (or lineages); everyone hoped that the relationship between the couple would be deep and lasting. In the long run, however, the permanence of this relationship might depend more on how successfully the "business" angle was managed than on the strength of the couple's feelings for one another. One man on Lamotrek, according to Alkire, was forced to leave his wife, to whom he was deeply attached, simply because her family was forcing him to spend so much time working for them that he found himself neglecting his responsibilities to his own blood lineage.[30]

In the past, then, couples had a limited life of their own. They were hemmed in by in-laws and family, often remaining in their presence and always within the shadow of their interests. Life without these other ties was unthinkable and perhaps even unbearable to many who are products of an earlier set of attitudes and practices. A couple I know was given a honeymoon at a local hotel for three or four days following their church marriage ceremony but decided to return early because they couldn't stand the solitude. In years past, the freedom from the "interference" of relatives that Westerners ideally expected of a young family was hardly even a value in Micronesia.

The tension between the couple's marital relationship and their own family concerns has always been a fact of life in any Micronesian marriage. Many otherwise happy marital relationships have foundered because of competing interests between the families. As a priest, I have heard my share of tragic stories about how disagreement over financial obligations poisoned the relationship between the couple and damaged or destroyed the marriage. Often one of the parties, in coming to the assistance of his or her own family, will provoke resentment in the marriage partner, who feels that his or her kin are being neglected.

Divorce rates at the time of the arrival of the first wave of American anthropologists in the late 1940s were reportedly high. Lessa, working in Ulithi, wrote that the average married adult on the island had been divorced an average of two times for those who had reached the age of fifty. His figures suggest that divorce in Ulithi didn't just happen during the first years of marriage before young people settled down into a permanent relationship, but that it would frequently occur after several years of marriage.[31] Alkire, who studied on Lamotrek in 1962, reported even higher rates there: an average of over three marriages per person, with one or two individuals married as many as ten times.[32] Spoehr writes that people in Majuro "could be married once or twice before they settled down into a permanent union," but he admits that he might have found an even higher rate if he had had time to research everyone's marital history.[33] "Divorce was frequent on all islands and still is on Pohnpei proper and in Truk Lagoon," according to Fischer.[34] It was probably even more frequent in Palau and Yap, which have always been known for their high divorce rates.

Clearly, then, high divorce rates are not an outgrowth of modernization. Forty or fifty years ago, divorce was a frequent occurrence on all islands, with the possible exception of tiny islands under tight church control, and was not confined to the early years of marriage before the couple's relationship had stabilized. The high rates are understandable, given the tension that invariably existed between the marital relationship and the even more fundamental blood ties that bound each of the couple to his or her own family. Divorce today may be less frequent than it was in the past, although there are no figures to substantiate this. Almost certainly it is no more common.

Today, as the lineage is breaking up under the impact of modernization, nuclear families are beginning to achieve a measure of independence that was unimaginable and undesirable in past years. More young couples are setting up their own households on individually owned land, sometimes with very few or no relatives living with them. The movement to towns and now to other, distant islands only increases this trend toward independence. Although these trends may not be a deliberate attempt to ensure the young couple freedom from their in-laws, they are having that very effect. Intentionally or not, many young married couples today are making all the changes in lifestyle that will check the pressure of their relatives on them.

Moreover, the personal support base for the young couple today is shifting away from one's blood relations to one's spouse. Husbands and wives spend more time alone together than they might have in the past. One Chuukese man in early middle age, after telling me once that he was teased by his friends for appearing in public so often with his wife, admitted that he enjoyed nothing so much as cruising around town with her in his pickup. That admission was singular in a culture in which men do not display their feelings for their wives in front of others. Whether or not spouses are establishing stronger feelings for one another than in the past, couples are plainly transgressing the code of conduct that once governed their public behavior toward each other. Hand holding by couples and public dancing together, while not common, is occasionally seen today, as old restraints on signs of affection in public begin to crumble.

The recent steps in the direction of liberation of married couples from the influence of their blood relatives may reduce the tensions that have beset them in the past. The increased distance between them and these relatives gives them breathing space, after a fashion. But the reverse side of the coin is that they also have to do without the assistance that these relatives provide—by way of conflict resolution when trouble breaks out in the household or in protecting the wife and children from an abusive father.

6 Death

Laying the Dead to Rest

Yukiwo's death was not sudden. He had been suffering from kidney failure for several years and required regular dialysis at the Pohnpei hospital. When he developed liver cancer shortly before his death, he and his family faced a quandary. Should he remain in the hospital and continue dialysis, even though the doctors had told him that his liver condition would render this treatment ineffective? Or should he, knowing that he was to die anyway, discontinue the dialysis, leave the hospital, and return to his home island—in Chuuk, some four hundred miles away—to spend his last days in the company of his family?

When I visited him two days before he died, he was still in the hospital. His cubicle was packed with relatives, more than a dozen, who had begun their death watch. His relatives in Chuuk were unsure what to do —whether to fly to Pohnpei to see him before he passed away or to await what they hoped was his certain return to his home island. Many times during the past week they had called to ask that Yukiwo return to Chuuk to be with his entire family before he passed away. But the small group of his relatives on Pohnpei felt that he was already too weak to make the trip. His wife, who was Pohnpeian, preferred that he remain on the island where they had lived for the last ten years. In the end, he remained on Pohnpei, with family members flying in from Chuuk to be with him during his last days. In accordance with his wishes, he was buried on the land he lived on. At her death, his wife will be buried alongside him.

In the past Micronesians came home to die, just as women once returned to their own place to give birth. Those near death, even if married, were moved to their own land to live out their final days with their kin. Rubinstein tells of an eighty-year-old woman from Fais who, when begin-

91

ning to fail, returned to her natal land to live out her last days.[1] Her conduct was typical of people of her age group. Persons who had been hospitalized but felt themselves failing despite the treatment they received would check out and return to their families as their time drew near. If they could not leave the hospital for some reason, their relatives came to be with them, flooding the ward and sleeping on the floor or shuttling back and forth in order to keep them company until the end.[2] As one anthropologist put it, island people seemed to fear the prospect of dying away from their relatives more than death itself.[3]

If at all possible, people wished to be buried on their own land, the land from which they sprang. In many parts of Micronesia, a person's umbilical cord was buried on his or her land at birth. Is it pushing an interpretation too far to see both burials—the umbilical cord at birth and the body at death—as expressive of the mystical relationship that existed between people and their land? At one time, sea burials were very common in the islands, but even these had their symbolic connections with the land. A burial on one's own land was a special mark of recognition in those days. In the Marshalls this sort of burial was often accorded to chiefs; in more egalitarian societies land burial might sometimes be granted to those who died young and were especially mourned.[4] It was the practice in Chuuk to bury especially beloved persons underneath their dwellings.[5] Interment on or near house plots was once done even on the coral atolls, but this practice was later discouraged by missionaries, who established cemeteries. In the Marshalls—at least on Ebeye and Majuro—and on the atolls in the western Carolines, cemeteries have become customary today.[6]

A person who died away from home posed a real threat to those who lived near the place of death as well as to his or her own relations. The soul was believed to linger where death occurred, and "only kinsmen can provide the material items and rituals that will encourage the soul to depart."[7] DeVerne Smith tells the story of an outsider whose body was found in a Palauan village a few days after his disappearance. So afraid of his ghost were the villagers that they huddled together at night in the houses of friends for protection. The people of the village left the body of the stranger on a raft in the lagoon until his relatives arrived to claim it and bring it back for burial. For months afterwards, people avoided the spot where he had died for fear of encountering his spirit. Only after a Catholic priest came to bless the place did the villagers again sleep peacefully at night.[8]

As the sick or elderly person approaches death, any wishes regarding the disposal of his or her body and property are listened to respect-fully. These last wishes are regarded as sacred today as in the past, and the dying person is granted whatever he or she might request.[9] All the relatives of the dying person come from near and far to take up a death watch at the bedside of the moribund individual. They care for the dying person, bringing food and drink and helping him or her with other bodily needs, but mostly they wait for the end.

The sequence of events immediately following a death is best portrayed in descriptions from the coral atolls between Yap and Chuuk, for customs there probably represent what would once have occurred in most parts of Micronesia. These customs were still observed in about 1950 on these islands. At the time of the death, the relatives and friends of the dead person take up a formalized wail, with others in the community joining in as they arrive. The family of the deceased—usually the women, but in the Marshalls the men—clean the corpse, cover it with turmeric, and decorate it with garlands.[10] In earlier times a relative would cut off a portion of the dead person's hair. In Fais the lock of hair was braided into a string and worn around the neck by a female relative for the next several months; in other islands it was stored in a wooden box as a keepsake.[11]

When the family has cleaned and prepared the body, men and women begin singing funeral laments or dirges. These are not spontaneous outbursts of grief, but traditional songs handed down through the generations and ritualistically performed for the occasion. Although these laments "serve to orchestrate the public expressions of grief and loss" in a formal way, many of those who join in the songs often get caught up in the emotion of the event.[12] Such songs are still sung today on many islands and have been integrated into the new funeral rituals.

The customs surrounding the actual death of a person and the preparation of the body for the wake have changed to a greater or lesser extent depending on the island. Much of what was done on the postwar atolls of Yap remains in force there even today. Perhaps the most significant change is not in the rituals surrounding the actual death, but in the disposal of the body. Fifty years ago there would be little doubt how the scenario with which this section began would be played out. As his condition grew more serious, Yukiwo would have left the hospital to return to his own island to die with his relatives. If, for some reason, death caught him by surprise in the Pohnpei hospital, his family would have arranged for the body to be embalmed and sent back to his own island in Chuuk.

As things happened, several of Yukiwo's closest relatives flew to

Pohnpei to be with him near the end, so he was not without the comfort of many of his kin. His relatives cleaned the body, dressed it up, and possibly even snipped the customary lock of hair and sang one or two of the old dirges, as they would have years ago. Yet, the body was not sent to Chuuk for burial. The decision on where he would be buried was a negotiated one rather than an automatic one, taking account of blood ties and marriage obligations and trying to balance what was owed to different parties. Such negotiated settlements over burial sites have become ever more common today as mobility has increased and families migrate outside Micronesia to work and study and live.[13]

Despiriting Death

The funeral was over, and the relatives who had assembled were getting ready to leave for their own homes. Anna, the twenty-four-year-old daughter of the man who had died, was relieved that the celebration was finished. Although she missed her father deeply, she was happy to be returning to her husband and two children, who were living on a nearby island. Before she left, though, she wanted to spend a few minutes with her mother.

The two of them sat side by side for a while until Anna looked up at her mother sadly and told her that nothing was going to bring her father back to life. "You have a life to live, Mom," she said. "Clean up. Take a good shower and change that dress you've been wearing all week. Dad would want you to carry on without him."

Her mother said nothing. After a minute or so, Anna spoke again. "I'll be leaving for home today. The boat's here, and I thought I would leave right after lunch. I'd like to go inland over there—you know, to that little piece of land where dad used to go to farm—and get a few coconuts for our trip."

Anna's mother looked alarmed. "Don't you know that we're putting that piece of property off limits for six months? That was your father's favorite piece of land. He went there all the time. Now we're putting tied coconut fronds on the trees to keep people out in honor of your father. But you can't go home today anyway. Didn't you know that we women aren't supposed to travel by sea for a month after a death in our family? My mother told me that it had to do with the sea spirits. And this dress —I'm supposed to wear it until the mourning period is over. Don't you know that in the old days we didn't take showers during the mourning period?"

"But Mom!" Anna replied. "Those old customs don't make sense any more. No one believes those stories old people used to tell about spirits hanging around the grave. We're all Christians today."

Death rituals throughout most of postwar Micronesia showed strong similarities from one island to another. They shared the same fundamental structure: a four-day cycle in which each of the days had a significance of its own, concluding in a graveside ceremony of ancient origin. There were variations on this structure, especially in Yap and Palau, on islands that lie outside what anthropologists and linguists call Nuclear Micronesia. There the number of days in the death celebration cycle was more liable to vary and other elements were added, but the form of the funeral was still fairly similar to what it was in other island groups in the area.

The similarity in death rituals seems to be rooted in common ancient beliefs regarding the spirit of the deceased. Micronesians once believed that the soul left the body with the last breath—usually through the top of the head, according to the people of Ulithi, but those from other islands sometimes tried to capture the soul as it was expelled through the mouth.[14] The soul was thought to remain in the vicinity of the body for the next three or four days, after which it was speeded on its way to its final destination by a ceremony.[15] While it hovered around the corpse, the soul was a dangerous but a potentially beneficial presence. Dangerous because it could frighten and harm people, but beneficial inasmuch as it could provide valuable information for the family. Hence, it had to be mollified and appeased by the family through food gifts and other offerings.

Funeral celebrations everywhere, then as now, were intended to heal the social wound left by the departure of one of the members of the community. A young Marshallese college graduate expressed it nicely when she wrote: "Death represents a tear in the family and, by extension, social fabric that must be restitched."[16] Funerals bring together the survivors so that they can reaffirm and strengthen the social and emotional bonds that unite them. For ancient Micronesians, however, funerals performed another important function: that is, to transform the dead person's soul into a benevolent ancestral spirit.[17] Close relatives of the deceased played an essential role in this process. "Only kinsmen can provide the material items and rituals that will encourage the soul to depart," Smith writes of Palau in the past.[18] It is difficult to overstate the importance of discharging this task well in view of the belief in the dangers posed by souls in their transitional state between the world of the living and the world of the dead. Especially dangerous were those who committed suicide or died a violent death.[19] Souls that were aided in the progression between the two worlds, in contrast, would be forever well disposed to their living relatives.[20]

During the soul's wanderings for the four days between the death and the final ceremony, or frequently even later, people expected that the soul might visit one of the lineage members. In former times the family would prepare one of its more suggestible members to receive the spirit and become an instrument for the utterance of its messages. Spirit "possession" was frequent at those times and was always regarded by the family as a blessing. There is an explicit record of such spirit possession for Chuuk and for Ulithi, but it was probably also practiced on other islands.[21] In Palau, the soul of the deceased person was also consulted by way of trance-possession, but through the services of a *kerong*, or medium. There the relatives sought to divine the cause of death, with an eye to determining whether it was caused deliberately through sorcery.[22] This voluntary spirit possession, already on the decline everywhere in the 1950s, was practically nonexistent by 1970. Spirit possession following a death has occurred sporadically since then, but it can no longer be called voluntary, and it serves an entirely different purpose.[23]

The funeral ceremonies in the past concluded with a graveside ritual on the fourth day that seems to have been, in effect, a dismissal of the soul of the deceased. At one time the family lit a great bonfire in front of the house early in the morning of the fourth day to send the soul of its departed member on its way. All the personal belongings of the dead person—mats, clothes, and especially cherished goods—were thrown onto the fire in an effort to discourage the spirit from returning to the house in the future and causing some misfortune. This custom, which was recorded for Satawal in the 1930s, was apparently widespread in the central Carolines, Chuuk included, and may have been practiced in the eastern Carolines and the Marshalls as well.[24] An anthropologist working in Chuuk witnessed, in 1947, a ceremony in which a female relative of the deceased brought a piece of the dead woman's dress, placed it on the sand in front of the house, and burned it. This ceremony, a vestige of the older practice of burning all personal belongings, was believed to hasten the peaceful departure of the soul of the dead person.[25]

In the postwar years, on many islands, the custom has been altered. Lessa records that in Ulithi personal effects such as "knives, coconut graters, cups, bowls, sleeping mats, loincloths, combs, necklaces" were placed in the grave when the body was buried.[26] The custom of burying grave goods with the body continued through the 1960s and 1970s, although it seems to have lost its association with its original purpose of encouraging the departure of the soul. In a funeral that took place in Palau in the early 1970s, a dozen strong men hauled to the grave site an enormous casket that had been nailed securely shut. Only later did the mourners learn that, at his request, the dead man had been buried together with his motorcycle, thus denying it to a rival who had long coveted the machine. Another story that has made the rounds for years is recounted by a priest in Yap who, when blessing a body at the grave, heard the muffled words of the old song "In Heaven There Is No Beer" being emitted from the casket. The sound was coming from the dead person's transistor radio, which had been turned on when it was placed in the coffin to be buried with him.[27]

A custom that is still followed in some places even today is marking off the property of the deceased and prohibiting anyone from intruding on the property or using it for a specified period of time. For three months, around 1980, after the death of an old man who worked at our school in Chuuk, we were denied the use of our boat dock, which happened to be on his property. It was also forbidden to pick coconuts or breadfruit from the trees on his land during the same three-month period. This ban, too, may be related to the desire to pacify the soul of the deceased. Gladwin, describing the tying of coconut fronds to the trunks of trees bounding the property of a recently deceased person, explains this custom as a strategy used to give the spirit more freedom to roam, especially when it was invited to return during the longer family mourning period.[28] The end of the mourning period, which coincided with the lifting of the taboo, was marked by a family feast. This practice was also followed in Yap, where the ban on use of the dead person's lands lasted for a whole year.[29] In the Marshalls, too, such prohibitions were observed, although not usually for as long a period.[30]

For peoples in the western Carolines funerals were considered unclean and polluting. This perception was not simply because of the physical corruption that occurs at death, but because of the dangerous situation created when a soul is released from its body and hovers about before its final departure.[31] In Palau females in the family were confined to the house, where they were prohibited from cooking or washing for a few days, while the village followed its own taboos against loud noises and boisterous conduct.[32] In Yap, throughout the entire period of the "smell of the dead," certain taboos were in force. Many of those in the dead person's clan would abstain from eating fish for three days.[33] In Ulithi and Fais, presumably as well as the other islands in the central Carolines, the mourning period brought taboos for villagers lasting ten days as well as the longer mourning period of five lunar months imposed on the family. Those who washed the corpse and dug the grave, because they had been polluted from their contact with the body, were supposed to sleep apart from everyone else for a period of ten days.[34]

During the 1970s the taboos described above were still generally observed on those islands. Smith, during her fieldwork in 1973, recorded that Palauans still respected these prohibitions, and Labby, working in Yap a few years earlier, found the same to be true there.[35] By the early 1980s, however, a dramatic change was noted in Yap. Although no exchange of food could have had any place whatsoever in the traditional Yapese funeral as long as the "smell of the dead" was in the air—that is, for several days after the death—people were beginning to ignore the taboo as competitive food gifts were introduced into the mortuary ritual. The burial of a prominent community leader in the early 1980s featured contributions that included a hundred sacks of rice and dozens of slaughtered pigs.[36] Yapese admit with a shake of the head that today people commonly eat at funerals, something that they never would have done in the 1970s or earlier.[37]

Spirit beliefs, under assault from Christianity and modernization for years, have been slow to change in the islands. Despite the persistence of many of the beliefs, the funeral practices that they undergirded showed considerable evolution even before World War II. Many Micronesians may have held on to their traditional beliefs in the souls of the dead, but for various reasons they were unwilling to observe the customs that sprang from these beliefs. In the postwar years, as funeral practices in Micronesia have continued to be uncoupled from their original association with the spirits, these practices have been subject to even greater change. The despiriting of funeral customs has been as much responsible for the change in these funeral practices as any other social or economic force.

Smoothing Stones and Feelings

It was mid-afternoon when the mourners began drifting into the Catholic cemetery on Majuro. By five o'clock the church parking lot was packed with cars, and vehicles spilled over onto both sides of the road. Two or three hundred people, many dressed in black, milled around the graveyard waiting for the erak to begin. Even more were expected because the deceased was a prominent person in the community, although he had never held public office. Finally, someone stood and addressed the crowd, who now began to move closer to the newly decorated grave. A priest, draped in a white stole, then began a long prayer in Marshallese, at the end of which he sprinkled the grave. Then the mourners filed up to the grave, one by one, and each was handed a small basket woven of palm leaves filled with white pebbles. Each person would empty the contents of the basket alongside the edge of the grave and return to his or her place. When all the people had filed up and emptied their baskets at the graveside, two or three members of the family came up and leveled the mounds of stones that had been left near the grave. They smoothed them out with their hands until the pebbles beside the grave were nearly as level as the cement covering the burial spot.

A representative of the family then came forward to thank everyone for coming. In the course of his brief talk, as I was told later, he apologized to all for the poor preparations for the erak *and for the failure of the family to provide anything to eat or drink at this time. He added a perfunctory apology to all members of the Majuro community for any way in which the family might have offended them. Finally, he invited all those at the graveside to join the family in a small dinner to be given at the former residence of the deceased. With this, people began drifting off toward their cars.*

The *erak* is the final event of the funeral celebration in the Marshall Islands. It is centered on the simple ritual of inviting family members and respected members of the community to spread small, sea-washed rocks around the grave. The "smoothing of the rocks," as the word *"erak"* suggests, is symbolic. In the first place, it signals an end and brings a sense of completion to the funeral ceremony, lasting several days, in which the family and community bid their farewell to the deceased. At another and deeper level, however, the "smoothing of stones" means the easing of tensions that threaten to divide people, straightening out the relationships within the family, reaffirming the unity of the group in the face of the disruption caused by the recent loss of one of its members.[38]

Every island culture in Micronesia had some ritual to serve as the final act in the funeral ceremony. Often this ritual, which signified closure and finality, was performed at the grave site. The type of gesture varied from one island to another, however. The Kosraean funeral ends, a few days after the burial, with the *kuhlyuhk*, or "the making over of the grave," at which men pour cement over the grave to form a raised slab over the tomb.[39] In Palau the final ceremony is called *omengades*, or "the sealing of the grave." This sealing is accomplished by paving with stones the area surrounding the grave.[40] In Ulithi, in the early postwar years, a permanent stone slab was erected over the grave, much like the cement structure made on Kosrae. In Chuuk and Pohnpei, by contrast, there is no special ritual at the graveside on the fourth day. On Pohnpei the fourth day is simply called the "day of cleaning up" and is dedicated to preparation for the family members' departure. In Chuuk this day, which is called the *erek*, features the reading of the will and once was spent on a family meeting intended to bring about reconciliation and harmony among all members.

Originally, the purpose of this part of the funeral in the central Carolines was to hasten the departure of the soul of the deceased and to ensure that it left pleased with the family's regard for it. This may well have been the function of this day in other parts of Micronesia also.

With the decline in the old spirit beliefs, or at least the reluctance to continue ritualizing these beliefs, the emphasis shifted to ensuring that family relationships were in good order. Funerals became occasions to repair damaged family bonds. Throughout Micronesia a funeral is a rare opportunity for straight talk and tears within the family, as individuals accept blame for problems they may have caused and apologize for their harsh words and actions. In the central Carolines the whole family gathers to hear members vent their frustrations, speak flatly of the ways in which others in the family have hurt them, and say other things that they would simply avoid mentioning at any other time. At the funeral of a young Chuukese man several years ago, the boy's father and grandfather, who had not spoken to one another for several years, voiced their feelings about the events that led up to the rift between them and finally, in words choked with emotion, were reconciled amid much weeping.[41]

Funerals serve this purpose well because they are times of emotional intensity anyway. In describing the funeral of a young Marshallese man in 1946, Spoehr tells of the overt anger of the mother of the deceased at one of her daughters for arriving late for the funeral, even to the point of trying to strike her publicly.[42] This expression of raw emotion, which might be interdicted at other times, was permitted on such occasions and was channeled in the "smoothing of stones" that is conducted at the end of the ceremony. It surfaces as a person's readiness to talk about his or her personal feelings toward others in the family in an uncharacteristi-

At the church cemetery in Majuro. (Francis X. Hezel)

cally straightforward fashion. This kind of honesty is expected at the time of the family reconciliation.

A Marshallese woman in her fifties once told me how she experienced the *erak* when she was still a girl on one of the outer atolls. The whole community of a couple hundred people would gather in the afternoon to await the arrival of the *iroij*, or high chief, and the pastor. At their arrival they would all proceed to the grave to pour the stones on the grave and smooth them out afterwards. They would then return to the clearing where they had first gathered and arrange themselves in a large circle, seating themselves on the ground on palm branches. The community discussion would then begin, with each person speaking out about matters that had long bothered him or her. This part of the meeting would continue for as long as was needed. After the reconciliation all were invited to the concluding funeral feast.[43]

The apology at the recent *erak* in Majuro, described at the beginning of this section, was merely a brief formality. There was no open exchange on the problems that the group faced nor any evidence of a reconciliation within the family, much less the community. It is as if the smoothing of stones had ceased to signify any interpersonal reordering of relations. In Chuuk, too, people admit that at recent funerals there is no family meeting to sort out its problems before the final family meal. The frank discussion and the open display of emotion that once was a distinctive feature of this final part of the funeral ceremony seems to be omitted ever more frequently today. In societies that discourage a public expression of emotion, especially negative feelings, the *erak* or its counterparts provided a rare opportunity to vent feelings in such a way as to mend injured relationships.[44] If this custom were to vanish, as seems to be happening in Chuuk and the Marshalls, then the funeral may be losing one of its most valuable functions.

The Return of the Standard Funeral

"How do I find the Mendoza house?" I asked the man at the gas station.

"Should be no problem," he answered quickly. "Isn't that where the funeral is being held? Just look for the place near the bridge where all the cars are parked. You'll be lucky to find a spot to leave your car."

He was right. It was very easy to find the house. The line of cars and pickups must have run a quarter of a mile. Then there were the dark red, nearly black trails of pig's blood on the road where the animals were carried off the trucks. There was no mistaking the sound of sakau being pounded in the distance, so I headed in that direction. I reached what must have been the Mendoza compound after a five-minute walk. There were people everywhere around the house. Young men were carting sakau *plants to a pile outside the meetinghouse; others were staggering under the weight of what looked like three-hundred- or four-hundred-pound pigs. A large stone oven had been built about fifty yards away from the meetinghouse. Several boys stood around it stoking the fire. Up the hill a little way was what looked like the grave in the making, with six or seven young men either digging or sitting around smoking. Inside the meetinghouse four stones were ringing to the sound of sakau pounding, and coconut shell cups were being passed back and forth. The place was a babel of sounds: laughter, throats being cleared, hawking and spitting, the grunting and squeal of pigs outside. On the platform at the front sat two high chiefs, one on either side, their legs folded underneath them. A small table, stacked with food and with a coffee pot and cup, was set up next to each of the chiefs. From the small house a few feet down the driveway, I could hear the monotone of women saying the rosary, punctuated every so often with sobbing or a drawn-out wail.*

I felt a gentle tap on the shoulder and turned around quickly to find a former student of mine smiling at me. "So what do you think of a Pohnpeian funeral?" he asked.

The funeral in Micronesia is rapidly becoming homogenized today, as it may have been at one time in the very distant past. Nearly everywhere the signs of a funeral are the same. The blue or white tarpaulin in front of a house, the women carrying bundles of firewood to cook the rice and boil the coffee, scores of cars parked tightly alongside the road, men hauling sacks of rice and boxes of chicken and turkey tails from their pickups—all these are sure indications that there is a funeral close by.[45]

The wake, too, shows the signs of standardization. The men gather outside drinking coffee, gossiping, or perhaps digging the grave or offering suggestions to those who are doing so. Inside the house seated around the coffin are the female relatives, many dressed in black, with some of the older women even wearing mantillas or veils. Depending on the religious denomination of the family, they may be reciting the rosary or singing and praying psalms. At times a wail or sobbing will break out, and the women closest to the head of the casket will begin sobbing as they throw their heads on the edge of the casket close to the face of the dead person. Newcomers will file into the room slowly, stand briefly over the casket to view the body, and drop a dollar bill or two into the small basket set near the corpse.[46] When they complete this ritual, they will leave the room. As they do, someone will hand them a roll or doughnut or biscuits wrapped in a paper napkin and a cup of coffee or punch. Outside they will mill around and chat in small groups for an hour or two, or perhaps spend the night there if they are closely related to the dead person. Occasionally, a church group will arrive, its members crowding into the room in which the body is laid out to sing hymns and offer prayers for the deceased. At some point the leader of the group will identify the group and offer a few words of condolence to the gathering or perhaps even do a bible reading followed by a short homily.

Young women will circulate around the crowd filling cups with coffee or sweetened ice water. As the evening wears on, women will begin passing around plates of food to those who are staying for a longer time. For most of the family it will be a sleepless night, for they will be entertaining the guests and providing for their needs as well as for more distant family members.

The Micronesian funeral is a miracle of rapid organization in a society better known for studied deliberateness in its activities. Somehow people and resources are pulled together from near and far in a matter of a few hours. Word is put out on the radio announcing the death within minutes of the event. Almost immediately relatives and friends gather and organize into work parties. Women take up their cooking stations, families decide on appropriate contributions, food gifts begin pouring in, the casket is purchased or work is begun on building one of plywood, and the location of the grave site is determined. The next twenty-four hours, or the next several days if the body is embalmed, is a time of feverish activity for the family and close friends.

The relatively recent practice of embalming may protract the wake a few days, but it is not the main reason for longer funerals today. Even after the burial, the modern Micronesian funeral may be extended several more days. In many places the length of the funeral celebration has changed from four days to nine owing to the influence of Catholicism, which introduced novenas for the dead.[47] Some Protestant communities, not to be outdone by Catholics, have lengthened the funeral celebration to nine or ten days. In Palau, where the sealing of the tomb was once done on the fourth day, it is now usually done on the ninth day in keeping with the timetable of the novena.[48] This is also the common practice in Yap, on both the mainland and the outer islands, and in most parts of Chuuk. In the Protestant Marshall Islands, likewise, the church service for the dead person is often held several days after the burial. Catholics in the Northern Marianas have taken a further step by recently adding a second family novena to the first, more public one, thus extending the length of the celebration to eighteen days.

The food served to relatives and guests who remain during this period is simple fare as opposed to feast food, and the family can expect to receive food gifts from relatives throughout this period. Even so, longer funerals strain the resources of the family. The burden of feeding guests for several days in addition to the obligation of providing for the funeral feast often puts the family into debt. It has become common for families to take out loans for family funerals. One person estimated that the average cost of a Marshallese funeral to the family of the deceased would be in the order of $3,000.[49] My own guess is that the expense incurred by a family in Pohnpei or Kosrae would be at least that.[50]

During the course of the funeral, the family is usually responsible for providing one feast. In Palau and Yap, with their concern for pollution and the restrictions imposed on cooking, the "feast" is in reality a food

Women mourning at a Palauan wake. (Julita Tellei)

exchange. In most island groups the feast concludes the funeral, occurring either at the *erak* or at the end of the novena, although in Pohnpei the feast takes place on the first day of the four-day celebration.

While the features of the funeral in all parts of Micronesia are moving toward uniformity, the celebration is also escalating in magnitude in most quarters. Funeral feasts nearly everywhere have grown in size and expense because of rapid modern communications and transportation. A funeral today is not just a community event involving perhaps a couple hundred fellow villagers, but one that can summon several hundred people, sometimes more than a thousand or two, from all over the island group. Consequently, a funeral on the larger islands is less a family celebration than a display of the family's resources and a bid for public recognition. Since funerals play to a much larger audience than they used to, there is much more at stake.

Pohnpei is a good illustration. When people describe the funeral feast, or *mwurilik*, held on the day of burial, they say that formerly it was arranged in such a way as to satisfy the family's needs. There may have been a high-titled chief at the funeral, but his presence did not drive the celebration. Family members, then as now, brought pigs, *sakau*, and yams

Squeezing *sakau* on Pohnpei. (Micronesian Seminar)

to the funeral, but just about everyone remarks that the number of pigs presented at a funeral in the 1960s and 1970s was much smaller than now. The earth oven in which the food was cooked was not opened until after the burial, and the food from the oven was truly used for a funeral feast rather than simply for ostentatious display and partition to the titled persons who attend.

Today the Pohnpeian funeral feast has, in the words of one anthropologist, become the "quintessential representation of custom."[51] As many of the former community feasts and first-fruit offerings have become extinct, funeral feasts have taken on their function to become the foremost occasions for the recognition of chiefly authority.[52] Few funerals occur on Pohnpei these days without some high chief, a Nahnmwarki or Nahnken, in attendance. Thus, the "public performance of power and hierarchy" in the funeral has come to supersede other considerations.[53] The large piles of pig carcasses outside the meetinghouse (*nahs*), the dozens of *sakau* plants that are presented in front of the platform in the *nahs*, and the yams brought to the funeral by guests are all divided up according to the rules for partitioning food at Pohnpeian feasts. As a result, there is a grand scale and formality to the funeral feasts that surpasses anything that might have been carried out on such occasions in the past. Funeral feasts, then, have been expanded and invested with much of the ceremony that once found expression in other feasts. It is almost as if the culture, fearing that other chiefly feasts will decline or vanish altogether, chooses to graft the recognition of "power and hierarchy" onto family funeral feasts. Funeral feasts might well be considered the perfect carrier, if only because funerals will never vanish.

Pohnpei is not the only place such a transfer has happened. In Yap the food exchanges, or *mitmit*, that were so integral a part of the culture and that were formerly associated with weddings have been transferred to funerals. There, too, the funeral has become much larger and much more expensive than it once was. This is to be expected, for the Yapese funeral carries a much larger cultural burden than it did in the past.

In every island group in Micronesia the funeral feast has escalated in the past few decades, even though this change has been largely unrecognized. In the minds of most people, the funeral feast is the embodiment of the traditional culture pure and simple. To adapt or diminish it in any form is seen as tantamount to striking a blow against the soul of the culture. Nonetheless, a few attempts have been made to reduce the considerable cost of funerals in resources and time. Forces in Chuuk and in Kosrae have been working toward this end, but progress has been slow.

7 Sexuality

From Nightcrawling to Dating

It was nearly dawn when Ioane and Yvette stumbled boozily, arm in arm, down one of the side streets in town. The first roosters were already crowing, and a few early risers, wrapped in towels, were preparing to take their morning shower. An occasional car would slow down as it passed the couple, the driver giving them a quick sidelong glance to see who they were. Ioane sometimes waved at the driver, wrapping his arm more tightly around Yvette and nearly pulling her off her feet as he yanked her toward him.

Ioane had been watching Yvette for months now. He had first seen her working as a clerk in a small store, but they hadn't spoken to one another at that time. Every now and then he caught sight of her in the town disco, and his eyes would follow her as she moved to and from the dance floor, but it was a month after he first saw her that they actually spoke to one another. After that they would chat for a time when they met by chance at the disco. Tonight was the first night Ioane had really been out with Yvette. They met at the disco again, but this time they were together the whole evening. They drank and talked and danced until closing time. Then they bought a few beers and went to a place alongside the river where they could be by themselves. It had been a romantic evening, especially satisfying for Ioane, who had been watching Yvette closely for so long. Now he was walking her home, even now dreaming of their next evening together.

In spite of all the fabled sexual freedom among South Sea Islanders, Micronesians in the 1950s would have been shocked at this scene. Many would be even today. Myths of insouciant romance aside, sexuality in the islands was tightly controlled in the past. Young people were allowed a certain measure of latitude in this area and were expected to have liaisons, but within what were regarded as reasonable limits. Some of the early anthropologists pointed out that the number of unmarried women in a village available for roving young bachelors was often extremely limited, thus acting as a control on sexual behavior.[1] Even where the supply was greater, sexuality was no more unrestricted than any other area of island life. Young people—and even the not-so-young—were permitted their sexual affairs, but it was expected that these would be conducted clandestinely, out of the public view. Discretion was the order of the day.

Nightcrawling was the rule, not the exception, in most parts of Micronesia. A young man who became enthralled by a young woman might watch her for a time without speaking to her directly. He would look for opportunities to signal his interest to the girl, usually in the most subtle ways. Now and then he might find occasion to exchange a word with her, but usually he would look for an intermediary to carry a message to the young woman of his dreams. There were other ways of communicating with one's sweetheart as well. When I first arrived in Micronesia in 1963, my students gleefully exposed me to a whole body of lore on what type of flowers might be worn behind which ear to deliver what messages to one's beloved. A favorite strategy in Chuuk, I later learned, was for the young man to befriend someone in her family so that he had a ready excuse for visiting her house. All of this was aimed at arranging an assignation with the girl in a way that would draw as little public attention as possible. Boys might boast of their conquests with close friends and talk of their current lady love, but they would not have dared to air this publicly.

In a small community, there were few opportunities for a boy and a girl to be together undisturbed for any length of time. To pursue a sexual affair without being detected was a risky adventure, something that undoubtedly added to the thrill. Unless the girl could find some way to meet the boy in the bush, he was required to visit her in her own house after everyone else in the family was asleep. Sometimes he might be able to arrange for her to leave the house, but very often he was obliged to sneak in and hold his tryst with the young lady in a house filled with her relatives. The Pohnpeian, Kosraean, and Chuukese languages have words for nightcrawling, the act of pursuing amours by slipping into the girl's house without disturbing the other members of the family.[2] In Chuuk the renowned lovestick was employed in such situations. According to the time-honored story, a boy would insert his lovestick, carved in his own pattern, through the nipa walls of the house to prod the young lady, who would signal the boy to enter or leave immediately, depending on her inclination.[3]

An assignation of this type could be a harrowing adventure, especially if the young man should wake up the family while he was there. A friend of mine once told how, during his courtship of the woman he later married, he had paddled to a nearby island to see her one night. While they were clandestinely visiting in the house, her uncle suddenly awoke, causing the young man to dash for his canoe and paddle furiously home. Each island has its repertoire of comical stories about the near escapes and misadventures resulting from nightcrawling.

A sexual relationship did not give the couple proprietary rights over one another. A young man did not publicly associate with his girlfriend even if he was seeing her every night and the whole village knew that they were conducting an affair. Regard for public opinion was strong, and custom dictated that such liaisons were to be conducted clandestinely. Young people could take advantage of the liberties they were conceded by their society, but they could not flout convention as they took their pleasure.

The couple could have sexual relations every night in secret without being regarded as married. Once they began sleeping through the night in the same house, however, they were considered as good as married. Smith recounts that Palauans who regarded a young man as a desirable match for their daughter might drug him and get him to oversleep so that he would be compelled to declare his intentions in the morning.[4] Lessa tells of the lengths to which one young man from Ulithi had to go to avoid being publicly detected by the family of the girl he was visiting. Awaking late, he hid in the rafters of the house all day until nightfall, when he could at last sneak out undetected.[5] In Micronesia, openly establishing a joint residence was tantamount to a public declaration of intention to marry.

Micronesian permissiveness in the matter of sex had its limits. Martha Ward, who lived on Pohnpei for a time during the early 1970s, writes that local people judged as irresponsible Peace Corps volunteers or military men fathering children with young girls.[6] I once heard a Pohnpeian adult rant indignantly about one American who made a habit of seeking out young girls as sexual partners without any regard for the way in which such things were done on the island. His objection seemed to be both the age of the girls and the openness with which the American solicited them in the community. Even in Pohnpei, an island that has long been viewed by Peace Corps volunteers and others as a garden of fleshly pleasures, not everything goes.

Promiscuity, while tolerated, has never been condoned in island Micronesia. Jack Fischer, who spent several years on Chuuk and Pohnpei between 1949 and 1954, once ridiculed as a "daydream" the view that Westerners might have of the islands as an "idyllic savage paradise where everybody spends his time making love with everybody else." Fischer makes a point that is often missed: "Even in pre-marital affairs faithfulness is valued and openly promiscuous men or women, especially the latter, are censured and held in low regard by the community. And while many parents condone some pre-marital sexual activity in their children they usually disapprove of any that does not involve a potential spouse for the child, especially if the child is a daughter."[7] On Ifaluk during the early postwar years, Burrows and Spiro report, an affair between young lovers was formalized through an exchange of gifts as a pledge of commitment to one another. The girl often did not allow her boyfriend to have sexual intercourse with her for the first few nights, until she was satisfied that their relationship was more than a casual affair.[8]

On most islands, a young woman who decided to move in with a man, whether local or foreign, might easily have obtained the blessing of her parents, especially if it looked as though the affair might end in marriage. Her sexual relationship, while it might not last forever, was expected to have some stability. Nowhere would she have been encouraged to change bed partners weekly or monthly.[9]

Sexual gratification was in principle accepted by Micronesian societies, but in practice it was more tightly regulated by these same societies than might at first appear to be the case. The separation of the sexes, the restricted access of young men to young women, and the premium placed on discretion in conducting sexual affairs were controlling forces in the past. Yet, all have been weakened to some extent by social change within the last thirty or forty years.

The education expansion that has occurred since the early 1960s is one important factor in this change. Coeducation, especially at the high school level, has given girls and boys much more direct access to one another than formerly. They take class with one another, participate in clubs and organizations with one another, and recreate with each other much more freely than would have been permitted in an earlier day. An especially visible landmark of this change has been the gradual acceptance of Western dancing into cultures that afforded almost no room for mixed-gender recreation for the young. The high school dances I used to help chaperone in Chuuk during the early 1970s were an ordeal for us and the students who attended them, however eagerly the students looked forward to them. Boys would nervously eye the girls at the other side of the hall even if they had fortified themselves beforehand with as much alcohol as they could get away with drinking.[10] A few brave souls might venture out onto the floor after the fourth or fifth number, but it wasn't until halfway through the evening that most of the boys self-consciously set foot on the dance floor. The last number, played over and over on the record player, was the signal for everyone to join in the fun.

Bars that offered music and dancing to young patrons were first established in Palau during the early 1960s, soon after the ban on alcohol was lifted for Micronesians. I remember how surprised I was, even then, to see girls on the back of motorcycles clinging to boys who could have been my students as they roared off when the bar closed at one or two o'clock in the morning. Other islands were slower to allow such changes, but by the end of that decade every island group except Kosrae had its bars and music. Their patrons were mostly males, although even then some young women were braving social convention to serve as dance partners. By the late 1970s, with the spread of the disco craze to Micronesia, a plethora of more respectable places opened, attracting with their strobe lights, enhanced sound systems, and, frequently, live bands a young clientele that was out for something more than to get drunk as quickly as possible. They wanted to dance and date and enjoy the lifestyle of the young that they had experienced in the United States or heard of from returning college students. The disco craze was soon followed by the rise of the nightclubs in Majuro and Ebeye, almost entirely patronized by young people.

Over the years Micronesian town-dwellers have come to accept the fact that Western dancing and dating are here to stay, even if they cannot bring themselves to endorse the practice. People are getting used to seeing boys and girls hang around with one another during the day and in the evening. As young people cultivate new expectations, parents find it difficult to monitor their daughters' comings and goings as closely as they might have years ago. The quality of parental supervision varies considerably from one community to the next, however. My impression is that parents in Chuuk and Kosrae continue to watch their daughters closely, while most of the other islands have relaxed their control a great deal.[11]

Today there is far more openness in the relationship between boys and girls. Girls and boys go out on dates quite openly, sometimes making a show of returning home quite late at night. At one time they would have hidden from onlookers, but couples like the one described at the beginning of this section now seem to be indifferent to the eyes of others.[12]

Martha Ward writes of the reports that have reached her about Pohnpei in the early 1990s: "I hear that young couples hold hands and eat together in public. Dating customs are changing. Young people who have gone off the island return wanting movies, restaurants, bars, and a separate young adult life-style. It is said that girls exchange sexual favors for a night out dancing."[13]

The difference, in Pohnpei and nearly everywhere else, is not young people's sexual behavior nowadays—that has been a constant in island life —but the lack of discretion with which they now practice it. Nightcrawling in today's island towns is becoming a lost art.

The Sanctuary of the Family

It is early evening and the family is seated on the floor of the main room in their wooden house in the village. The TV set, which has been playing continuously through the meal, has been largely ignored by everyone except the three small children, who have been watching some cartoons. Several video cassettes lie scattered on the floor. Matthew, the eighteen-year-old son, picks through the videos and finds one that he wants to watch. He ejects the cartoon that is playing, provoking loud complaints from the small children, and flips his video into the VCR. As he does, the patter of the older members of the family gradually is stilled as they wait to see what kind of a movie they will be watching. His older sister, a young woman in her early twenties, has just come in from showering. She sees the family quiet down, then pauses a moment at the door and finally takes a seat next to her sister, a high school student of sixteen. Her eleven-year-old brother, who has been paging through one of his textbooks as if he were considering doing his homework, puts the books aside and gazes intently at the screen. Their father, lying on the floor, slowly rises to a sitting position as the movie begins. Only their mother is missing; she is outside washing the dishes in a large plastic basin. One of the children calls out to her, but she tells him that she is busy and makes no effort to join them.

The title explodes onto the screen: "The Ranch Girls." A minute later the action begins with a shot of a young woman slipping off her blouse and skirt to join a blonde-haired, muscular man in bed. The oldest daughter, who has spent two years at a U.S. college, laughs when she sees where the movie is going. "Another one of those skin flicks, Matthew? Can't you ever find anything decent?"

Matthew lowers his head and smiles weakly without answering. His younger brother shifts uneasily on the floor. Their father looks quickly around the room, then lets his eyes wander up to the ceiling where he fixes his gaze on an imaginary spider web, or perhaps a gecko. The family falls into sudden silence. The only sound besides the loud, long moans from the TV set comes from the chatter of the small children, who are unaffected by what is showing on the screen.

Discussion of sexuality has never had a place in the sanctuary of the Micronesian family. Parents did not usually speak of sexual matters with their children, not even mother to daughter or father to son. The cross-gender barriers within the family were even higher, especially between brothers and sisters. Not only were they forbidden to speak of sexual matters directly, but they were expected to avoid any language that might even suggest sexual activity or bodily elimination. At one time the Chuukese language possessed an entire vocabulary of circumlocutions for words that hinted at certain parts of the body and their functions.[14] This polite, almost Victorian language was always used in mixed company in Chuuk and on the central Caroline atolls.[15] Chuukese distinguished the kind of speech that could be used in the dwelling house (that is, in the presence of women in the family) from speech that could be used in the cookhouse (where more relaxed speech was permitted) or in the men's house (where men could say just about anything). Other island cultures had similar prohibitions regarding the use of suggestive language in mixed company.

Although Chuukese no longer resort to the old circumlocutions in their speech, they studiously take pains to avoid any sexual innuendos in the presence of their female relatives. Others are expected to show the same *délicatesse* when speaking to a man in the presence of his "sister." I recall one memorable incident at Xavier some years ago when one of our students did not have the sense to do so. He used a vulgar expression when a Chuukese boy and his female cousin (a "sister" by local kinship reckoning), both of them also Xavier students, were within earshot. After brooding on the insult suffered by his cousin for more than an hour, the offended Chuukese boy charged into the study hall with a machete in hand and had to be wrestled to the ground by two strong outer island boys. We all learned that day, twenty years ago, just how binding the family prohibitions remained in Chuuk.

There were other taboos on sexual display within the family as well.

According to Goodenough, a man's relationship with his mature daughter in Chuuk was once as formally correct as the relationship between a man and his chief; he was to show her the utmost signs of respect and avoid any casual contact with her, steering away from anything that might be seen as the slightest indication of intimacy.[16] In those early postwar days, long after the introduction of Western clothing, Chuukese women were supposed to cover their breasts in the presence of certain male relatives.[17] On other islands similar restrictions were enjoined. Pohnpeian women, for instance, were not to display their underclothing where it could be seen by their brothers or close male relatives.[18] Menstruating women were to keep all evidence of their discharge hidden from the eyes of men in their family. Moreover, there was a universal ban on brothers and sisters sleeping under the same roof once they had reached puberty. Palauan women were compelled to set up their own dwellings, while in the rest of the Carolines young men generally moved out of the family dwelling to stay in men's houses or other buildings that might serve as male dormitories.[19] On certain islands, it would have been shocking for a brother and sister to share the same food or beverage or cigarette, or even taste food cooked over the same fire or drink from a single cup.[20] There was an old-fashioned formality to the relationship between men and women within the family. Boundary lines were drawn and barriers erected to prevent any unseemly familiarity between them.[21]

Although anthropologists have debated at times the reason for the strong cross-gender prohibitions within the family, it seems clear enough that, aside from their value as a token of respect, these restrictions were employed to prevent sexual liaisons between members of the family. Much of the elaborate machinery designed to keep sparks from catching fire within the family, in turn, has its origin in the island notion of sexuality, for people believe that the sexual urge is simply irresistible for a healthy male. Martha Ward captures this belief when she writes that islanders regard physical love as so overpowering that uncontrollable desire can be brought on by a "glimpse of an inner knee, a liquid look."[22] When a couple are alone together, it is assumed that they have been satisfying their overpowering sexual urges. In the island way of thinking, the only effective way to resist this urge is by avoiding all occasions for sexual contact—that is, by ensuring that women are not alone with men. The cultural restrictions on social contact within the family would have greatly reduced the possibility of such occasions.

Even today the mutual respect between males and females in the family remains unabated, with members still avoiding sexual references across gender lines. Just a few years ago I decided to test the force of the old taboos by mischievously remarking to a Micronesian friend of mine how pretty his female cousin was. His reaction was swift and strong. Although he was the gentlest and warmest of persons, he told me to shut up and never say anything like that again. I remembering smiling to myself afterwards, satisfied that at least one of the traditional values had remained secure against all the assaults of modernization.

The value may be as firmly rooted as ever, but many of the behavioral manifestations of it have changed over the years. Brothers and sisters, once prohibited from sleeping in the same house, now often share the same quarters. Goodenough noticed the change when he returned to Chuuk in 1964, seventeen years after his first visit. When he was doing his fieldwork there in 1947 on the island of Romanum, the ban was scrupulously observed: there were no instances in which adult brothers and sisters —or even those who used these kinship terms of one another—lived under the same roof. By the time of his return, it was not unusual to find them living in the same house.[23] The old prohibition has fallen into disregard in other islands as well. Even in the more conservative corners of Micronesia such as the atoll of Ifaluk, brothers and sisters began sleeping in the same dwellings sometime after World War II, when the use of men's houses as male sleeping quarters was abandoned.[24]

Likewise, many of the other practices that once served as safeguards of family integrity and signs of cross-gender respect have fallen into disuse. Today on Pohnpei women's undergarments are hung on the line to dry in full sight of everyone in the family. Brothers and sisters, especially in more modernized areas, no longer feel the need to avoid eating from the same plate or drinking from the same cup. But in what may be the most important change of all, mass media have introduced an element of explicit sexuality into the very bosom of the family, where it was once excluded. Video rentals, especially, open the family up to the world of R-rated movies—nothing of great importance if young men were watching by themselves, but a shocking departure from custom when the assembled family, males and females together, watch a love scene in an R-rated movie, as in the vignette above. In some families someone might grab the remote control and fast-forward through the steamy parts of the video to spare everyone embarrassment, but in others this does not happen. Instead, the family may sit frozen when sex scenes begin, responding only with nervous laughter or perhaps awkward silence. Yet, even such a reaction is a gauge of the enormous encroachments that recent change has made on the customs that once protected a key value in the Micronesian constellation: cross-gender respect in the family.

With the relaxation of the taboos within the family, one might expect to see an increase in incest.[25] Indeed, there has always been some incest on the islands—there were two cases in Pohnpei when Fischer arrived there after the war and an isolated case or two on the atolls of the central Carolines—but its occurrence seems to have been very rare.[26] It appears to be less rare today. A 1985–1986 survey of child abuse in four of the island groups in Micronesia turned up several reported cases of incest, and I know of several other instances of young women so regularly molested by their fathers or uncles that they had to be sent off in secrecy to live with relatives on another island.[27]

Whether the apparently growing problem of incest can be attributed in any way to the breakdown of the old restraints on sexual matters within the family is uncertain. Micronesians everywhere still honor the old value of cross-gender respect and avoidance, but many of the forms that used to embody this respect seem to have been lost in recent decades. These forms may prove to be more essential than they might have seemed.

Sex at the Service of the Family

"Let me introduce you to my husband," she said. We shook hands and chatted for a while about life in Honolulu. Her husband said that he had been born and raised in Hawai'i. Like so many others here, he told me, he was little bit of this and a little bit of that: his ancestry was part Chinese, part Hawaiian, part Portuguese, with a little Filipino, Scottish, and Italian thrown in. I explained that I knew his wife when she was a student at Xavier High School about fifteen years before. She had put on a few pounds since then, I said, but it didn't take long to see that she was the same effervescent person she had been when I taught her English and history.

"Didn't your wife want to return to Palau once you were married?" I asked him.

He frowned and sneaked a quick glance at his wife, who was absorbed in conversation with someone else. "We went back for a year to try it out. I liked it and wanted to stay for a while, but she couldn't wait to leave. Whenever they had a family event, her relatives would come around to ask if we could help out. I had no problem with that. I had a good job with a hotel there and was getting a nice salary. I was glad to contribute to those family parties. They were all new to me and I was getting an eyeful, but my wife kept complaining at the way her relatives were eating into our savings. She told me that there would be no end to it until we got so far away that they couldn't reach us."

"Is Hawai'i really beyond the reach of her family?" I asked.

He chuckled as he replied. "Not really. Her family calls a couple times a week, and we get plenty of requests for help. But she's trying to talk me into moving to New Jersey. I have a job offer there, and she thinks that we should be safe on the East Coast."

While sexuality was rarely spoken of within the family, it was generally understood that the sexual conduct of its members was very much a family concern. Sexuality, like every other area of their lives, lay securely under the aegis of the family, whose interests it was meant to serve. The family urged certain controls on the young boy or girl: the importance of observing exogamous marriage rules and avoiding even the appearance of any sexual contact with relatives. Children were also warned against sexual experimentation at too young an age; they were told they would become sick if they had sex too early. In Ifaluk, for example, girls were not to have intercourse before their third menstruation, while boys were not to engage in sex before they were about sixteen.[28]

Sexuality, while providing for the young a zone of adventure stamped with a rare sense of individuality, was expected, in the end, to be used for the advancement of the family. Sexual relationships might afford deep personal satisfaction in an area closed to all but one's closest friends. They might provide the intoxicating thrill of the illicit and slightly dangerous. Even so, it was generally understood that sexuality, like everything else in one's life, was ultimately to be placed at the service of the family.

There is a long tradition in Micronesia of the use of sex for family advancement. On Pohnpei and Kosrae during the wild years of the old whaleship trade in the nineteenth century, girls sold their bodies to seamen to gain access to cloth, iron tools, and other valuables that their families might not otherwise be able to acquire. Prostitution was the one means that commoners had to break the trade monopoly enjoyed by the high chiefs on these islands.[29] In Palau of the last century, women were chosen to work in the men's clubhouses on the basis of their attractiveness and sexual skills. Their short employment, which included providing sexual services for clubhouse members, was generously rewarded with the gift of Palauan valuables, which brought social recognition and higher status for their families.[30] Much the same road to advancement existed in Yap, where girls also once served in village men's houses in exchange for "money" and prestige. Even in Chuuk, generally regarded as rather puritanical compared with its neighbors, girls were encouraged to use their sexual allure to win a good match—that is, a man who could provide land and prestige to the girl's family. Sexuality, even apart from eventual marriage, has always been recognized as a valuable tool for enriching the family and advancing its status.[31]

The belief that sex is supposed to serve the interests of the family was fully embraced during the years following World War II. There was never any doubt that this was still very much the case in Palau, even though Palauan women had ceased to serve in the clubhouses for over half a century. Only after they had consulted with their families would Palauan women settle into sexual relationships. Their husbands or boyfriends, even if they were foreigners, were absorbed into the Palauan exchange network. Such a man was expected to support his wife or girlfriend's kin group at the time of the customary events, although it was understood that he could not draw on the same large pool of relatives that Palauan men had at their beck.

This belief is still very much operative today in the lives of most Micronesian couples, even those who live abroad, but there are signs of erosion, as the story with which I began this section illustrates. The Palauan woman married to a non-Micronesian seemed more eager to protect her man from the relentless demands of her family than to exploit him to advance the social status of her blood family. She might have chosen him as her spouse without the measure of parental approval that would have been expected in the past. She clearly regarded him more as a provider for their nuclear family than as a source of potential wealth for her kin. To reinforce her position, she urged him to move to the mainland United States to attempt to keep him beyond the long reach of the Palauan exchange network. In this respect, she was simply doing what more and more young Micronesians are doing today: setting up a household at a distance from her kin (and sometimes from his) to limit the demands placed on them by their families. Hence, the flow of resources back into her family, although not blocked entirely, will be a much thinner stream than would have been the case in earlier times.

Although this young Palauan woman is not typical, she is by no means uncommon these days. I know another Micronesian woman, married to an American and living on Guam, who has become the gate-keeper of their household and the last line of defense against what she calls her preying kinfolk. She has taken it upon herself to inform her cousins and even uncles, usually in language that cannot be misunderstood, that they have overstayed their welcome in the house or that they may not borrow the money they have asked for. Like the woman in the vignette, she has taken on the role of guardian of her husband's and children's interests.

All these changes could perhaps be attributed to a new understanding of marriage, which is itself the product of the rise of the nuclear family. Yet, it could also be argued that they might be traced to the growing individualism that is another product of the decline of the extended family. Today young people not only conduct their sexual relations outside the gaze of the family, as they would have done in the past, but they increasingly keep the relationships that develop from these encounters beyond the ken of the family. More frequently today girls seem to bestow their favors on boys who provide something personal for them—a night on the town or a nice gift—rather than something that translates into credit for their families. In short, sexuality is becoming a commodity used less to serve the family than to advance one's own personal interests.

8 Political Authority

A Hibiscus in the Wind

Kasiano had just been caught. The local newspaper, always slower than the coconut telegraph to pick up the latest, juiciest tidbit, had come out with the story only the day before. "Misuse of public funds" is what they called it in the newspaper article. "Malfeasance" was the term that a prominent government lawyer had used. The bald facts were that Kasiano had dipped into his municipal public works funds and helped himself to nearly $25,000 that had been set aside to rebuild a village dock. People who knew Kasiano would shake their heads and mumble something to the effect that it wasn't the first time this kind of thing had happened. After all, no one ever did find out where all that money earmarked for the youth center went a couple of years ago. But Kasiano was not just another villager; he was the ranking chief of the northwest section of the island. Since people showed him the usual forms of respect due a high chief, it was very unlikely that any of his people would publicly support the charges that were being brought against him. As for Kasiano, the paper quoted him as claiming that he was entitled to use the money for his own purposes. The money was his to appropriate since he was chief, after all. Isn't public money the present-day equivalent of the local food that his people would once have offered him in tribute, he asked.

While Kasiano is not being presented as typical of island chiefs, the kind of incident illustrated above has happened more than once in modern-day Micronesia. Even more important, the story illustrates some of the tensions that have arisen regarding the role of the traditional island chief in today's nation-state. What authority, if any, does the traditional chief possess in today's new island society? What are the obligations of the chief to his people and vice versa? How have expectations on both sides changed in the years following World War II?

121

The terms "chief" and "traditional leader" are notoriously ambiguous when applied to Micronesia. Because of the different forms of traditional political organization found on various islands, the terms meant different things in different places. A chief was one thing on Pohnpei and quite another on one of the atolls of the central Carolines.

In precontact times Pohnpei and Kosrae were the most highly centralized and stratified societies in Micronesia, and the Marshalls was right behind them.[1] Each of these places had paramount chiefs, with lesser sectional chiefs to provide a support base for the high chiefs. The people provided tribute to the paramount chief in return for the right to use the land they worked. In Yap and Palau, in contrast, the highest authority was the village chief, who was assisted by a council representing all the ranking clans in the village. Villages might have a higher or lower status, depending on their success in warfare and other accomplishments. Some villages might acquire considerable influence and hold a privileged position in the alliances or islandwide networks that were continually being reshaped, even though they never exercised direct political authority over another village.[2] There were three or four main centers of power in Yap and Palau. Least stratified of all were Chuuk and the atolls of the central Carolines (together with the precontact Marianas). Small geographical units on which matrilineal groups had settled were ruled by the head of the ranking matrilineage. The political authority over an island comprising several of these units was very weak and subject to continual renegotiation. On many atolls political leadership was shared between the leaders of the top-ranking three or four clans.[3]

Chiefly authority everywhere was rooted in the claim to land. The words of a Tongan noble about his own islands apply just as much to Micronesia: "The land was our power base and we used to have the respect of the people because we owned the land."[4] In general, political authority was bestowed on a representative of the clan that was recognized as having the strongest claim to the land, whether through earliest arrival or by virtue of conquest. Although people from other clans later shared in the use of this land, the residual rights to the land that were held by the senior group grounded its claim to political authority and to the homage, tribute, and other signs of respect that usually accompanied this authority.[5] These claims were usually supported by myths memorializing the authority of the ranking clan, often divinizing this authority by linking it to the gods.[6]

Rank and status ran through every aspect of island life, so much so that it was unnecessary to flaunt them by personal flamboyance. It would have been all but impossible for a first-time visitor to one of the coral atolls to determine who the island chief was, so unostentatiously did island leaders conduct themselves.[7] Even on the larger, more hierarchical islands, chiefs were expected to assume a humble demeanor. There were no scepters, thrones, or palaces to be found in Micronesia. The status of chiefs could be more easily inferred from the respect that people paid them than from their clothing or other personal accouterments. Chiefs were deferred to, addressed in honorific language, awarded the seats of honor and choicest foods at feasts, and on some islands offered regular tribute or first fruits from their people inasmuch as they possessed residual rights over the land that their people worked.

The powers of chiefs varied from place to place. Even so, the common expectation everywhere was that the chief was to serve the people by what today would be called community building. Chiefs did this, first of all, by initiating public projects—including the construction of community buildings and docks, the paving of public paths, and village cleanups. At one time chiefs were also expected to stimulate productivity in the community by encouraging their people to plant and harvest more. Chiefs managed the community landholdings, which would have been the equivalent of today's public land. They were also entrusted with the responsibility of keeping the peace within the realm by reconciling conflicts between families and factions in the community.[8]

The obligations of chiefs to their people were every bit as real, though not always as visible, as their entitlements. "A chief is a hibiscus in the wind," as a Pohnpeian proverb put it, meaning that the chief is expected to bow and bend in response to his people's needs the way a wind-blown hibiscus stalk might.[9] Other islands might have had other metaphors to express the solicitousness that a chief was expected to show for his subjects. The chief was expected to be a care provider for his people besides being a caretaker of its communal holdings. He was to provide for his people when they were hungry, lead the way to new lands when the population had outgrown its present area, and protect them when they were threatened by outside forces.

Chiefs were expected to give generously to their people. A popular Marshallese saying states that "the paramount chief has three stomachs: one for food, one for storing people's gossip, and one as a storehouse of goods for the people."[10] A good chief was expected to "regurgitate" his goods to provide for the community, even at his personal expense. Marshallese paramount chiefs during German rule would purchase tools for their workers and pay the passage to Jaluit, the site of the hospital, for anyone needing medical attention.[11] This expectation was widespread throughout Micronesia: chiefs on Ifaluk were said to be distinctive only in the value and number of gifts they offered, while chiefs on Yap apparently outdid the generosity of those who were supposed to be offering them tribute.[12]

Admittedly, this idealistic depiction may better represent what chiefs ought to have been than what they were. Still, many people fondly remember in their former traditional leaders a sense of noblesse oblige that they hint may be missing today.

Whatever the case, it is clear that Micronesian chiefs are still respected today despite the social disruption that modernization has inflicted on island life. Indeed, they may be paid even more respect than they enjoyed before the war, for on many islands people regard them as a valued link with the past that must be maintained, whatever the cost. Many times on Pohnpei I have witnessed people falling all over themselves to find a padded chair or bring a special plate of food to a high chief, even when he was merely attending a civic or church meeting and had no special role in the event. Installation ceremonies for new chiefs in Palau, replete with many of the symbols of the past, are always well attended. Even in the central Carolines and Chuuk, where chiefly authority was much more limited, the forms of respect for chiefs continue to be observed. On Ulithi, for instance, any turtles caught at sea are brought to the main islet of Mogmog and presented to the ranking chief, as people there have done for hundreds of years.

While the institution of chieftainship has survived, the nature of the relationship between chiefs and their people has changed in at least two important respects. First, chiefs do not seem as strongly bound to their people by reciprocity as they were in earlier years; they receive but do not give as freely as they did in the past. Second, the dynamic exchange between chiefs and their people that allowed others to share political authority has partially broken down. One often hears it said today that chiefs are meant to lead, while commoners have no responsibility other than to obey. This statement would have been far from true in earlier times.

The incident involving Kasiano described above, a situation that has been repeated many times over the last thirty or forty years, suggests that many chiefs today see their title as a path to privilege rather than an invitation to serve their people. The ideal chief, in the eyes of most Micronesians, is the person who is prepared to impoverish himself to provide for his people. The flow of goods and wealth was two-way in the past: from the chief to his people as well as from them to him. By way of illustration, Carucci notes that when Marshallese chiefs sailed to other atolls to pick up their share of the copra profits once or twice a year, they did not go empty-handed; their canoes were filled with goods that their people might be able to use. Carucci quotes an old Marshallese informant who described how the chief's heavily laden canoe would progress from island to island, dropping off food and supplies on the way out and picking up food crops as tribute on the return trip.[13]

At one time the paramount chief on Pohnpei or the Marshalls was expected to assist those commoners who worked the land to make it productive. This role may have entailed chiefly blessings on the land in pre-Christian days, as some authors suggest; certainly it meant granting people the right to use the land to feed their families and benefit the community.[14] The chiefs might be given a token amount of profit from crops or copra sales, but their portion seems to have been modest compared with what chiefs are receiving today. In the Marshalls during the nineteenth century, for instance, the chief's share was about 10 percent of the market value of all copra sold; it has risen to one-third of the commercial value of the land in recent times.[15] The increase is especially striking in the case of rental fees for Marshallese land on Kwajalein, where payments run into the millions of dollars.

On Pohnpei these days, more of the tribute given to the paramount chiefs for title feasts and other ceremonial events comes in the form of nontraditional goods. When titles are bestowed on affluent Pohnpeians, the latter often reciprocate with gifts of money or store-bought goods— as when a chief was presented with a large branch, with bills attached to every twig and shoot, or given the keys to a pickup truck loaded with cases of food.[16] In former times, the "payment" to the paramount chief bestowing the title was made in yams or *sakau* or pigs—all of which could be divided up and redistributed to others at the end of the feast. Money and cash-bought goods cannot be redistributed as readily, if only because it seems so much more psychologically difficult for chiefs to surrender cash.

The old authority system, despite its elaborate shows of respect toward chiefs, allowed ample input from commoners before decisions were made, and it had strong controls on the authority of the chief. So much so, in fact, that two social scientists working in the central Carolines during the early years of U.S. naval administration concluded that there was no need for U.S. naval authorities to proceed with their planned public elections. They were convinced that the island society they were studying was already as democratic as the United States. The only time they ever heard the island chiefs give orders to anyone, they wrote, was at a community work project where "utter anarchy" reigned and everyone else was shouting orders as well.[17]

A story I heard years ago illustrates this point very well. A highly respected village chief in Chuuk once stood up in a men's house to give a speech laying out a course of action that he was proposing to the village. Hardly had he begun spelling out his plan when his audience dissolved into small groups, the men murmuring to one another even as the chief continued his speech. The chief talked on for another twenty minutes, but by the end of his talk he had swung from his original proposal to a very different plan that he judged more acceptable to the people of the village. As he had been speaking, he was also weighing the response and making appropriate changes in the plan he was presenting. Thus it is that a Chuukese delegate to the 1975 Micronesian Constitutional Convention could justly claim that on his island "the chiefs tell the people what to do and the people tell the chiefs what to do."[18]

Even in Pohnpei, where chiefs enjoyed greater power than on most other islands, political authority was shared, and checks were employed to insure against overconcentration in a single person.[19] Chiefs who did not respond to the people's needs or afford them the opportunity to contribute to the decision-making process—in other words, chiefs who did not bend in the wind—were often disowned by their people. When a Marshallese paramount chief, who had long neglected his people during their forced migration because of U.S. nuclear testing on their island, belatedly tried to visit them, he was told that he was not welcome on the island and shown his way back to the ship.[20]

It may be that the status of the chief has been frozen. In Micronesia there seems to be a popular but unfounded notion that the traditional chief was a despot with supreme and unchallenged power. This has never been true in Micronesia, although many local people and outsiders evidently believe the myth. To judge from the number of stories about chiefs like Kasiano that are heard today, the controls on the authority of the chief and the boundaries of this authority have changed in the past fifty years. Those checks that may still be effective come less from the traditional structures of political authority on an island than from the modern political system, which has introduced new boundaries.

The Dual-Chief System

The meetinghouse was filled to overflowing for the islandwide celebration. People sat tightly packed on the floor, while dozens more stood outside the low walls of the building. Hanging from the rafters like bunting were long folds of cloth in different bright patterns that would be offered to the women later. The master of ceremonies stood toward the front of the throng. Behind him, on chairs arranged in an arc, sat perhaps twenty island dignitaries. The magistrate and the municipal judge were seated at one end next to a couple of prominent pastors. Nearly all the rest of the seats were occupied by the island chiefs, most of them fanning themselves with their programs. Off to the side slightly behind the row of chairs, a well-dressed middle-aged man crouched, careful to draw as little attention to himself as possible. He was the congressman who represented the island in the national legislature. After one of the pastors rose to give the invocation, the master of ceremonies called on the congressman to address the assembly. The congressman stood, his body still bowed, and paid his respects one by one to the traditional leaders present. With apologies for his presumptuousness, he began his brief remarks hesitantly. After thanking the island leaders for inviting him to the celebration, he made a few observations on the importance of the celebration and pledged his support for the development program that the island leaders endorsed. He concluded his short talk with another word of thanks and returned to his place, seemingly grateful to be out of the limelight. The day belonged to the people and their chiefs, he had told the crowd.

Two weeks later, a group of eight of these chiefs appeared at the office of the congressman in town. He hurried out to greet them and usher them into his office, while one of his staff scurried around to find chairs for everyone in the delegation. When everyone was finally seated, someone brought in coffee for everyone. From his seat behind his desk, the congressman surveyed the group while he chatted for a while. Then, after a brief lull in the conversation, a spokesman for the delegation of chiefs finally announced the purpose of the visit. They had come to seek funding for some public works projects that could not be built without assistance from the congress.

The above incident, which has been reenacted time and again throughout the islands, illustrates the split of political authority that has occurred in Micronesia. While local chiefs, still respected today, have their locus of authority in the village, elected government officials now enjoy considerable authority of their own, thanks to the resources they command. Today's society is one in which political authority is divided between the two. In effect, a "dual-chief" system operates in the islands today.

The modern political system in Micronesia today, intertwined as it

Congress of Micronesia in session (1965). (TT Archives, University of Hawai'i Library)

has become with the traditional political system, was a creation of the U.S. administration in the early postwar era. A year or two after the U.S. occupation of Micronesia at the end of World War II, the first elections were held for municipal offices throughout the islands. Magistrates, often different individuals from the traditional chiefs, were chosen by ballot to exercise formal authority over islands or clusters of villages. Over the next several years, district councils, which in time would evolve into legislatures, were established in each island group. Finally, in 1965, the modern government was expanded to a new and broader level when the territory-wide Congress of Micronesia was formed.[21]

For sixty years before the war, Micronesia had been ruled by foreign administrations, but these administrative bureaucracies were staffed almost entirely by expatriates. Even though these colonial administrations represented the supreme authority in the islands, the traditional system they blanketed operated much as it always had. Beneath the flurry of executive orders and decrees that flowed from offices staffed by foreigners, chiefs did what they always had done, even when their authority was hedged in by colonial governments. The colonial administrations used whatever means they had in order to domesticate chiefs and fashion their councils into suitable instruments for indirect rule. At times, the Japanese chose new chiefs to suit their purposes and seated their hand-picked men in the chiefly council. When this happened in Palau, the people adapted by developing a dual-chief system: the Japanese-appointed man represented the community in all official council meetings, while the "deposed" chief continued to function behind the scenes as the real community leader.[22] The officially sanctioned chief, in representing the community and its needs to the colonial government, brokered outside resources for the community in a pattern that continued long afterwards.

A form of this "dual-chief system" became institutionalized in the islands during the U.S. trusteeship. Micronesian elected officials on every level—municipal, district, and territorial—represented their communities in the modern government, even as the chiefly system continued to operate at the grassroots level. By the time that the Micronesian islands became fully self-governing, in about 1980, the parallel political systems were deeply etched into island life. A modern political system staffed by Micronesian officials overlay the patchwork of traditional chieftainships in the islands.

At first, during the early years under the U.S. Navy, island peoples experimented to find a formula that would integrate the traditional authority system into the modern one. The people of Palau and Yap and the Marshalls used the first elections in late 1947 to reappoint the traditional chiefs who had been deposed by the Japanese, electing them as magistrates on many islands. For a time, people in many island groups cautiously admitted traditional leaders into the legislature, but they later found this system unworkable. During those early postwar years Micronesians seemed to be scrambling to get the right formula. In the end, in every island group except the Marshalls, they decided not to integrate traditional leaders into the modern political system. The most common explanation, heard from one end of Micronesia to the other, is that an elected office cheapens the traditional authority of their chiefs and diminishes these chiefs in the eyes of their people. In fact, however, there are probably other unspoken reasons. To have chiefs seated beside commoners in a participatory government system would reduce the commoners to silence and possibly impotence, something that most people would surely not want to happen. Whatever the reason, in nearly all island groups traditional leaders and elected government officials have gone their separate ways.[23]

Although respect is paid to chiefs and chiefly authority is still recognized in traditional areas, chiefs do not have the same sway over local affairs that they once had. A Yapese friend of mine who is an astute observer of cultural matters claims that the authority of chiefs has declined steadily in Yap since he was a child. Palauans I talk to say the same about their traditional leaders. This stands to reason, if only because the resources traditional leaders command today are of less importance than they once were. Except in the Marshalls, the hold of chiefs on the land has been weakened greatly through years of colonial rule.[24] But there is another, even more important reason for the decline in chiefly authority today: money, the resource that has surpassed even land in importance today, flows from outside sources. Traditional leaders have little control over this stream of money; it is the elected officials who have their hands on the faucet. The modern government and those who serve it make nearly all the major decisions at the islandwide level and above.

The dual-chief system was invented to allow hereditary island chiefs to operate according to custom at a time when colonial governments threatened to throttle the traditional political system. As this system has become firmly rooted in Micronesia during the last fifty years, traditional chiefs have remained masters of their own domain—namely, the traditional sector with its emphasis on subsistence production.[25] Yet, that sector represents an ever shrinking part of total island life today, largely owing to the comparatively enormous pool of cash funds that Micronesia's "shadow chiefs," its government officials, can make available to their people. It is ironic that the dual-chief system, established to preserve and protect the authority of traditional leaders, should have had the effect of diminishing their real political authority in the end.[26]

Some of these traditional leaders, sensing that they are losing ground, hustle to establish a broader power base for themselves. Some go into business, usually opening a store or partnering in a tourist venture; others obtain a good job in the upper echelons of the civil service. Still others defy the informal taboo against chiefly involvement in the modern political arena and run for elected office. When this happens nowadays, the traditional chief will almost always lose.[27] The election returns are a sharp reminder that the people would prefer to keep their chiefs far from the hurly-burly of the modern political arena.

Even where the traditional leaders have been unable or unwilling to parlay their role into a new power base, they are treated with a respect bordering on reverence. Elected and appointed officials in the modern government with access to many more riches than the chiefs themselves could ever command fall in line to pay them homage, as in the story at the beginning of this section. Oddly enough, the greater the measure of political change and the smaller the resource base traditional leaders can claim, the more tenaciously people seem to cling to them. The prestige of traditional leaders seems to have increased even as their direct political authority has diminished.

While officials in the modern government keep the schools and hospitals operating, manage the funds for public services, and keep the nation-state on course, traditional leaders may seem to be dealing with far more humble matters: organizing village events and feasts, and dispensing titles and honors, for instance. The truth is, however, that the respect paid to chiefs at the most basic levels of society makes them indispensable aides in advancing the national program in any Pacific nation. They can perform special grassroots services that the government does not have the means or interest to accomplish. In addition to keeping the peace and re-solving conflicts among the people in their chiefdom, as they have always done, they can broker local economic development projects, offer public support and endorsement for current movements, and serve as a conduit of information between the central government and their communities (as they did in colonial days). One high chief on Pohnpei, by recently lending his support to a watershed conservation project, ensured that good-sized audiences would attend the public meetings and that the measures being proposed would get a fair hearing.

Much of what chiefs do today can be summed up as providing legitimacy for government leaders and their programs. Without their support for government-sponsored projects and programs, these would have little chance of getting off the ground. Chiefs also provide legitimacy for government officials, especially those who are elected. They may do this, as on Pohnpei, by granting prestigious traditional titles to governors, congressmen, legislators, and other highly placed government officials. In Yap, in contrast, the chiefs meet to approve and validate a candidate for elected office; without their approval a candidate could not hope to win. On Kosrae, where church leaders stand in for the traditional chiefs the island once had, support from these modern-day "traditional leaders" is required of any serious contender for political office.[28]

Perhaps one of the most important functions of traditional leaders in the islands today is to restore proper balance to the hybrid political system that has emerged in the last half century. The old political systems in Micronesia, from the most hierarchical to the least complex, were all organized to permit authority to be shared widely by any and all who had an interest in the decision making. The figure of the paramount chief, in those islands that had one, may have seemed to tower above all other persons, but in reality he was the "personification of power" rather than an autocrat.[29] The chief was, in a sense, the subject of the people he ruled. To guard against the concentration of power in the hands of an individual (or a single polity), Micronesian societies developed a complex system of checks and balances on every level. The cross-cutting authority system in Yap, with its three major alliances and its twofold division into "men's chiefs" and "young men's chiefs," is a good example.[30] Another example can be found in the Palauan system of dualities, in which one power bloc was countered by another at every level.[31] These systems successfully guarded against any leader who might be inclined to make a power play to acquire supremacy over the entire island group, as happened in Hawai'i and Tahiti in the nineteenth century.

The once balanced traditional political system has been upset by the introduction of the modern government, headed by elected officials with enormous cash resources at their disposal. At a time when this new political system threatened to wipe the other political players off the board, Micronesian societies appear to have developed their own defenses against the threat of such a monopoly. Traditional leaders, whose authority seemed to be on the wane, have been reaffirmed by their people and today are treated with as much respect as ever—or more. Petersen writes that people on Pohnpei perceive their traditional chiefs as a force that can be used to keep the national congress in check, but his statement could be broadened considerably.[32] The people of Yap, Chuuk, Kosrae, and Palau also appear to be using their traditional leaders as a bulwark to keep in check the entire modern political sector—governors, state legislators, magistrates, other elected officials, top-level civil servants, and all else who wield power in its newest form.

Traditional chiefs, then, are a counterbalance to the growing authority of the modern leadership in today's island societies. They can serve this function to the extent that they are kept safely out of the modern political system, despite the occasional inclination of a chief to run for elected office. This interpretation may explain the decision that Micronesians made repeatedly in early postwar years and have ratified time and again that traditional chiefs should not become elected officials in the modern government.[33] (Only in the Marshalls, where paramount chiefs regularly run for the national legislature, is there no separation of these different

Meeting of the early district legislature in Chuuk (1957). (Library of Congress of FSM)

political realms.³⁴) In this way, traditional leaders can be viewed as performing today their age-old function of protecting their people—not
from external enemies or improvidence in food production, but from the
harm that could befall them if the modern government system ever held a
monopoly on political authority.

Making the Voice of Authority Heard

*The new head of the accounting department, a young man in his early
thirties, had been in his position for less than six months. From the day
he first walked into the office, he sensed that he would have trouble working with his staff. His staff was deferential toward him, but in a chilly
and remote way. Then he began having difficulty getting work assign-
ments from his staff. Even when he explained in the gentlest manner that
he needed the report by the end of the week, he would get it a week or two
late without any explanation of why it wasn't done on time. Sometimes,
when he asked someone to take on a special project, the person would
promise to do it but back out suddenly at the last minute. He couldn't
help wondering whether there was a conspiracy among the office staff to*

force him to quit in frustration. Was it his young age? His outer island background? Were they jealous of him for his quick rise to the head of the department? Or displeased that one of their own group had not been regarded as suitable for the top position? For several minutes he stared down at his desk wondering what to do.

The problem of the exercise of authority in present-day Micronesia reaches beyond traditional chiefs and elected officials, touching the management of government offices and even private businesses. It is a problem that vexes office heads, school principals, and even church pastors. How does the person who finds himself or herself in charge of a team of employees acquire the right to rule? How does he or she win the acceptance needed to provide real leadership for his or her coworkers?

A person's rank has always been based on the status of his or her family's land and, at least in some islands, on the titles he or she possesses. It could also depend on ties through kinship or marriage to other prominent individuals in the community, not to mention personal achievements and services to the society. Within the family circle, rank was determined by gender and age, so that older persons enjoyed a higher status than younger family members and males generally a higher status than females. Rank has always conferred a measure of authority in the islands.

Any island society, with its social network of well-defined statuses and roles, had a shared understanding of who was in charge of what. There were master navigators and those called on to lead fishing expeditions, not to mention those regarded as expert craftsmen, boatbuilders, and healers. These were people whose competence was recognized by the community. No doubt there were overlapping spheres of authority at times and even contested positions, but the traditional leaders would have negotiated a resolution in such cases.

New roles were created through the years as the islands were affected by the cultural influences of the Western world. An anthropologist who worked in Majuro soon after World War II identified a handful of what could be called new specialists—persons who had skills in a certain area and were recognized by the community as having special responsibilities in connection with this area.[35] The island pastor was one such person, and the medical aide, who had received some training in medicine, was another. In those early days the schoolteacher, who served under American officials, was one of the few persons on the island who knew English. Hence, his status and the authority that derived from it were secure. Each of these persons held distinctive credentials for the position he occupied. As was true of those with traditional leadership roles, the community in some form approved these persons, endorsing them even if it did not appoint them, and sanctioned their roles.

These roles are muddier with today's dual political authority systems and sprawling, less clearly defined communities. No longer is there a single candidate for health aide or only one person capable of teaching in English in a Western-style school. Many people have been trained to assume any given position; five or ten or twenty individuals might have the background necessary to take an accounting job, for example. The governor might have appointed a young man as the head of the state accounting office, giving him a clear title to the job, but for this man to become the effective head of an office team, he must gain acceptance from those he works with. His appointment by the governor doesn't guarantee this. A former student of mine who was named as principal in one of the schools in the Federated States of Micronesia told me that he had similar problems gaining the confidence of his teachers. For a year or longer he struggled in his new position, feeling all the while that the staff of his school never really accepted him as their leader.

Government bureaucracies are supposed to function in such a way that people's roles are defined by position in the organization and not by personal characteristics; such attributes as status in the community, title, and family ties should not affect one's performance at all. The bureaucracy ought to be impersonal, in theory at least, and its staff should be interchangeable functionaries who fill the slots assigned them. Ideally, any person could be replaced by anyone else with the necessary skills for the position with no impact on the system whatsoever. This, at least, is the theory, although what are labeled as bureaucracies in Micronesia operate very differently.[36]

Many government officials today recognize that in order to succeed in a government post it helps greatly to have other claims to respect beyond the official title of the post that one bears. To have a high traditional title or to be an ordained minister or high church official gives a person a leg up on others, often making it possible for him or her to win acquiescence from office mates, which might otherwise be more difficult. Young men from highly ranked families usually find their office mates deferring to them in many subtle and not so subtle ways. To gain legitimacy is not the problem for them that it is for others of lower rank.

Another strategy, akin to the first, is to ensure that one's office subordinates are all persons who owe one respect and obedience for cultural reasons. I remember once asking a mission employee in Chuuk to find two strong young men to help trim the trees on the property. He reported to work a little while later with the two young men, whom I recognized as his own son and nephew. When they finished the job two days later and came in for their pay, I couldn't help teasing the man about hiring his own relatives. I asked him why he didn't distribute the wealth around a little and recruit people from another family. I tweaked him with a saying that had become popular among critics of the government: "*Ke pach, ke tento*," loosely translated as "If you're connected, you get the goods."[37] Turning serious, the man explained that hiring his relatives made eminently good sense for a Micronesian straw boss because it was easier for him to get them to do what he wanted. Since they were already subordinate to him anyway because of family ties, he could count on them to heed his instructions and felt free to criticize them if they did not work well. What Westerners call nepotism many Micronesians have regarded as a sensible strategy for compelling obedience and getting the job done.

School principals and other appointed officials can be very effective when their work team is controlled in this way. For years I had been hearing stories of how well managed one of the public schools on Pohnpei was. People often remarked with amazement on how successful the principal was in limiting absences among the teachers, a major problem in most public schools. Then, one day, someone casually mentioned that he hires people who are related to him, nephews and other members of the family. If this is the case, his success in enforcing attendance standards is less surprising, for he would have gathered around him a work force of people who already have family ties to him and must heed his demands.

These were the transitional ways of dealing with the hard problem of gaining acceptance for a position of authority in the modern sector of an island society. They are still in use today, but they are under heavy attack by Western institutions as well as by young Micronesians embracing modern values with their emphasis on equal opportunity.

There is a growing awareness that new norms have to be established for new types of authority today. Rank still means a great deal, but the old ranking system, with its emphasis on age, gender, title, and importance of the lineage, is opening up to include new markers. Expertise in one's field is beginning to count for something today, but it is often measured narrowly by degree and speciality area. Hence, credentials are understood to be paper ones. This may account for the enormous emphasis—excessive in the eyes of many Westerners—placed on degrees in Micronesia. A degree is the new title used to legitimize authority in Micronesia today.

Yet, the fact is that a degree doesn't always legitimize authority—as with the young man who finds himself in charge of the accounting department. He clearly has the title, but the community endorsement for him in his new position may be a long time in coming. Meanwhile, he needs to use the time-honored means to win acceptance: sit back and be prepared to listen, avoid anything that appears to his staff as self-promotion, and adopt the self-deprecatory techniques that have served islanders so well over the years.

9 Population and Migration

The Demographic Revolution

We were sitting around chatting at the baptismal party when I asked Joanna, the mother of the infant who was baptized just an hour before, how many brothers and sisters she had. She told me that there were ten in her family altogether, six girls and four boys. She was one of the youngest girls, she added. Then she started ticking off the names of her brothers and sisters, and where they were living now. When she saw the fatigued look in my eyes as I tried to keep up with her account, she laughed and told me that if I thought that was hard to follow, perhaps I ought to try keeping her mother's family straight. There were sixteen children altogether, she said, although only thirteen had survived childhood and only eight were still alive now. She was ready to begin a recital of their names and life histories but stopped when she saw me roll my eyes. Instead, she pointed to her young son and said, "You see little Jeremy here? He'll be one of three, no more than three. My husband and I have already agreed that we don't want a large family like the ones we grew up in."

Joanna is typical of many in her generation in wanting a small family, but she has come from a line in which large families were the rule for two generations. If one were able to trace her family line even farther back than a generation or two, one might find that the women back then had far fewer births than Joanna's mother and grandmother. A century and a half ago they might have had only one or two, if that many. Demography has changed direction several times in the recent history of the islands, just as it is doing once again.

In 1954 the population of the Caroline and Marshall Islands was 55,000. This is about the same size as the estimated total population in the early 1800s, before the islands began to experience intense contact with the West.[1] Forty years later, in 1994, there were more than 170,000 people residing in the islands—over three times their population in 1954.[2] Despite the heavy emigration in recent years, there are probably about 180,000 now at the end of the twentieth century. Thus, when considering forces that have created change in the islands, one must not neglect the demographic revolution of the postwar years.

The population upheavals in recent centuries began with the arrival of foreigners in the early nineteenth century. The diseases they introduced —including influenza, measles, smallpox, and venereal diseases—had the effect of reducing the aboriginal population size of 55,000 by one-third by the end of the century. Pohnpei, which lost about 4,000 of its population during the smallpox epidemic of 1854, continued to diminish for the remainder of the century, although much more slowly. Palau's population, in its decline from nearly 10,000 to 4,000 during the century, mirrored Pohnpei's. The Marshalls seems to have lost about a third of its people during the 1800s, finishing with a scattered population of about 10,000.[3] Kosrae's population underwent the most precipitous decline, plummeting from 3,000 at the coming of the first Europeans in 1830 to barely 300 fifty years later.[4] Yap's population, which at first seemed stable, began its long dip at the beginning of the twentieth century. Only Chuuk and the isolated outer islands of Yap, which had avoided intense contact longer than any other island groups, were spared.

By the beginning of German rule at the turn of the twentieth century, the population of all island groups except Yap had stabilized. Throughout the Japanese administration in the 1920s and 1930s, the population held steady at about 45,000, although the islands were later engulfed by a large expatriate population as preparations for World War II began.[5] Although the war was a catastrophe for the islands, it did not claim more than a few hundred Micronesian lives, far fewer than the Japanese and American lives lost in the conflict.[6]

Following the war, the island populations showed a dramatic new increase, in large measure a result of better medical care. The U.S. Navy inoculated the entire population immediately after the war, hospitals were established on all the main islands, dispensaries were set up on some of the remote outer islands, and a cadre of young Micronesian medical officers and nurses trained to provide health care for their people. The newly discovered antibiotics helped combat serious infections, yaws, tuberculosis, and respiratory diseases. As improved medical services were increasing the life expectancy of adults, they were also boosting the infant survival rate so that many of the newborn children who would have died in the past could now reach maturity. While better diet and living standards were increasing fertility, some of the cultural practices that once ensured longer intervals between childbirth fell into disuse. The customary prohibition of sexual intercourse between a new mother and her husband, once lasting a year or longer, began to shorten or disappear altogether.[7]

Between the end of the war and 1954, the population had already grown from 45,000 to 55,000.[8] For the next forty years the population of the islands soared. The annual growth rate of the population was over 3 percent, often closer to 3.5 percent, for most of this period. Chuuk's population doubled between 1950 and 1972, and the doubling time for Pohnpei, Kosrae, and the Marshalls was even shorter. Only in Yap and Palau, where the doubling time was closer to forty years, was the population growth rate more moderate.[9] The Micronesian population, which had shown decline during the nineteenth century and little growth during the first half of the next century, went into a steep ascent during the postwar years. The population problem shifted from insufficient growth to excessive growth, as overpopulation became targeted as a serious concern.

The migration from rural villages and atolls into towns, which was in full force through the 1960s and early 1970s as people followed the jobs and pursued educational opportunities, only made the overcrowding worse. Between 1955 and 1973, Koror's population grew from about 30 percent to 60 percent of the entire population of Palau. Its population exploded from 3,500 to over 7,600. During those same eighteen years, Weno's share of the Chuuk population doubled from 15 percent to 30 percent, while Kolonia's percentage of Pohnpei's nearly tripled (from 9 percent to 25 percent). The migration into towns was even more dramatic in the Marshalls, where the two urbanized atolls of Majuro and Kwajalein, which together accounted for barely a third of the whole Marshallese population in 1958, contained nearly two-thirds in 1973. The population of the two atolls leapt from 4,700 to 15,800 during those fifteen years.[10] Kosrae and Yap were the only islands that avoided serious overcrowding problems.

Overcrowding, however, was not the most acute problem that faced those who moved into town. They soon found that the tight unity that could be found in most rural villages was impossible in a town with thousands of people. Since it was a potpourri of migrants from different islands without shared kin ties, a town could not offer the sense of close affiliation that people had learned to expect in the village. Neither could it provide the social controls to check the reckless behavior of young drunks and other miscreants.[11] Those same strategies that kept the peace so well in smaller villages didn't necessarily work in the town. The town was not just a larger and upscale version of a village; it was a very different sort of place that presented a new set of problems.

Early attempts to curb postwar population growth through family planning were not very successful, owing to the cultural attitudes toward children. Children had always been regarded as a blessing—the more children the luckier the family—since they were seen as workers rather than consumers. Besides, children were also a form of social security for the family; it was they who would provide for the parents in their old age. More children meant not only more hands to help out for the family, but added insurance that the parents would be properly cared for when they became too old to work, even if some of the children moved off island or neglected their parents. I have known families that had sixteen or eighteen surviving children, and one family that had twenty. In every case, the parents considered themselves fortunate to have had such large families, which offered them a house full of workers as well as a foolproof social security policy.

By the late 1980s, there were signs that attitudes were beginning to change. The average family size was dropping, since the typical woman was having fewer children during her childbearing years.[12] People were ready to start reducing family size on many islands. At a conference on population pressure in Chuuk, some participants admitted that they were beginning to find it difficult to feed everyone in their families on the limited land available. Those who tried to support a large family on a modest salary had an even harder time. Some adults were ready to take advantage of the family planning aids that were then being made available everywhere. Struggling to provide for their large families, they had started to realize that children could be a burden as well as a benefit. As happens all over the world, it was those in the most modernized sector, the town-dwellers, who appreciated this fact first.

The combined populations of the Federated States of Micronesia, Palau, and the Marshalls are approaching 200,000, but much more slowly than during the earlier postwar decades. The population growth rate of the Federated States has slowed from over 3.5 percent to about 2 percent

Children on Ebeye, Marshall Islands. (Saul Riesenberg Collection, MARC)

a year.[13] The Marshalls, which until recently was measured at over 4 percent, seems to have dropped even more sharply. According to the preliminary figures from the 1999 census, the annual growth rate during the past decade was only 1.3 percent.[14] Palau's local population has shown almost no growth for over twenty years, although imported workers from Asia have pushed up the total population there during the 1990s.[15] The birth rate is showing a steady decline in all these places, as people realize that their resources are being stretched dangerously thin.

With disease and death no longer limiting family size as they once did, parents are employing other means of controlling family size. The mother in the vignette above, who, born into a family of ten, has decided to have only three children, is typical of most young educated women today. Young mothers are not hesitant to declare that they will have no more than two or three children. Small families are becoming the rule rather than the exception in many parts of Micronesia.

Once again the population trends in Micronesia are being reversed. Modernization, in the form of improved medicine, has contributed heavily to the dramatic population increase during the postwar years. But it is also modernization, especially the heavy dependence on a cash income and wage employment, that has been responsible for the decline in the birth rate in recent years. Population projections for the islands based on growth rates in the early 1980s seem unduly alarmist given the actual growth rates in recent years. Yet, the fact remains that the population of the islands now is more than three times what it was at the end of World War II and probably far higher than it has been at any time in history.

Chasing Jobs Abroad

I had barely walked through the door of one of Guam's biggest depart-ment stores when a woman walked up to me, reached out and took my hand, and mumbled a Chuukese greeting. I recognized her as a former parishioner at the cathedral on Weno and asked about her family. Just as she began telling me how many of them were now on Guam, two young men smiled and nodded as they walked by. Was one of them the boy who replaced his father as boatman for the church on Toloas, I wondered. There was no time to pursue the inquiry because two or three more former friends walked up and offered their greetings. As I strolled through the store, ten or fifteen more people nodded in my direction or came up to say hello. It occurred to me that no matter where I was in the store, I was never more than an aisle away from someone I knew (or should have known) from Chuuk.

A half hour later I was driving across the southern part of the island on what looked like a deserted road. The road slashed through the scrub grass and red clay of the boondocks, one of the few places on Guam seem-ingly ignored by developers. I remember thinking that here at least I would stumble into no Chuukese. As I slowed down on a curve in the road, I approached a ramshackle shanty, constructed of odd pieces of tin and scrap wood, the only dwelling along that lonely stretch of road. From it a man emerged. When he saw me leaning out of the window of my car, he waved and smiled. "Ingeiti Jesus Christus, Patire," he called out in the familiar Chuukese greeting.

A visit to Guam is always an encounter with familiar faces in the most surprising places. Every gas station, store, or fast food place I stop at is sure to have a Micronesian or two working there. Micronesians sell fish and pounded breadfruit and *tuba* alongside the road, and they can be seen packed together in the back of pickup trucks heading to and from work. Since the late 1980s, shortly after the Compact of Free Association went into effect, Chuukese and other FSM citizens have become a permanent feature on Guam.

Through the 1990s thousands of Chuukese have left their homes to take up residence on Guam, while hundreds more have moved to Saipan, Hawai'i, or the mainland United States. Pohnpeians, Yapese, and Kosraeans have also been emigrating, although not in the same large numbers as Chuukese. The predictions that have been heard since the 1970s that Micronesia would witness an exodus as occurred in Tonga, Samoa, and many of the other islands in the South Pacific have at last been realized. The exodus may have been slow in coming, but it arrived with stunning force.

In reality, the outflow from Micronesia began long before, when Palauans began leaving home for other destinations. Already by 1953, just two years after the transfer of the Trust Territory to civilian rule, there were a hundred Palauans on Guam "in quest of education, high wages and bright lights."[16] They owned the small bars and diners along Marine Drive that later passed into the hands of Koreans. Over the next two decades, an estimated 1,000 Palauans left their islands to live abroad, many of them on Guam but others in America.[17] Since 1972, when Micronesians became eligible for U.S. federal college grants, the flow of emigrants from Palau has grown into a torrent. An estimated 240 Palauans have left each year, creating a total emigrant pool of thousands of Palauans and leaving Palau's resident local population on a no-growth plateau for the last twenty-five years.[18]

From the beginning Palauans have followed the jobs with a special zeal that was found nowhere else in Micronesia. The competitiveness so deeply ingrained in Palauan society has always been a strong inducement to search for higher-paying jobs. Where Palauans led, others soon followed.

During the early 1970s, as financial aid became available to Micronesian students, hundreds of young high school graduates headed to the United States for college studies. In 1966 there were only about 200 Micronesians attending college, nearly all of them in Guam. Eleven years later, Micronesian college students numbered 2,400, most of them enrolled in schools in Hawai'i or on the U.S. mainland.[19] The vast majority of these Micronesians returned to their islands after college, since new jobs were still to be found in the islands. Moreover, they could not remain in the United States legally once they had finished school. Outer island Yapese, who had limited opportunities in Yap or on their own highly traditional islands, were the only ethnic group other than Palauans to reside in the United States in any significant numbers during the early 1980s.

After the Compact of Free Association went into effect in the Federated States of Micronesia and the Marshalls in 1986, the first serious emigration from these groups began. Since the Compact contained a provision granting Micronesians an open door into the United States to reside and work, they could look for the jobs that were not available back home in Guam's economy, which was then developing rapidly under the impact of Asian tourism. In those first years, FSM citizens came to Guam at the rate of nearly 1,000 a year, with Chuukese accounting for more than double the combined total of all the other states.[20] Then they began spilling over onto Saipan, an island some two hundred miles north of Guam, before moving beyond to Hawai'i and the mainland.

Wage employment in all parts of Micronesia, which had been sharply rising through the 1970s, slowed at the end of the decade. By the early 1980s the job boom was over, even as hundreds of college-educated Micronesians were entering the labor pool. Some new jobs were added during the next few years—about eight hundred a year throughout Micronesia —but not nearly enough to satisfy the aspirations of the swelling ranks of the high school graduates.[21] During the late 1980s, as the number of new jobs decreased to about four hundred a year, emigration from the Federated States and the Marshalls began in earnest. Ten or twenty years earlier, most of the high school graduates who could not find jobs in town might have slipped back into the village to live off the land, but needs were changing now. Admission into the cash economy was becoming an imperative for the young.

As Guam's economy slowed down in 1991 and growing local resentment made the new immigrants feel unwelcome, Micronesians began choosing new, more distant destinations. Marshallese, from the start, had moved east to Hawai'i in preference to Guam, and before long they were establishing small communities in California. The destinations became more numerous and more geographically diverse, as recruiters came to the islands to find cheap labor and immigrants shifted to wherever work could be found. In the past few years, dozens of Pohnpeians were hired to do fruit picking in Oregon, while others were recruited to become physical therapists in a home for the aged in South Carolina. There is a large contingent of Micronesians working at Sea World in Orlando, Florida. Hundreds of Marshallese are working in Arkansas on a gigantic poultry farm. The recruiters continue to target the islands even now as a source of cheap and reliable untrained labor for large businesses in the United States.

Meeting the plane on Majuro. (TT Archives, University of Hawai'i Library)

The extent of emigration in the last two decades can be measured by comparing the size of the emigrant community in 1980 with that of the present. In 1980 there were only a few dozen Chuukese nonstudents living on Guam. There were no more than 300 Marshallese, apart from those still attending college, living abroad. The estimated size of the total emigrant pool from the whole of the Federated States of Micronesia was perhaps 1,500. Palau, in contrast, which had been sending out a couple hundred people a year over the last decade or more, had an estimated 4,000 of its people living in Guam, Saipan, and the United States by 1980.[22]

The most recent (1998) count of FSM citizens who have emigrated to Guam, Saipan, and Hawai'i puts their number at 12,000.[23] With the inclusion of an estimated 4,000 residing in the mainland United States, there are about 16,000 FSM people who have left home to make their living abroad. In less than twenty years, therefore, the size of the emigrant pool has grown from a negligible fraction of the FSM population to over 13 percent of all FSM-born people. The Marshalls may have about 5,000 people living in Hawai'i and on the U.S. mainland now, and the Palauan emigrant community has grown to an estimated 6,000 or more.[24] If these estimates, which are partially based on surveys from recent years, are accurate, there are more than 25,000 Micronesians living abroad today. In other words, one out of every eight Micronesians now lives overseas.

What is pushing Micronesians to leave their islands in such numbers? For the most part, they are emigrating to find the jobs they are unable to procure at home, as they readily admit. Most will take entry-level jobs as bellhops, chambermaids, warehouse clerks, busboys, waitresses, and security guards to support themselves. Contrary to popular belief, this outflow of people does not represent a genuine "brain drain." College graduates with good job prospects nearly always return to the islands after school to pick off the best positions. It is those with no more than a high school diploma, those with little hope of finding work in the Micronesian towns, who crowd the airports waiting for the plane that will bring them to a new land of opportunity.[25] Lately, even those with almost no formal education seem to be on the move. Within the past two or three years, several young men who dropped out of elementary school have been sent to Guam by their families to find work as common laborers in construction or as security guards.

Micronesians sometimes leave for other reasons as well. Some are seeking better education for their children and health care for their families. Distressed at the poor quality of public services or disgusted by the seemingly endless convolutions of local island politics that hinder any progress, some are reaching out for a better life somewhere else.

Over the centuries Micronesians have always found it necessary to adjust population levels to the resources available in a place. An American friend of mine noticed that on Satawal, where he lived with his wife for years, a maximum of about 800 people seemed to be all that the coral atoll could comfortably support. When the population reached this upper limit, young men were sent off to marry girls from other atolls (where, it was expected, they and their families would make their residence).[26] Throughout history the delicate balance between population and resources always had to be monitored and maintained. Today the resources in question are not just land and the food that is grown on it, but jobs with which people can support themselves and their families. The resource toward which more and more Micronesians are turning—job opportunities at home—is unable to keep up with the growing population and its rising aspirations. Emigration is the means now being used to redress the imbalance.

Settling In Overseas

A Jesuit priest and friend of mine who worked in the outer islands of Yap drove me over to a house in a remote village on Guam. We were looking for Antonio, a young man from one of the outer islands who had been living on Guam for six or seven years. The last time I had seen him, he was living with three friends, all of them about his age and from the same island. When we arrived at the house, our first indication that something had changed was the absence of the usual mound of Budweiser empties just off the porch. A well-fed dog barked as we approached the front door and called inside. That's surprising, I thought; they never had a dog before. Two children, perhaps three or four years old, emerged from the kitchen with a man old enough to be wearing some of the traditional island tattoos. He greeted us and told us that he was Antonio's father-in-law. Last year, Antonio had brought his wife and two children to Guam. Because his wife was a high school graduate, she quickly found a job. Since her employment would have left the children untended, her parents had also come to be babysitters for the family and to care for the house. Meanwhile, two of Antonio's original housemates still lived with them; the other had moved to another home and was thinking of bringing his own family to Guam just as Antonio had done.

The first generation of FSM emigrants to Guam was a wild one. Many of the first wave were young men, usually in their twenties or thirties, who had never been off island before. They often lived together in groups of four or five or more, all related or from the same island, pooling their income to cover the rent and other expenses. They worked at low-paying jobs, sometimes at the same establishment or at least in the same kind of work. The several young men from an outer island in Chuuk who lived together in one household worked as security guards; most of those in another group worked at the same fast-food steakhouse. More than half of the Micronesian households on Guam surveyed for a 1988 study were composed entirely of young males.[27] Since the young men in the household were roughly the same age, there was usually no real leadership. People would drift in and out of the house, staying for a while and leaving when they received an invitation to board in better surroundings somewhere else. Cleaning and ordinary care of the house was often overlooked; beer cans were piled high just outside the house in witness to the partying that was a common feature of this young bachelors' dormitory life.

All-night drinking bouts and drunken-driving arrests were all too often part of it also.[28]

Don Rubinstein, a social scientist studying the Micronesian migrants on Guam, observed an evolution in the form of their households. In the second stage of the pattern he identified, one of the young men would bring his wife in to join him, possibly with one or two of their small children. The married couple, sometimes joined by another couple, became the nucleus of the household. Its remaining members, however, were an aggregation of loosely related kin—"a kinship tossed salad," as Rubinstein calls it.[29] Migrants during these early stages would characteristically change residence as often as three or four times a year. It was only when the household began to take a more stable form, one that mirrored households back in their own home islands, that the migrants truly settled down. They would apply for low-rent government-subsidized housing or take out a long-term lease on a flat. By this time the household had taken on most of the features that it would have had in the islands. A couple, now recognized as the "owners" of the house or apartment, gathered around them an extended family similar to that with which they might have lived back home. They would bring in some of their older children, enrolling them in the local public schools. To take care of the children, they would invite a set of grandparents, giving the family additional generational depth. An assortment of other persons related to either the husband or the wife, chosen according to more traditional norms, also joined the household.

As the household filled out, some of the earlier problems migrants had encountered solved themselves. With a stronger authority system in place in the family, the young were better supervised and less likely to run wild on weekends. The head of the family, often still young by Micronesian standards, was himself expected to act responsibly now that he was entrusted with the care of the whole household. The children had the full-time attention of an older adult, and no matter what the attitude of the local people toward migrants, everyone enjoyed a familiar cultural environment, at least within the confines of their family, that afforded them a certain measure of comfort.

As the number of migrants on Guam grew, they developed their own community support systems. From the beginning, Chuukese and outer island Yapese Catholics congregated on Sundays at the Campus Ministry Center that serves the University of Guam. There they would attend mass, lingering afterward to pick up the latest news from their home islands and to plan the events of the coming week. The young men sometimes organized basketball or softball games in the afternoon. During these same years several Chuukese-run Protestant churches sprang up on Guam, with pastors who had moved to Guam from Chuuk ministering to the congregations. Years before, the church had been an important social focal point for Palauans, who, even as they were still moving to Guam in large numbers, opened a Palauan Evangelical Church on the island.[30]

Micronesians who have settled in Hawai'i or on the U.S. mainland have had to make the same kind of adjustments with similar results. Today there are several towns and cities that have flowered into significant settlements for emigrating Micronesians. Often, there is a community college that Micronesian students once attended in significant numbers or a business recruiting Micronesian labor that served as the original magnet for the migrant population. Corsicana, Texas, a small town not far from Dallas in which 500 or 600 Micronesians are living, is the home of Navarro College, a favorite destination for Chuukese and Yapese students several years ago. A small community eventually gathered around the students who chose to stay after finishing school. Kansas City, which houses Park College, another favorite of the Micronesian college-bound in past years, now has several hundred Micronesian residents, including perhaps 300 Pohnpeians. In more recent years, instant Micronesian migrant communities have been springing up as large numbers of islanders were recruited for a single business. The scores of Marshallese brought into Arkansas to work on the poultry farms around the state is one of the most striking examples.

The emigrant community in Costa Mesa, a blue-collar town in affluent Orange County, California, was for years the "official" Marshallese overseas community. Twenty years before the Compact opened the door to Marshallese job-seekers in the United States, students were attending Southern California College, a private school run by the Assemblies of God. The Marshallese population of Costa Mesa grew rapidly after the Compact went into effect—from 300 in 1991, and 400 in 1995, to an estimated 800 in 1999.[31] Parents brought their children in from the islands to give them a better education than they could have received back home. The Costa Mesa community also picked up Marshallese who had originally settled in other parts of the United States. Already by the early 1990s, the migrant households in Costa Mesa were almost mirror images of those in the Marshalls in their size and composition.[32] Most of the men held jobs as machinists, while many women worked in assembly-line jobs making medical devices.

A young Palauan family living in the U.S. (Julita Tellei)

In the earlier years of the community, Marshallese formed an organization known as "Jake Jobol Eo" (Share and Share Alike) as well as a
women's club.[33] With the fees they collected, the organizations sponsored
cultural events and helped people meet the expenses of weddings and
funerals. Through these clubs and the Marshallese churches, a calendar
of community-wide activities was offered to the emigrants, including the
traditional programs of competitive singing and dancing at Christmas,
and celebrations of first birthdays (*kemem*). The Marshallese community also gathered for very different kinds of celebrations. On Memorial
Day weekend, I walked into a gym in Costa Mesa in which hundreds of
Marshallese were watching an all-Marshallese basketball tournament.
Teams from distant places—Hawai'i, Arizona, and Oregon, among others
—represented the other Marshallese communities invited to celebrate the
weekend in a renewal of old cultural bonds in their new home.

Micronesian emigrant communities, once they have reached a critical
mass, build up their own community support systems, as the Costa Mesa
community has done. Sometimes they do so through newly formed organizations like Jake Jobol Eo, but more often it is through the churches. In
Arkansas and throughout the South, Marshallese are said to open their

own churches very soon after their arrival. Often they acquire rights to an old, unused building that they renovate for use in their worship. Besides providing a place of worship in their own language, the church serves as a social center for the migrants. Through the wide range of activities it offers, the church builds up a sense of community among its members while offering them a bridge to the larger American society that they have hesitantly joined.

An International People

While we waited in the Guam airport to board the Monday morning flight through the islands, the departure area began filling up with passengers. During the half-hour before boarding, I had a chance to say hello to some of the people. Most of the passengers, as usual, appeared to be bound for Chuuk, although all for different reasons. The most conspicuous were a rather large entourage, all dressed in as many black articles of clothing as they could find in their personal wardrobes, with three of the party carrying floral arrangements and Styrofoam crosses. They were the family and relatives of a young man who had died suddenly on Guam, and they were accompanying his body back to Chuuk for burial. There were four children in their preteens who had just finished the school year and were going back to Chuuk for summer vacation. In another part of the departure area stood a man, his wife, and two children, all of them preparing to return to their home island for a big family reunion. Then there was a Chuukese man currently employed by one of the garment factories on Saipan. He was on his way to Chuuk to recruit two dozen women to sign on as seamstresses in his factory. Two college-age kids were making the trip to help coach the basketball team that would be representing Chuuk in the FSM Games at the end of the summer. All of the people I spoke to were Guam residents, and all were returning to Chuuk for a short visit.

Over the past several years, the flights from Chuuk to Guam have always been crowded with people intending to resettle on Guam, to say nothing of weekend shoppers and temporary visitors. Far more surprising, however, is that the return flights to Chuuk have been almost as crowded. Anyone who thinks that Micronesian emigrants abroad simply vanish one day never to be seen again need only scan the departure area of a return flight to the islands to discover that this is far from the case. The above sketch of a departure area on Guam gives a sample of the variety of people returning to their home island, if only for a time, and the many different reasons they have for visiting.

Even Micronesians who have settled in Hawai'i or on the U.S. mainland will return occasionally, despite the distance and the expense. Family funerals will bring them home, either to acompany the body of a relative who has died abroad or, more commonly, to attend the funeral of someone who has passed away in the islands. There are other reasons Micronesians return home for a visit, even from thousands of miles away. Now and then sports teams or dance groups may come to perform for the benefit of their fellow islanders while renewing old ties. Marshallese have sometimes sent their children back home to attend elementary school for a year or two before enrolling them in a U.S. junior high school. Even this short stay has the effect of forging bonds between the emigrants and the relatives they have left back home, just as adoption once did. Sometimes the reverse might happen: the emigrant may return to his or her home island to find one or two relatives to bring back to the United States to live with the family.

Goods flow back and forth between the home islands and the new communities as freely as people. A few years ago, Chuukese would send fish and pounded breadfruit to their relatives on Guam in ice chests that would be returned a few days later, filled with frozen chicken and other treats that could be bought cheaply on Guam. Chuukese on Guam would also send back cartons of secondhand clothes, most of them purchased for next to nothing from Catholic Charities or the Salvation Army. Marshallese in Costa Mesa and Hawai'i also send back clothes and food, but they add luxuries such as perfume, keyboards, computer games, and other electronic equipment.[34]

Goods are exchanged between migrants and their relatives back home just as they would be if all were living on the same island. Money flow, however, has up to this time been predominantly in the direction of the migrant communities. The authors of a report on the Marshallese community in Costa Mesa estimate that the value of remittances from the Marshalls to California is four times greater than the flow in the opposite direction. For the Marshallese living in Enid, Oklahoma, the ratio is estimated to be seven to one.[35] Much the same could have been said of the migrants from the Federated States of Micronesia in Guam until recently. Only in 1994 for the first time was an inflow of remittances measured for FSM citizens; it was put at a little more than one million dollars in that year.[36]

Surveys of migrant communities reveal a good amount of return migration. One Palauan who graduated from Xavier High School in the mid-1960s returned to Palau only a few years ago after living for twenty years in Hawai'i. The present Ibedul, the highest-ranked chief in Koror, had been serving in the U.S. Army for several years when he was recalled to Palau to assume the title.

The exchange of goods and money and the flow of persons back and forth across the "highway" stretching from the home islands to faraway destinations in the United States, sometimes resulting in the return of longtime migrants, are clear indications that migrants do not make a decisive break with their homeland when they move overseas. They still belong to their home islands. Far from cutting their bonds with their homeland, they do what they can to nurture these ties by promoting cultural events and by encouraging awareness in the young of where they come from. Marshallese tell stories to their young that are probably very much like the tales Bikinians told their youth long after they had been forced to evacuate their island for atomic testing.

Many Micronesian migrants would like to maintain title to land at home and at least some stake in their home island, just as most Samoans and Tongans did as they scattered through the United States and other countries. To do so, they are compelled to continue the exchanges with their family members at home and to visit from time to time in order to reaffirm kin bonds. Kinship, after all, is not simply bestowed at birth; it is created over time through shared food and presence. This process continues today, just as it always did, but now over a distance spanning the Pacific.

The growing number of emigrants are not dropouts or permanent exiles, those who have chosen the United States rather than their own countries. Although they are no longer residing in their political states, they remain tied to their peoples and cultures even at a distance. Emigrants are the most distant members of their nation, which has come to embrace more than the single political jurisdiction in which they were born. They are the international wing of a people distributed from one end of the Pacific to the other.

Summing Up

The preceding chapters show a web of change in which dozens of inter-related innovations are touching every part of island life and affect-ing nearly every social institution, although not all of them to the same degree. This change is not only pervasive, but it runs very deep. It reaches down to the very roots of the island societies, altering the land-kin-ship foundations on which island societies rest: it has loosened lineage ties and altered the fundamental relationship between people and their land.

In traditional island life, any person's livelihood depended on access to the land, which was often equated in island parlance with the food it produced. One could normally gain this access only by cultivating member-ship in the kin group to which one belonged, since this group held the rights to the land one hoped to live on. The tight link between land and kin was one of the most elemental facts of life for a traditional Microne-sian. With the emergence of a cash economy based on wage labor, how-ever, Micronesians could actually envision feeding themselves apart from the traditional land-kin linkage. And many did so. Enough, at least, to tip the balance toward the radical social changes that flowed from the liber-ation of the household from the larger kin group.

The single household has become an economic unit in a way that never would have been possible in earlier times. But this fundamental eco-nomic transformation triggered a chain of social explosions. As the house-hold, headed by an adult with a salaried job, drifted toward economic independence, the social bonds that joined the household to the extended family were correspondingly weakened, even if not altogether lost. In all Micronesian societies, the strength of kinship is correlative to the respon-sibility members have for feeding one another. To put it another way, shar-ing food with someone doesn't just express kin ties with that person, it forms them. The opposite is also true, however. As the extended family loses the responsibility for feeding the household, it also surrenders many of the social obligations and rights that it once enjoyed with respect to members of this household.[1]

The reader has only to recall some of the changes that were described in the chapters of this book to comprehend how far-reaching the consequences of the emergence of the household have been. In the first place, the child-rearing system is stripped of some of the other members of the lineage—aunts, uncles, grandparents—who could have been counted on to help bring up children and resolve conflicts within the broad family circle. As all these people cease to eat together, or at least to eat from the same pot, they surrender authority over one another's children. Especially crucial is the withdrawal of the maternal uncle from the support system, for he once shared with the father, in an ingeniously balanced system, responsibility for the care of children belonging to his lineage. As the maternal uncle withdraws from the system, the balance is upset, and so disciplinary authority tends to be concentrated in the father today. The result is a widening gap between fathers and sons, leading to what I have referred to as the "absent father syndrome."

Even the close relationship between brothers and their married sisters is being altered, since they no longer share the same resource base. A woman's husband, not her brothers or blood kin, is expected to provide for her needs in today's island society. As a result, brothers are much slower today to intervene in their sisters' domestic squabbles, even when they are being seriously mistreated by their husbands.

Adoption practices also are transformed. Adoption is used less often than it once was to bond lineages to one another, since the lineage is of declining importance today. Instead, it functions as a means of providing parents for a young child who may have few other options, thus becoming a welfare stratagem for the child instead of a tactic for cementing relations between families.

The fragmentation of the extended family, in weakening the centripetal force that binds members to their land and kin, contributes to the growing mobility of islanders in the modern world. Today it is easier for individuals and households to move out to live on their own, sometimes in a different part of the world, without feeling the same sense of betrayal that they might have felt in the past. The most striking illustration of this mobility and increased search for independence is the single mother with her children who sets up a separate household, a phenomenon that would have been unthinkable in the past but that is beginning to happen today. This same fragmentation of the lineage is rapidly stripping women of their most important nondomestic roles, all of which have been traditionally rooted in the extended family, leaving them shorn of everything but responsibility for the household work and the care of the children.

The shift in the direction of a cash economy is having profound effects on land practices as well. Increasingly today, land is being commodified and alienated as it never would have been in an age when land was unrivaled as the primary resource. More than ever before, its worth is measured in monetary terms and it is being converted into cash. At the same time, the traditional corporate ownership of the land is yielding to individual ownership as the importance of the lineage wanes. Traditional land inheritance patterns, once anchored firmly in the matrilineage on most islands, are giving way to a father-son inheritance pattern. This change is understandable, considering that a man's responsibility today is to provide for his children rather than for the lineage group that would have claimed his main allegiance in the past. As land passes out of lineage control, women, who were once widely regarded as the guardians of the land, are losing the power they had to determine how land will be distributed in the extended family; men are quickly gaining a monopoly on this prerogative.

The decline in the importance of the land-kin axis has also had its effects on some of the major events in the life cycle of islanders. These changes, while seemingly inconsequential, are indicative of the sweeping impact that modernization and the new family forms it has spawned are having on all aspects of island life today. Pregnancy and birth were once the occasion for new mothers to seek support from their own kinswomen. Today, however, women are less likely to return to their own families and land to give birth, or even to expect that their sisters or mothers will be there to assist them in delivery and early care of their children. Instead, these women usually head for the hospital to deliver, sometimes even traveling abroad to give birth. At the other end of the life cycle, there are parallel changes. Burials today occur with increasing frequency not on the deceased's own lineage land, but at the spouse's grave site or elsewhere. Burial practice is just one more manifestation of the shift in allegiance occurring today—away from the blood kin and toward the nuclear family. Blood ties may have been stronger than marriage bonds in the past, but the current is running strongly in the opposite direction today. Generally, the family has less say over its son's or daughter's choice of marriage partner today, is likely to be more distant from the household the new couple sets up, and stands to gain much less material support from the couple than ever before.

Individualism seems to be another by-product of modernization and the changes it brings to a more traditional society. Although many people attribute the growing individualism in such a society to the alluring portrayals of this value in the media and to increased encounters with Westerners, I've always wondered whether intense exposure of this kind is sufficient to explain the change in any given traditional society. A systemic change is required, it seems, before the modeling can have any effect on society's members. In the tension that invariably exists between the individual and the social group, traditional Pacific societies have always come down strongly on the side of subordinating the individual's interests to those of the community, even at the cost of suppressing the creative impulses of the individual. Micronesian societies have repeatedly eschewed creativity at the expense of chaos; they have continually chosen conformity for the sake of consensus. Individualism, although capable of releasing powerful innovative energies, can threaten the fragile unity of the small island population. Yet, a source of livelihood independent of one's kin is the first step in the release of the individual from the powerful ties that bound him or her to the extended family. As Karl Marx insisted, people must be freed from the structures that constrain them materially and economically before they can begin to develop their individuality in other, more personal areas of life.

The signs of growing individualism are everywhere today. Young people are freer to choose their own spouses, sometimes even without parental approval, for reasons that are personal rather than family-related. Similarly, sexuality is less circumscribed by family mores and interests so that boys and girls are able to enjoy it without regard to its consequences for the family's interests. Sexuality is becoming more a personal pleasure, less a device to secure benefits for one's family. All this may be regarded as a form of liberation or a plunge into license, depending on the viewpoint taken. The same ambiguity surrounds the changes that have touched the lives of women in recent years. In the islands today women may more easily pursue their own careers without reference to the traditional gender roles that once limited the kind of work they were allowed to perform. As they do this, however, females run the risk of developing an adversarial relationship with males. They can be viewed as competitors rather than partners once both sexes begin drawing from a single job pool— something that never would have occurred in an earlier day when gender roles were distinct and complementary. Married families, too, enjoy more latitude to define their own lifestyles and work patterns, even when these are in opposition to traditional patterns. In a few instances, women are

Western goods and modern values: Uncrating a new refrigerator. (Library of Congress of FSM)

taking wage jobs and supporting their families while their husbands assume a large share of the household chores.

Finally, the resource shift occurring in recent decades has had its effects on the authority system. Traditional chiefs nearly everywhere have surrendered most of the land rights that they once held—not just the residual rights to all the privately used land in their chiefdoms, but rights to the unused portions of land that they once held in trust for the community. Not only have they lost their major stake in the traditional resource (land), but chiefs have been denied access to the new resource (money), since the modern government, with its elected leaders, controls these assets. Yet, even though traditional leaders enjoy less real power today as their hold over resources has diminished, their prestige in the eyes of their people appears to be higher than ever. People are turning to them to check the threat of an overconcentration of power in the hands of the officials of the modern political system. Even if the old mechanisms for redistribution of local resources and authority sharing between chiefs and their subjects are breaking down, Micronesians seem willing to allow the chiefs to monopolize the reduced authority they have as long as they serve as a buffer against the modern government. Today there exists a dual authority system, with the traditional chiefs and the modern government serving as the two poles of this system.

All the interlocked social changes described in this volume and summarized in this chapter are usually attributed to the vaguely defined but seemingly irresistible force that is known as modernization. These changes, which imply both the acceptance of new behavior or customs and transformation in people's values and attitudes, are often seen as the result of multiple outside forces working on the society during a period of intense exposure to the West. Indeed, dozens of forces have been acting on these island societies during the last half century: formal education, college opportunities abroad, the influence of American movies and television, improved transportation and the increased mobility of islanders, political status changes, a large influx of American and Asian residents, and growing tourism, among others. No doubt these have all had their impact. Nonetheless, one must question whether these forces, even collectively, would have been potent enough to create a fissure in the tight kin-land unity that is the bedrock of island societies. The Japanese were unable to accomplish this in the prewar years despite the huge foreign population and the intense educational campaign they undertook to "free" the individual from the restraints imposed by the extended family. To create the seismic rumble that the islands have felt during the last few decades, a basic systemic change was probably required. This change would have been the shift toward a cash economy and all that it implies. The other forces, even if they were not the point of the drill against the rock, have undoubtedly widened and deepened the openings that the new cash economy created.

It would seem that the single change that has had the most profound effect on the islands in the last fifty years is the introduction of the cash economy as a genuine societal force. For at least a century before this period began, Micronesians were bartering with European and American merchants and traders for imported goods: cloth, tobacco, ironware and guns, among other things. For much of this time they had some access to Western currency and understood how to use it. But throughout this whole period, they were purchasing or bartering for what might be called luxury goods rather than basic commodities. The currency or foreign exchange that they earned supplemented their subsistence lifestyle; it did not replace it.[2]

Even during the height of Japanese development in the late 1930s, Micronesians were far from being able to support themselves with their cash earnings. It was only during the U.S. trusteeship, especially after the rapid escalation of jobs and salaries during the 1960s and 1970s, that the inflow of cash reached a critical threshold, allowing at least some families to support themselves almost entirely on their earnings.[3] It was during this period, then, that the cash economy was at last able to provide an alternative to the traditional land-based economy that had hitherto been the only available means of livelihood for island peoples. This is not to say that the subsistence economy disappeared. Indeed, it is still an important factor in island life, accounting for perhaps half of the food eaten by Micronesians. Today the two economies exist side by side, with a great deal of interflow between them, but the enormous systemic changes that the cash economy has had on social structures in the meantime cannot be ignored.

Can one really trace all the social changes of the last half century to a single source: the emergence of the cash economy? Yes and no. Other forces of change, including those mentioned above, have left their marks on the islands and have affected the way in which Micronesians see the world today, but attitudinal change alone would seem inadequate to explain the magnitude of social change that has been described in this volume. The evidence points to the key role of the cash economy as a necessary condition for the most fundamental change, especially that touching land and family, over the past decades.

If this long summary of social change seems darkly apocalyptic, remember that one could generate an equally long list of cultural features that have remained intact over the last half century. The preceding chapters illustrate some remarkable examples of cultural persistence. Traditional leaders, for instance, continue to command respect, even if their power base is shifting and the function they serve today is different from what it once was. Many of the external practices at funerals have endured over the years, even when the spirit beliefs that inspired them have been forgotten. Another example of cultural persistence can be found in the exchanges between the families of the husband and wife at betrothal and marriage. Although the forms may have altered to some extent, the practice itself appears to be as strong as ever. All these examples illustrate the adaptability of the island cultures.

Even so, some will be tempted to see the land-kin bond as a bulwark, the last line of defense against modern Western culture and all that it stands for. To them this volume is a confirmation of what they may have suspected and feared: the dam has already burst, releasing the flood-

(Saul Riesenberg Collection, MARC)

waters of change to wash away the cultural landscape. In this bleak view, once the barricade is crossed, a cycle of predetermined change is initiated with all the inevitability of death and the same end result for the culture. Yet, the facts today suggest otherwise. The cash economy and the traditional subsistence economy not only coexist, but they feed into one another in sometimes unusual ways. Who would have dreamed forty years ago that *sakau* bars would be selling the local drink to Pohnpeians or that Chuukese would be exporting packages of pounded breadfruit to Guam for sale at roadside markets? Societies adapt, often in marvelous ways, to what might seem to be traumatic changes at first sight. Even as the lineage's authority over its members continues to decline, Micronesians are busily restoring old types of food exchanges or inventing new ones, to keep the lineage operative in the lives of its members. They are also finding more excuses for the extended family to gather on special days, much as Americans did long ago when they established Thanksgiving Day or Christmas as occasions for family reunions.

While the impact of change in the last half century has been great, it has not been annihilating. Although the social change during this period has meant the loss of certain traditional features in the island societies, it

(Micronesian Seminar)

has not unraveled them like a tapestry, leaving nothing but an armful of loose threads. Those same changes have added new elements to the cultures, altering the relationship of elements to one another in such a way as to create a new design, yet leaving many of the old themes in recognizable form.

In truth, this volume is a book without an ending. I have tried to map here some of the more significant changes, displayed against a background of traditional practices, that have occurred in Micronesia during the past half century. In doing this, I hoped to point to the general direction in which these modern island societies are heading. Human societies have a way of confounding social prophets, however, and I would not be foolish enough to attempt to predict how far these changes will go, how they will be integrated into existing cultural patterns, or what these societies will look like fifty years down the road. Whatever happens, you can be sure that the Micronesian societies of the future will integrate the new and the old into strange and colorful patterns, sure to enchant future generations and confuse the old.

Notes

Chapter 1: Family

1. An extreme example of the older extended family unit was a Mortlockese family, living on Weno, capital of Chuuk, in the early 1970s, whose compound consisted of five buildings providing a home for fifty-one persons.

2. Changes in the form and function of the Chuukese family since World War II are summarized in an unpublished paper based on the research of a young Chuukese, Innocente Oneisom; see Oneisom 1992.

3. In earlier times each estate in Chuuk had a single large dwelling in which the women of the lineage and their husbands slept. The house was partitioned off into sleeping compartments along the side, one for each married couple and one for the unmarried girls who had reached puberty; the young men slept in the men's house, or *uut*. The central part of the large dwelling was used as a living room and for minor cooking. The main features of this lineage house were similar to the large dwelling houses that could be found on other islands, particularly Pohnpei and Palau, but the Chuukese lineage house was built on the ground, while the dwellings in the latter places were raised. By the late Japanese prewar colonial period, the large lineage dwellings had almost entirely disappeared from Chuuk, although similar dwellings were still being used in other island groups like Pohnpei. See Goodenough 1961:67–68; LeBar 1964:108–111.

4. The earth oven, which demanded arduous work and considerable strength, gave way to the iron cooking pot everywhere in Micronesia, in some places more quickly than in others. By the end of the Second World War, the earth oven had fallen into disuse except on ceremonial occasions (see, for example, Oneisom 1992:8–9). The iron pot had been introduced in the nineteenth century by whalers and traders, but by the time of Japanese rule (the 1920s and 1930s), it was standard household equipment, so much so that "ironpot" was taken into many of the languages as a loanword. The cooking pot was generally used to feed the large kin groups that had always constituted a single eating unit but afforded flexibility in this regard (Hezel 1995:205). By the early 1960s, when I first arrived in Chuuk, the iron pot was often used to cook breadfruit that would be distributed to the entire lineage group, but it sometimes served to prepare food for a single household.

5. Food is an element of life that carries special importance and symbolic value for all Pacific Islanders, as is repeated time and again in the literature. Throughout Micronesia, however, the distribution of food has always been far more consequential than the act of communal eating. At Pohnpeian feasts, for instance, the actual consumption of food is either minimal or nonexistent during the celebration itself. Likewise, on most other islands in Micronesia little attention is paid to whether one eats now or takes the food to be consumed later. However, the preparation of "plates" for guests is serious business.

6. This structure disappeared in Chuuk for a time after World War II, but it later reappeared

as the islands recovered from the impact of the war. Today meetinghouses are ubiquitous in Chuuk.

7. The Chuukese *uut* once served as a canoe house as well as a meeting place for the lineage; as such it could be located at quite a distance from the lineage dwellings (Goodenough 1961:68).

8. Residence rules in postwar Chuuk were the subject of a dispute between two noted anthropologists, John Fischer and Ward Goodenough. Although their formulations of residence rules differed, both anthropologists recorded matrilocal marriage in the majority of cases —71 percent according to Goodenough (1956) and 58 percent according to Fischer (1958). For a brief treatment of the subject of residence rules in Micronesia, see Marshall 1999: 137–139.

9. See, for instance, Burton et al. 1996 and Hage 1998.

10. The culture-language area extending from Kiribati through the Marshalls and the eastern and central Carolines all the way to the atolls southwest of Palau is termed Nuclear Micronesia. It does not include the Marianas, Yap proper, or Palau. The last two islands especially show distinctive cultural features that are not shared by the rest of Micronesia, as will be seen again and again throughout this book.

11. Spoehr 1949:155–160.

12. "Ponapeans today speak of the matrilineages as the localized groups of the past," Glenn Petersen writes in treating older matrilocal patterns on Pohnpei (1982:131–132). The outer islands of Pohnpei State, however, show stronger patrilineal features and a decided preference for patrilocal residence (Marshall 1999:115–116, 138–139).

13. Anthropologists have reconsidered the matter in recent years and now agree that, even though the father's side of the family is especially strong in Yap, there is no patrilineage as such. Hence, they now renounce the use of the term "double descent" for Yap. See Marshall 1999:116.

14. It should be noted, however, that the other atolls more distant from Yap are generally matrilocal, reflecting the features of Chuuk.

15. Marshallese residential groups may have been bilateral—that is, drawn from both father's and mother's kin—whereas in Chuuk such groups were once predominantly matrilineal. Nonetheless, the cultural geography of the estate was much the same: a common cookhouse once served all the dwellings on the property (Alkire 1977:69–70).

16. Despite what seems to be an earlier tendency toward nuclear family households in Palau, there was an obligatory exchange of food between households affiliated with the same lineage. Smith 1983:37; Force and Force 1972:25–26.

17. Yap was even more exceptional in that different gender-age groups even within the nuclear family ate from "separate pots"—that is, food that came from different taro patches and was cooked separately.

18. Even when people did not live together, they often shared food on a regular basis, with food gifts passing back and forth between relatives. Throughout Micronesia, such gifts not only express indebtedness to kinfolk but actually define who shall be regarded as kin (Flinn 1992:56).

19. Today there are instances in which several closely related nuclear families have moved into the same building, each using a room or two as its own private area. Usually this arrangement involves parents and their married children with their families. Each small family unit may be furnished with its own television set and other amenities, sometimes even including cooking facilities. There are a number of such homes on Pohnpei, and Julie Walsh reports the same for the Marshalls (personal communication, 23 October 1998).

20. "Micronesian" here denotes any person from Palau, the Marshalls, or the Federated States of Micronesia. Figures are drawn from the annual reports to the United Nations on the Trust Territory of the Pacific Islands for this period and are compiled in Hezel 1984.

21. Figures are found in Hezel 1989:64–66.
22. This incident was reported to the author by Ted Lowe in the course of the latter's field-work in Chuuk in 1996–1997.
23. The Pohnpeian word for respect, *"wahu,"* literally means a valley or the physical space be-tween objects. Throughout Micronesia in the past, respect was expressed in two spatial modes or dimensions: on a horizontal plane by maintaining a polite distance from the one in authority and on the vertical plane by keeping oneself lower than the authority through ritualized gestures such as bowing and crawling.
24. See, for instance, Gladwin and Sarason 1953 and Goodenough 1961.
25. This, at least, is the interpretation of Ted Lowe, who studied changes in family dynamics in Chuuk; Lowe, personal communication, September 1997.
26. This illustration is cited in Fischer and Fischer 1957:133.
27. The term for maternal uncle in Palau is *"okdemaol,"* in Yap *"wa'ayengin,"* in Pohnpei *"uhlap,"* and in the Marshalls *"wulabe."*
28. Smith 1983:192.
29. Marshallese use of the word *"tam,"* "outrigger," in reference to the father was cited by Leonard Mason, who did fieldwork in the Marshalls in the late 1940s (personal commu-nication). For a brief description of the parent-child relationship on Majuro, see Spoehr 1949:194. Spoehr draws attention to an exception in the general informality that governs these relationships: the relationship between the father and his eldest son is character-ized by heightened respect in the Marshalls. The same is true of other island groups in Micronesia.
30. See, for instance, Lingenfelter 1975:42 and Labby 1976:50.
31. Fathers and sons in Chuuk sometimes work together even today, it should be understood. Sons may help their fathers in building a house, making repairs on a house or boat, and even doing food gathering at times. Yet, joint work does not seem to be done today as commonly or as comfortably as in the past. Although other explanations are sometimes offered for this change, I would contend that as the broad lineage support system dissolved, the father-son work team was redefined. As households assumed the responsibility of sup-porting themselves, the son no longer worked with the father but for him. As so often seems to be the case, economic changes in the support system bring about corresponding alter-ations in social relationships. In this case, the father became the source of material sup-port and so was invested with much more authority than formerly.
32. Ted Lowe first brought the difference between same-sex parent-child relationships to my attention; Lowe, personal communication, 1997.
33. In the thirty years between 1970 and 1999, there have been more than a thousand deaths by suicide in Micronesia. During the 1990s an average of nearly fifty persons died by their own hand each year in Palau, the Marshalls, and the Federated States of Micronesia. The general suicide rate for that period has been 27 per hundred thousand, more than double the general rate in the United States. The age-sex specific rates for males aged fifteen to twenty-four ranged from 70 per hundred thousand in Palau to 206 per hundred thousand in Chuuk (Hezel 1989).
34. About 70 percent of the suicides in Chuuk and Pohnpei were brought on by a conflict with a parent or older sibling (Hezel 1989:50).
35. For further development of this explanation for suicide, see Hezel 1987b and 1989.
36. This incident is recounted in Barnabas and Hezel 1992:18–19.
37. An overview of the positive features of child rearing in the extended family is presented in Hezel 1989:60–61.
38. In Chuuk at least, there are no such strict authority lines between cousins, so the relation-ship between them can be much more casual than between brothers. Generally speaking, cousins in Chuuk can be drinking buddies; brothers cannot. The same appears to be true

in other island groups. Holly Barker reports that brothers in the Marshalls do not usually feel comfortable drinking with one another, since they must be on guard in their behavior toward one another (personal communication, 31 March 1999). Augustine Kohler says the same of Pohnpei but adds that younger brothers do not like serving as lackeys for their older siblings at drinking parties (personal communication, 2 April 1999).

39. Barnabas and Hezel 1992:27.

40. Surveys of alcohol and drug use in the Federated States of Micronesia and the Marshalls have been produced by Micronesian Seminar (1997a, 1997b). For a similar survey of alcohol and drug use in Palau, see Futterman and Lyman 1998.

41. This is something that I heard said again and again, from women as well as men, during my years in Chuuk.

42. Smith 1983:118.

43. Julie Walsh and Holly Barker, personal communication, 6 February 1999.

44. Anthropologists point out that although patrilineal descent groups "can afford to lose a considerable degree of control over their female members," the close interdependence of brothers and sisters is essential in matrilineal societies. "No male can found a new segment unless he is able to pair off with one or more sisters . . . and no female can found a new segment without a male from her own group" (Schneider 1961:11, 26, quoted in Marshall 1999:109–110).

45. Yap may be the single exception, for a married woman there looked not to her brothers for protection from abuse by her husband, but to sisters of her husband's estate (Egan 1998: 171–172).

46. I am indebted to Don Rubinstein for bringing to my attention the economic grounding for the brother-sister relationship. This bond, like so many other social ties in island societies, is rooted in the economic support system.

47. Smith 1983:205.

48. Flinn 1992:65.

49. Alkire 1965:60.

50. Adoption rates for different island communities vary widely, from rates comparable to those in Palau, Pulap, and the Polynesian outliers of Pohnpei to a low of 15 percent on Yap and only 5 percent on Kosrae. Kirkpatrick and Broder report a rate of 15 percent for two villages in Rumung, Yap, surveyed in 1972 (1976:203). Scott Wilson was able to identify sixty-two cases of formal adoption on Kosrae in 1964 for a rate of about 5 percent (1976:85). Rynkiewich reports a rate of 25 percent on Arno in the Marshalls in 1969–1970 (1976: 110). Lessa writes that, during his fieldwork in 1949, 45 percent of all Ulithians were adopted (1966:11). The rate of adoption on Nukuoro in 1965 was given as 61 percent, according to Carroll (1970b:154); and that of Kapingamarangi, its sister Polynesian outlier, was 52 percent in 1966 (Lieber 1970:171). Differences in the understanding of the term "adoption," besides the cultural variations in island groups, may be responsible for the wide range.

51. Anthropologists have long debated the motives for adoption. Some have seen it primarily as a means of sharing scarce resources (children) with couples who have none; others have tended to see it more as an expression of solidarity. Today most anthropologists are inclined to see adoption as serving both functions and others besides. For a concise and helpful discussion, see Marshall 1999:117–121.

52. My understanding of adoption here reflects the two major volumes on adoption in the Pacific published in the ASAO Monograph series: Carroll 1970a and Brady 1976.

53. Rubinstein brings this out in his dissertation on Fais; see Rubinstein 1979.

54. Oneisom 1992:12.

55. Barnabas and Hezel 1992:21. Nearly everyone interviewed in this study commented that adoption on Pohnpei has greatly decreased since the 1960s.

56. Kirkpatrick and Broder (1976:203) compare their own sample of seventy-eight persons in

two villages in 1972 with the sample of 2,100 persons collected in 1947 by Hunt, Kidder, and Schneider (Hunt et al. 1954).

57. Both anecdotes are found in Marcus 1991:7.

58. In 1985–1986 a survey of child abuse throughout the region was completed with a grant provided by the U.S.-funded Juvenile Justice Program. The study, coordinated by the Micronesian Seminar under the direction of Mariano Marcus, resulted in four reports on major island groups and a summary report authored by Marcus (1991).

59. This is reported as increasingly common among more affluent Marshallese and Pohnpeian families. Barnabas and Hezel 1992:21; Julie Walsh, personal communication, 21 October 1998.

60. Johnson 1998. Within the last few years, Palau has also witnessed adoptions of some local children by American couples (Elizabeth Rechebei, personal communication, 14 December 1998).

Chapter 2: Land

1. Hezel 1985.

2. The survey of land sales on Pohnpei during the early 1980s was done at the request of the Micronesian Seminar by Frank Castro, then head of the Land Office on Pohnpei. The data compiled include the names of the buyer and seller, land area, type of land, location, date of transaction, and price. Since the sale of land, even to other Pohnpeians, is expressly forbidden by the state constitution, most of the transactions have recorded the sale price in a slightly veiled form.

3. Fischer 1958:104.

4. See, for instance, Goodenough 1961:49 and Fischer 1958:184–189.

5. Alkire 1977:88.

6. Ibid.

7. Smith 1983:121.

8. Alkire 1965:47.

9. This often-quoted saying is cited in Lingenfelter 1975:98.

10. This observation was made by Julie Walsh, quoting a senior government official in Majuro (Julie Walsh, personal communication, 23 October 1998).

11. Force and Force 1972:15. Most of Europe once observed the same practice, as when the head of an estate was known by the title "Master of Hestviken" or "Lord of Crown Heights." The West has almost entirely lost this tradition, which remains in force in several parts of Micronesia.

12. Smith 1983:244.

13. Quoted in Parker 1985:66.

14. Egan 1998:87–88, who quotes an informant as saying: "An individual who is not in any way attached to the soil of the land where the fundamental resources for life sustenance can be obtained . . . has taken to his feet to walk for his food, going around from household to household. [He] is therefore voiceless!"

15. Parker 1985:107–109; Smith 1983:122.

16. The quote is from Tony DeBrum, a man in his fifties who recalls the shift in attitude he describes (Julie Walsh, personal communication, 23 October 1998).

17. Fischer 1958:100.

18. There were a few exceptions to the general rule that all land was once corporately owned, notably in the outliers of Pohnpei. Damas, for instance, claims that land parcels on Pingelap were sometimes held by an individual (1994:94–95).

19. Tobin 1958:7. Actually land rights in the Marshalls are divided among three parties: the high chief (*iroij*), the head of the family unit residing on a piece of land (*alab*), and the people residing on the parcel (*dri jerbal*).

20. Kaneshiro 1958:296.

21. Rufino Mauricio, a trained archaeologist who has done fieldwork on Pohnpei, claims that the paramount chiefs held this land in trust for the people they ruled (personal communication, 25 November 1998).

22. The German colonial administration, as one of its major goals, attempted to break the power of the chiefs over the land—successfully in Pohnpei, much less so in the Marshalls (Hezel 1995:131–135). Twenty years later, the Japanese administration, taking the reforms one step further, tried to wrest the land from the communal ownership of kin groups so that it might be held by individuals (ibid.:192).

23. McCutcheon 1985:69–70.

24. See, for instance, Useem 1946:39–40 on practices in Yap.

25. Tobin 1958:25–26.

26. See, for instance, McCutcheon 1985:74–75.

27. Fischer 1958:115.

28. McCutcheon 1990:7.

29. This popular belief was only a slight exaggeration, according to Ehrlich (1978:131, 150). Listing Nanpei's chief landholdings in 1912, Ehrlich claims that they represented about "twenty-five per cent of the land on Pohnpei to which titles were issued by the German administration."

30. McCutcheon 1990:22.

31. McGrath and Wilson 1971:187–188. Since their article was published in 1971, however, the preference for group ownership may reflect people's unwillingness to let go of old land patterns rather than a return to these same patterns in reaction to individual ownership.

32. Flinn 1992:63.

33. Quoted in Smith 1983:43.

34. Land in Yap is usually, although not always, passed down patrilineally, as Marksbury explains (1979:177–178). The father-son inheritance pattern is the dominant one, but land may also be received from a paternal uncle or a brother.

35. Smith 1983:124.

36. Smith 1983:127.

37. Smith 1983:131.

38. This brief summary of land litigation was offered by Mitaro Dannis, senior land commissioner in Chuuk, at the Chuuk Land Conference, held in Chuuk in February 1993. See Hezel 1993.

39. Sokichy Fritz, the chief justice of the Chuuk State Court, made this remark at the Chuuk Land Conference; see Hezel 1993.

Chapter 3: Gender Roles

1. The content of this section, originally presented in a talk at the Waigani Seminar in Port Moresby in 1986, is taken from a published version: Hezel 1987a.

2. This example was furnished by Anne Lior in a video interview for a Micronesian Seminar television program on women's roles, 1 April 1994.

3. Taken from a video interview with Tina Takashy, 30 March 1994.

4. Smith 1983:309.

5. Kihleng makes the point that while most female titles were derivative from the husbands' titles, there were exceptions (1992:171). A woman could receive recognition by virtue of her own lineage position, the social position she had achieved through her deceased husband, or rarely through her own contribution to the community.

6. DeBrum and Rutz 1967:22.

7. Hezel 1987a:70.

8. Hezel 1987a:73.

9. Spoehr 1949:139–148.
10. Wilson 1968:72–90.
11. Ted Lowe confirms what I observed in Chuuk during the 1970s and 1980s: the growing importance of rice as a main staple in the diet (personal communication, 23 September 1996).
12. Rubinstein 1979:186.
13. Shineberg 1971:188, quoted in Kihleng 1996:61.
14. The 1960 figure is taken from Hezel 1984:38; it was derived from official government employment records reported in U.S. Department of State 1981:51. The 1990 figure was extracted from unpublished FSM social security records. Most of the increase in employment occurred during the 1960s and 1970s, for employment had already reached 18,783 by 1979 (Hezel 1984:38).
15. The FSM census for 1994 shows a total of 21,756 employees in the Federated States, 15,265 of whom were male (FSM 1996b:204). Palau's figure is taken from PNCPC 1998:27. Corresponding census figures cannot be found for the Marshalls.
16. Rubinstein reports the use of these two terms for men and women on Fais (1979:186).
17. This account of the women's protest outside the Truk (now Chuuk) Legislature in April 1979 is taken from Marshall and Marshall 1990:73–74. The Marshalls' book is a fascinating study of the women's movement for prohibition in Chuuk.
18. There may be some divergence of opinion on this point. The Marshalls' volume (1990) suggests that the women's movement in Chuuk may have been the harbinger of a social revolution in which women were claiming a larger and more public stake in their community. My emphasis here, supported by many of the Chuukese women I spoke to years after the protest, is slightly different in that I see this movement as an extension of the traditional roles that women have always played in Chuuk.
19. The bars on Pohnpei were closed by the district administrator in the wake of the killing of a policeman as he was trying to break up a drunken brawl. The march occurred some months later when the business community brought pressure to have the bars reopened. These events are recounted in Marshall and Marshall 1990:126–127.
20. For a fuller discussion of this campaign, see L. Wilson 1993; Roff 1991; Aldridge and Myers 1990.
21. The relative strength of women in Chuuk was a point missed by no less an authority than Thomas Gladwin, a trained anthropologist who had lived on Chuuk for several years. Gladwin explains in a brief article how wrong he was in assuming even after "four years of constant association with the Trukese . . . that the man is in a securely dominant position in the society" (1953:307).
22. Women were not accorded these four roles in every island group, however. Pohnpeian women, at least in the recent past, did not seem to serve as custodians of the land. Women in Yap Proper did not enjoy the functions of keepers of the peace and community counselors that their counterparts on other islands enjoyed.
23. This example was used by Eugenia Samuel in an interview for a television program with the Micronesian Seminar, 1 April 1994.
24. The sister or her children bore the title of *mafen* (trustee), according to Lingenfelter (1975: 55–57). See also Labby 1976:37–48 and Marksbury 1979:138–160.
25. Anne Lior, television interview, 1 April 1994.
26. Ibid.
27. Julie Walsh, personal communication, 23 October 1998.
28. For a fuller discussion of Palauan women's role in choosing titleholders, see Smith 1983: 307–309. The influence of Palauan women extends well beyond simply choosing who will be given a title. Implicit in this responsibility is the considerable sway women have over other matters in their lineage and, by way of the lineage, their influence in the community. The reason was put simply but powerfully by a Palauan woman quoted in L. Wilson 1993:157.

From womb to the tomb, Palauan men are taken care of by their sisters, by their female relatives. From when they are born, sisters take care of their brothers. When a man's wife has a first child, then his female relatives get together to give money to his wife's relatives. And then it comes time that he has an *ocheraol*—and that's when his sisters get together again and buy him a house. And when he's chief, they get together and give him money, and then he buys his boat or whatever else he needs. And then the sisters get together when he dies to give money for his children. So all the way from the womb to the tomb, the men of a clan are taken care of by the women. So that makes women really strong, really powerful in Palau.

29. The relationship between the male head of the lineage and his sisters was known as *lejman-juri*; see DeBrum and Rutz 1967:22–23.
30. Alkire 1977:31.
31. Rubinstein 1979:188.
32. Kimberlee Kihleng has written specifically about Pohnpeian women's production of cloth goods; see Kihleng 1992 and 1996.
33. See, for instance, Mason 1954:162–167.
34. Petersen (1982) gives a particularly good description of how the products of women's labor were once the basis for cultural exchanges on Pohnpei.
35. Marshall and Marshall 1990:108.
36. For these illustrations I am indebted to Eugenia Samuel (personal communication, 24 January 1999).
37. Females have made even greater strides in Palau, where they made up 45 percent of the work force as of 1995 (PNCPC 1998:27). Figures for 1960 were taken from a table in U.S. Department of State 1981:51, while those for 1994 come from the FSM census for that year (FSM 1996b:204).

Chapter 4: Birth

1. The Guam Public Health Office of Vital Statistics recorded 546 live births on the island to women from the Federated States of Micronesia, Palau, and the Marshalls in 1995. These represented 13 percent of all births on the island to ethnic groups that constituted only about 5 percent of the island's total population. Although many of these births were undoubtedly to Micronesian women residing on Guam, it is apparent from the statistics and anecdotal evidence that not all were. By 1997 the number of live births to Micronesians on Guam was listed as 661 (Government of Guam 1995 and 1997).
2. Smith 1983:164; Wilson 1976:185; Fischer and Fischer 1957:125. Smith, writing of this custom in Palau, says that women explain it as providing a rest from the hard work they habitually do in their husband's household, while men say that they fear the shame a possible death in childbirth could bring to their family.
3. Fischer and Fischer remark: "As the time for birth approaches, especially the birth of a woman's first child, the prospective mother on Truk and Ponape and related low islands usually wants to return to the home of her own family, if the couple is not already living there. This is because childbirth is feared and the woman wants to die with her family if she is to die" (1957:125). The same could be said for the Marshalls, as many informants attest.
4. See, for example, Lessa 1966:107.
5. Alkire 1982:34–35.
6. Spoehr 1949:206.
7. Lessa 1966:106.
8. The midwife in Yap was usually a low-caste woman, since childbirth was regarded as "dirty" or "contaminating." Even today when Yapese women deliver at the hospital, I was

told, they do so without the assistance of their blood relatives (Mary Figir, personal communication, 6 March 1999).

9. This man, who now holds a high position in the government, was said to have influenced other men to take the same stand. Often enough, though, the kinswomen of their wives came to them to help with the delivery.

10. As resident aliens, Micronesians from the Freely Associated States are ineligible for the full range of welfare benefits that U.S. citizens enjoy in the American territories, Hawai'i, and the mainland United States. Birth on American soil bestows these benefits to the child, and indirectly to his or her family, as well as the choice when the child reaches maturity of accepting U.S. citizenship.

11. Spoehr 1949:207. The author cites the German missionary priest August Erdland (1914:126), who worked in the Marshalls during the first decade of the twentieth century, on the length of breast-feeding in an earlier era.

12. Mary Figir, personal communication, 6 March 1999.

13. Gladwin 1953:77, citing Ann Fischer 1950:83.

14. Spoehr 1949:208.

15. Lessa 1966:107.

16. Lessa acknowledges that, even in the late 1940s, the taboo was "less operative than it used to be" (ibid.). He also points out that since the prohibition of sex between the married couple did not extend to other partners, some of the women might have been having relations with other men.

17. Chuuk data are found in Gorenflo 1995:72–81. Patterns in Palau are similar: the average birth rate for the years 1925–1935 was 26, while for 1958–1980 it was 30 (Gorenflo 1996:53–56, 62). There is no reason to believe that data from other islands would show anything other than the same slight increase.

18. Marshall and Marshall 1979.

19. In another study on the nutritional effects of bottle-feeding in a Chuukese village, Marshall and Marshall (1980) found that serious and life-threatening illness was more common among bottle-fed than breast-fed children.

20. Republic of the Marshall Islands 1990:16.

21. This incident and others were vividly presented in a video produced by the Republic of the Marshall Islands Health Services in 1985. The video was titled "Our Children Are Dying."

22. According to death records for Chuuk State for the years 1991–1996, 23 percent of all infant deaths were due to malnutrition. A tally of these death certificates was done by the Micronesian Seminar for presentation at the seminars on health care reform held in each state of Federated States of Micronesia during 1998.

23. For more detailed data on fertility rates, see Chapter 9.

24. According to a survey Thomas Gladwin made on the Chuukese island of Romanum in 1947, 56 of the 204 children born to all women on the island died in the first year. Hence, 22.5 percent of all live-born infants died before their first birthday. See Gladwin and Sarason 1953:78.

25. Gladwin and Sarason 1953:71.

26. Apollo Thall, personal communication, 21 January 1999; Labby refers to this ceremony, which he says was called "cutting off the hands of the spirit" (1976:5).

27. This double sense was noted especially in the Palau first-birth ceremony, which consists of daily baths over a course of time, the steaming of the young mother in a hut, and her public presentation to the family. Her achievement consists not just in giving birth to a child but in "displaying her power to earn wealth for her family"; see Smith 1983:171. The Pohnpeian first-birth ceremony, called "feast for breast milk," was less a celebration of the earning power of the woman than of her fertility; see Kihleng 1992:173.

28. Peoples 1985:137–138.

29. The gifts consisted of eleven trousers, six shirts, three towels, seven undershirts, seven briefs, and twelve yards of cloth (Peoples 1985:138).

30. Spoehr 1949:209.

31. Albia Rusin, personal communication, 4 September 1998.

32. Spoehr mentions the reciprocal gifts between the father's and mother's families (1949: 208). It should be noted, however, that others describing the celebration at about the same time do not mention these reciprocal gifts. Neither Albia Rusin, who was raised on Arno, nor Robert Kiste, who did fieldwork on Kili in the mid-1960s, makes any mention of these gifts.

33. Spoehr 1949:209.

34. Albia Rusin, personal communication, 4 September 1998.

Chapter 5: Marriage

1. Fischer and Fischer comment: "On Ponape and Truk infant betrothal was formerly practiced. This involved a formal agreement between the two families and an exchange of food and presents over a period of years. On Truk it is said that couples could break these arrangements when they became of age if they were determined to do so. The practice of infant betrothal was discouraged by the missionaries (and the German administration) and is now extinct" (1957:121).

2. Smith 1983:139–149; Gladwin and Sarason 1953:119.

3. The frequency of cross-cousin marriage varied greatly in those island groups where it was permitted. For instance, two-thirds of the marriages on Bikini in the early 1960s were between cross-cousins, while a mere 1 percent of those on Arno at that same time were cross-cousin (Kiste and Rynkiewich 1976). Demographic factors such as the size of the pool of potential partners may in good part explain the difference. See Marshall 1999:125–129.

4. Fischer and Fischer 1957:121.

5. Lessa 1966:104. On Lamotrek, however, marriages were usually arranged, according to William Alkire, an anthropologist who did fieldwork there in 1963 (1965:55).

6. Lessa 1966:104.

7. Smith 1983:139–140.

8. Fischer and Fischer 1957:121–122.

9. Gladwin and Sarason 1953:120. What Gladwin writes of Chuuk applies equally to most other Micronesian islands.

10. The prohibition of marriage between members of the same clan did not usually apply when one of the couple belonged to a distant branch of the clan living on another island. Pohnpeians, for instance, have the proverb *"Sohte pel en kot madau,"* meaning that clan taboos did not apply overseas.

11. In some places, notably in Chuuk, there was a test period before marriage that allowed families the opportunity to look over the in-marrying boy or girl so that they could make a better judgment on whether the young person met the standards for behavior demanded by the family. The custom of *kofot* allowed the exchange of the boy and girl between one another's families, where they lived for three months or longer (Goodenough 1961:121).

12. In his 1972 article on changing marriage patterns on Namoluk, an island in Chuuk State, Mac Marshall documents the shift in marriage patterns there, showing the increase in marriages off island by young people who have gone away to high school or college. He points out that these off-island marriages are "making it much more difficult for Namoluk parents to exercise control over their children's marital choices." Consequently, "the arranged marriages which have been the mainstay of the intricate set of interlineage alliances on the atoll are declining precipitously in number," and the cross-cousin marriage that was once preferred in order to ensure protection of lineage land is going out of fashion. See Marshall 1975:197.

13. The prohibition on marrying within one's own clan was occasionally violated even in the 1950s and 1960s, but the instances were few and became a topic of conversation in the community. My impression is that today transgressions are more common and far less remarkable than they once were.

14. The number of college students increased enormously after 1972, when Micronesians became eligible for Pell Grants and other U.S. federal programs aimed at enabling the less affluent to attend college. On the impact of these grants on college enrollment from Chuuk, for instance, see Hezel 1979.

15. One woman I know married secretly in the United States rather than return home first, because she was not sure that she could resist the considerable pressure that her family would put on her to marry a young man they had selected for her. In other words, she chose the modern equivalent of elopement.

16. Lessa asserts this of Ulithi in 1949 (1966:105), and Smith of Palau in the 1970s (1983:138); the same would almost certainly have been true of other islands. Informants from Pohnpei, Chuuk, and Yap say that enormous pressure, through public embarrassment as well other means, would have been placed on the young man to declare his engagement to the girl he had been visiting.

17. There are a few places in which the food exchange between a betrothed couple does not seem to occur, among them Pohnpei (William J. McGarry, S.J., personal communication, 28 October 1999).

18. Lessa 1966:105.

19. Goodenough 1961:49–50.

20. Labby 1976:42–43.

21. Mary Figir, personal communication, 7 March 1999. Although the reciprocal gifts continue in a single exchange, marriage is no longer the occasion for competitive ever-increasing gift giving, as it once was. Funerals seem to have replaced marriages in this respect, according to Egan 1998:26–31.

22. Peoples 1985:138–139.

23. Peoples gives detailed tallies of the gifts presented by each side in three weddings he attended on Kosrae between 1972 and 1975 (1985:141). See also Wilson 1968:42.

24. The notion of the creation of kin through gift exchanges, especially of food, is explained more fully in Smith 1983:96–135.

25. In this respect there are marked differences in the practices of the various cultural areas in Micronesia. Chuukese are comparatively quick to have a formal church marriage, Pohnpeians and Marshallese less so, and Yapese and Palauans notoriously slow in registering their marriages in this way.

26. One of the chapters of DeVerne Reed Smith's book *Palauan Social Structure* (1983) is titled "Marriage Is a Business." Similarly, a volume of essays on marriage in the Pacific (Marksbury 1993) bears the title *The Business of Marriage*.

27. See especially Smith 1983:109–112.

28. It also worked the other way around. For instance, if a woman's husband was compliant with his wife's request to support her kin, they might exert pressure to keep the marriage together even if she felt inclined to divorce so that she could marry someone else.

29. Smith paraphrases this adage when she writes of Palau that in the event of conflict "the cross-sibling tie must be honored above the marital tie" (1983:162). Chuukese have their own way of putting this, when they ask fellow lineage members who are under pressure to put their spouses' interests before their blood relatives': *"Nisengimwoch ika nisengitam?"* In other words, "What is more important to a person? One's spouse [who will mourn your death for only a short time before she remarries] or one's lineage [who will mourn you for years]?"

30. Alkire 1965:56.

31. The average number of divorces on Ulithi was reported to be 2 to 2.5 times per person; Lessa 1966:11.

32. Alkire 1965:54.
33. Spoehr 1949:214.
34. Fischer and Fischer 1957:123.

Chapter 6: Death

1. Rubinstein 1979:195.
2. Generally there are one or two close relatives staying with a patient in the hospital around the clock, but as the patient's condition worsens, the numbers grow. It is common to see ten or fifteen people hovering around a dying patient. Attempts on the part of hospital personnel to keep out relatives or even control the numbers have been universally unsuccessful.
3. Smith 1983:277.
4. Nelson Akeang, personal communication, 7 September 1998.
5. According to Gladwin and Sarason, burial under the floor of the house replaced the older custom of suspending the corpse in the house until it decomposed entirely, after which the bones were kept in the house for years (1953:160–161). The German administration put an end to this custom for health reasons.
6. The early Catholic missionaries in Chuuk established cemeteries there for a time despite the resistance of the people. Schoolchildren had to be forced to pass by the cemetery, so strong was their fear of the place. Evidently, the project in Chuuk was finally abandoned as hopeless. See Bollig 1927:20.
7. Smith 1983:277.
8. Ibid.
9. Lessa explicitly mentions this practice in Ulithi (1966:111), and I have found that it is observed in Chuuk up to the present. It also seems to be the custom on other islands.
10. Although women are entrusted with the task of cleaning and dressing up the body nearly everywhere in Micronesia, men take care of this task in the Marshalls, since women are said to be "too delicate to perform this duty without melting into a pool of sorrow." Nelson Akeang, personal communication, 7 September 1998.
11. See Rubinstein 1995:29 and Lessa 1966:112.
12. The quote is from Rubinstein, who makes the point that even ritualistic mourning can be a vehicle for expressing genuine emotion (1995:30). Lessa shows how deep this grief can be when he tells of women who were singing dirges for him to record breaking down in tears as they recalled some poignant memory of the death of a close family member (1966:112).
13. Hisashi Endo (1997) elucidates through case studies of Palauans who have died overseas some of the factors that are taken into account in making the decision on where such people are to be buried. Endo describes this decision as resulting from the process of what he calls "burial politics."
14. Lessa 1966:111.
15. Chuukese formerly believed in two souls: a "good" one and a "bad" one, although these were not differentiated by moral characteristics. The "bad soul" was thought to remain in the vicinity for an indefinite period but was not perceived as a serious threat. People focused most of their attention on the "good soul," which remained around the grave for four days before it left the area. Thereafter it could be contacted through the model canoe that hung in the lineage men's house. See Gladwin and Sarason 1953:166; Bollig 1927:13–14.
16. Stege 1997:31.
17. As Parmentier, writing of mortuary practices in Palau, puts it: "The ritual action . . . transforms the person's dangerously proximate ghost into a controllable yet distant ancestral spirit" (1988:281–283).
18. Smith 1983:277.

19. Smith reports this of Palau (1983:277), but my understanding is that the same was true on other islands.
20. There is a long and well-documented history throughout Micronesia of persons attempting to enter a trance state so as to become possessed by a spirit, especially that of a recently deceased person, in order to gain access to their secret knowledge. See Dobbin and Hezel 1996.
21. See Bollig 1927:16 and Lessa 1966:111–112.
22. In Palau the ritual, known as the *sis,* employed to find out the cause of death was once an important part of the funeral celebration; see Smith 1983:285–286.
23. See Dobbin and Hezel 1996:125.
24. On the custom as practiced in Satawal, see Hijikata 1941:11.
25. Gladwin, who describes this ritual in Chuuk, also mentions that the people carefully checked around the fire to see if the soul left footprints in the sand, for these were understood as signs of another impending death in the family or community (1953:166).
26. Lessa 1966:113.
27. Both these stories are attributed to my Jesuit colleagues—the first to Fr. Richard Hoar, who spent years in Palau, and the second to Fr. Neil Poulin, still working in Yap.
28. Gladwin and Sarason 1953:167.
29. Labby 1976:67.
30. Nelson Akeang, personal communication, 7 September 1998.
31. Parmentier 1988:282.
32. Parmentier 1988:287.
33. Labby 1976:66–67.
34. Lessa 1966:113.
35. See Smith 1983:285 and Labby 1976:66–68.
36. The radical change in the nature of the Yapese funeral celebration forms the main focus of a recent anthropological dissertation (Egan 1998).
37. Mary Figir, personal communication, 10 March 1999.
38. Stege quotes a Marshallese informant's explanation of the custom: "Number one, the rocks are for decoration. Number two they signal the end, the last goodbye. Number three, we are all gathered together in the gathering of the rocks. And so, any wrongs we may have committed against each other, any quarrels that stood between us, the rocks undo. It's like that saying, 'After the rocks are spread during the *arak* . . . we *arake* [or, put things to right] that which kept us apart' " (1997:34).
39. Peoples 1985:152.
40. Although a ritual with ti leaves called the *sis* is now performed about the fourth day and the *omengades* usually occurs several days later, Smith relates that in the late nineteenth century the *sis* and *omengades* occurred on the same day—the fourth day of the funeral celebration (1983:285–286).
41. Sadly, the young man whose death was the occasion of this reconciliation was a suicide victim. There were hints that his act of self-destruction was intended to put an end to the conflict between the two close relatives during the period of self-examination in which he knew the family would engage at his funeral.
42. Spoehr 1949:218.
43. Albia Rusin, personal communication, 3 September 1998.
44. It should be noted that in many Micronesian societies there are other institutionalized outlets for expression of anger, dissatisfaction, and other negative emotions today. Spirit possession among women and use of alcohol among men are two major outlets, both of which have greatly increased in use since 1960. Needless to say, neither is as productive or as safe as the *erak.*
45. This is not to deny that certain islands offer variations on these themes—for instance, the

trail of pig's blood on the paved road in Pohnpei or the pickups loaded with *sakau* plants, their stalks hanging over the tailgate.

46. At one time, I was told, the contribution of those attending a Marshallese wake was in the form of a bar of soap or later a small package of soap powder. Soap powder also seems to have been one of the standard items contributed at a Palauan wake in the past (Smith 1983:290).

47. Where the novena is observed, those ceremonies that were ordinarily done on the fourth day are carried out on the last day of the novena. In many islands, a mass is celebrated and food is prepared for the entire family; the family may or may not gather to reflect on its problems at some point during the day.

48. Smith 1983:286–287.

49. Nelson Akeang, personal communication, 5 September 1998. His figure tallied well with estimates that I heard from others in the Marshalls.

50. Peoples, who listed the cash value of total contributions at four funerals on Kosrae in the mid-1970s, calculates an average of $2,000 per funeral (1985:152–158).

51. Kihleng 1996:136.

52. Riesenberg lists a number of Pohnpeian feasts, many of which are no longer practiced (1968:83–90).

53. Kihleng 1996:136.

Chapter 7: Sexuality

1. In a well-known article on premarital freedom in Chuuk, Goodenough (1949) shows the considerable gap between theoretical sexual permissiveness and actual constraints in acting on this freedom. Not only are potential partners limited in some communities, but the fishbowl nature of island life makes it difficult for young people to find the privacy needed for such a relationship. Lessa makes the same point regarding Ulithi, contrasting the "bait of permissiveness" with the "cold facts of regulation" (1966:90).

2. Pohnpeians use the word *"aluenpwong,"* or "night walking," while Kosraeans use *"fwasr in fong,"* meaning the same thing. Chuukese employ the term *"tééfán"* or "house crawling."

3. The classic description of the Chuukese lovestick and its uses is to be found in Gladwin and Sarason 1953:106–107.

4. Smith 1983:138. The match did not necessarily stand the test of time. Smith relates that one such marriage lasted "one night and one day" before the boy departed for good.

5. Lessa 1966:84.

6. Ward 1989:38.

7. Fischer and Fischer 1957:123. Lessa reports the same thing for Ulithi: "Promiscuity is frowned upon; it is believed to promote barrenness in a girl and to betray a defect of character. . . . The same applies to a promiscuous boy. It is said that not only will he prove unfaithful but may become sterile through his inconstancy" (1966:88).

8. Burrows and Spiro 1957:291–292. In Ifaluk in the late 1940s, as the authors point out, even the relationship between lovers, as secret as it might have been, was formalized. It was expected that the male present his girlfriend with gifts in recognition of this relationship. A girl who had reason to suspect that her partner was unwilling to enter into this relationship would withhold her sexual favors from him.

9. In earlier times there was a form of regulated promiscuity on some islands, as on Ulithi, where a sex holiday, known as *pi supuhui*, was occasionally declared. At such times married and unmarried people would go off with each other to engage in sexual play for the day and night. Individuals might change sexual partners several times in the course of an evening. This practice was discontinued long before World War II, it is said (Lessa 1966:88).

10. A student counselor at Chuuk High School during the early 1970s told the story of six

high school boys who shared a single can of beer in order to work up the courage to approach girls publicly on the dance floor and ask them to dance. During my first year as principal of Xavier High School, in 1974, I learned that all but two of the twenty-six sophomores attending a school-sponsored dance had had something to drink in the course of the evening. Presumably, they drank to overcome their shyness about appearing with girls in front of their classmates and guests.

11.   A Catholic deacon on Pohnpei, after listening to my description of how strict Chuukese parents can be in supervising their daughters, told me that many of the Pohnpeian families in his section of the island were nearly as careful in the supervision of their own daughters forty years ago, when he was growing up. He then lamented the relaxed standards that he observed everywhere on Pohnpei today.

12.   Young couples in Chuuk today, although more daring than in the past, are still unwilling to expose themselves to public criticism. An anthropologist who did fieldwork there in 1996–1997 reports that lovers sometimes rendezvous in hotels on Weno or drive around the island in cars with tinted windows to protect themselves against prying eyes (Ted Lowe, personal communication, 10 May 1999).

13.   Ward 1989:152.

14.   In Chuuk the common words for "hole" or "stiff" or for certain colors that could have suggested the color of a woman's vagina were once banned in the company of women. Substitutes for these words were used in any social interaction between men and women, especially within the family.

15.   Lessa observed that on Ulithi, as on Chuuk, circumlocutions were used for bodily functions, sexual organs, and anything hinting at sexual activity. In the late 1940s, when Lessa did his fieldwork, the bat was never mentioned in polite company, because it is a figure commonly tattooed on the inside of women's legs; "rat" was used instead. Likewise, the term "loincloth" was avoided in mixed company. Instead, Lessa writes, "one speaks of banana bark when referring to a man's breechclout, and hibiscus when speaking of the female garment, these being the names of the materials utilized in their manufacture" (1966:80).

16.   According to Goodenough, a man was forbidden to engage in any sexual joking with his daughter or spend time with her privately (1961:116–119).

17.   Keeping their breasts covered, at least during the day, was another expression of modesty on the part of women toward their male relatives. During the evening, however, Chuukese women frequently went topless, even in the presence of these same relatives. See Gladwin and Sarason 1953:60.

18.   Barnabas and Hezel 1992:25.

19.   With respect to Palau, Parmentier wrote: "Restriction on the proximity of brother and sister compels these women to establish dwellings, called 'houses of senior women' (blil a ourrot), independent from those of male relatives holding the title" (1984:659). This and other material documenting the general prohibition in Micronesia against adult brothers and sisters residing in the same houses is cited in Marshall 1999:111–112.

20.   Marshall illustrates this with examples from Ifaluk and Pulap (1999:123).

21.   The extremes to which the family might go to protect its own good name in this regard are illustrated by a story DeVerne Smith tells of a practice she says that some Palauans observed in prewar years. To forestall any accusation that they had introduced their young daughters to sexual intercourse, fathers would sometimes bring in other men to deflower their daughters (Smith 1983:137). Fr. Bill McGarry told me that he had heard it said that on Pohnpei fathers sometimes did the same thing for identical reasons. While such a practice would be hard to imagine in Chuuk, given the strength of the father-daughter avoidance taboo there, it does indicate the importance that Micronesians everywhere gave to avoiding any suggestion of incest.

22. Ward 1989:40.
23. Goodenough 1974:85, cited in Marshall 1999:111–112.
24. Burrows and Spiro 1953:144.
25. Although most Micronesian languages make no distinction between degrees of incest, some forms of incest are clearly regarded as worse than others. Marriage within one's clan, although spoken of as "incest," is not as severely condemned as sexual relations within the closer family circle. Even here distinctions are made. Sexual relations between a father and a daughter or between a man and his stepdaughter are less serious transgressions than a sexual relationship between two siblings, or between mother and child, as Marshall points out (1999:131–133).
26. In the two known cases of incest on Pohnpei in early years, both men retained their honorary political titles; see Fischer et al. 1976:206. Violations of the incest taboo in the central Carolines were rare, it seems. See, for instance, Lessa 1966:90.
27. The 1985–1986 survey, carried out by various organizations under the supervision of the Micronesian Seminar, included four major island groups: Chuuk, Pohnpei, Yap, and Palau. Although the study did not purport to be comprehensive, some 115 cases of sexual abuse were reported. In most of these a young girl was abused by her father, stepfather, or uncle. Most of the victims were girls under the age of fifteen. See Marcus 1991.
28. Burrows and Spiro 1953:291.
29. Hanlon writes of Pohnpei: "In supplying the common people with trade goods in return for sexual favors, the ships came to rival the chiefs as providers for the society" (1988:99). Much the same could be said of Kosrae in the middle of the nineteenth century.
30. This Palauan custom is often misunderstood, especially in modern feminist literature on the islands, as Petra Steimle points out (1992:164). Women who served in the clubhouses, although they were sent by a village defeated in battle or as repayment for a favor received by a village, must not be understood as sex slaves. These women thought of themselves as honored to be chosen for this position and went willingly to serve in another village, where they cleaned the clubhouse, fetched water, trimmed the oil lamps, and provided for the sexual needs of the clubhouse members. They usually remained for six or seven months before returning to their own village. Such women did not return empty-handed. They were usually rewarded for their service with a piece of traditional Palauan money, which would be passed on to the head of the woman's family, resulting in considerable prestige for her and her kin. In addition, a woman might also receive an offer of marriage into a high-ranking clan in the village at which she served. Whatever the case, her status rose.
31. Chuukese women, for instance, have always been exhorted by their families to use their charms to secure land for the family (Parker 1985:70–76).

Chapter 8: Political Authority

1. Alkire 1977 is still one of the handiest pocket references on traditional political authority in Micronesia. The author provides a brief and clear description of the chiefly system in each of the major island groups in the area.
2. Even if village chiefs did not have the power of direct authority over those in other villages, they were sometimes able to exercise considerable influence in these villages through their networks with chiefs in those places. Pinsker points out that a century ago a village chief could request the chief from a village paired with his in the traditional alliance system to kill a young troublemaker from the other village. In such cases, the chief making the request could be reasonably confident that action would be taken (Pinsker 1997:151). Villages chiefs in Palau, working through traditional alliances, had recourse to the same kind of device.
3. On Ifaluk, for instance, political authority was shared by the five ranking chiefs, who met in council to decide on all important island matters; Burrows and Spiro 1957:186–187.

4. Quoted in Larmour 1997:281.
5. The importance of land rights in determining chieftainship is sometimes reflected in the local languages. Two words commonly used to designate district chiefs in Chuuk, *"soupwpwun"* and *"soufénú,"* can be translated as "master of the soil" and "master of the land." The Yapese word for chief, *"pilung,"* is derived from the word for "voice," since the chief is regarded as the "voice of the land" (Pinsker 1997:175).
6. See, for example, Carucci 1997:202. Carucci claims that chiefs in the Marshalls once customarily traced their ancestry to the gods.
7. Of one of the atolls in the central Carolines it was written that the only status markers found "between chiefs and so-called commoners were 'part-time distinctions,' visible only on formal occasions" (see Petersen 1999:155). Much the same could even be said of some of the more stratified high islands in the area.
8. Hezel 1997.
9. But there is another, more cynical interpretation of this proverb: chiefs will favor anyone who brings them food and other goods, regardless of what is required by custom (Riesenberg and Fischer 1955:15).
10. Rynkiewich 1972:65, cited in Carucci 1997:200–201.
11. Carucci 1997:203.
12. See Petersen 1999:155, 176.
13. Carucci 1997:203–204.
14. Carucci, writing of chiefs in the Marshalls, says that they were once regarded as "foreign deities" that "blessed" the land and made it productive; see Carucci 1997:200–201. Even on islands where the chiefs were not ascribed these divine powers, they were honored as benefactors inasmuch as they shared the land with their people.
15. Carucci claims that the paramount chief's share of copra produced was about 3 mil, or 0.3 cents, per pound of copra (1997:204). Since copra was selling for about 3 cents at the end of the nineteenth century, the chief's take came to about one-tenth of the value of the copra.
16. These examples of presentations to chiefs of nontraditional forms are from Hezel 1995:339.
17. Burrows and Spiro 1957:317, cited in Petersen 1999:155.
18. Petersen 1997:188.
19. Fischer and Fischer report that while they were on Pohnpei, in about 1950, chiefs "rarely made decisions without sounding out public opinion rather carefully" (1957:185). Chiefs sometimes sounded out their people in informal conversation or through formal discussions. When they used the latter method, the chiefs, "whatever their personal opinion, do not go farther than outlining the obvious alternatives of action, if that far. If the people present all agree on one course then the chief announces this as a decision. If they fail to agree he usually simply waits and perhaps brings up the matter again some other time" (ibid.).
20. Recounted in Stege 1997:61–62.
21. The establishment of the new "democratic" political system under U.S. administration is chronicled in Hezel 1995:277–282. For details on the creation of the Congress of Micronesia, see Hezel 1995:303–311.
22. Vidich 1949:195–197.
23. Palau, from the very beginning, refused to award elected offices to its traditional chiefs. In time, other island groups with the sole exception of the Marshalls seemed to adopt the same stance. In Chuuk local chiefs have been elected magistrates even up to the present day, as Pinsker points out (1997:164), but the political authority of these chiefs is so limited as to pose little threat to the principle of the separation of the two political spheres: traditional and modern. Whenever an amendment to the Constitution of the Federated States of Micronesia is proposed to establish a chamber of traditional chiefs as part of the national government, it is always roundly defeated, as Petersen (1997) explains.

24. The German administration pried the land on Pohnpei out of the hands of paramount chiefs when they gave individual landowners exclusive rights to their property through land deeds. The administration would have done the same on other island groups if it could have done so. This may have been the most dramatic change in landownership, but it was not the only one. Throughout the years colonial administrations nibbled away at the edges of private land, with the Japanese claiming as government property all land that had once been held by chiefs for community use. This land, which remained public land throughout the remainder of the Japanese mandate and the U.S. trusteeship, was returned to Micronesians in 1974. The land, however, was placed in the hands of the modern district government rather than those of the traditional leaders who once administered it on behalf of their communities (see also Chapter 2).

25. Accordingly, chiefs have often taken up the cause of environmental protection and resource conservation. Some of the chiefs on Pohnpei, for instance, have begun to campaign for the protection of the watershed and mangrove areas on that island.

26. Western influence, as one anthropologist notes, has "both diminished and increased the status and authority of Micronesian leaders" (Petersen 1999:174). While the prestige of these traditional leaders has grown, their real authority has been overshadowed by modern officials.

27. In the early years of the Congress of Micronesia, during the late 1960s and early 1970s, a few distinguished chiefs, such as Petrus Mailo of Chuuk, held seats in the congress. Since then, no one who might be called a traditional chief has been elected from the Federated States of Micronesia. Moreover, since the early 1970s none of the high chiefs on Pohnpei has been elected magistrate except for one person who was later impeached (Pinsker 1997: 167). Likewise, in Palau the highest chiefs have always failed in their bid to be elected for governorship or the national legislature. Only in the Marshalls have traditional chiefs been elected to public office over the years. The first two national presidents have been paramount chiefs, and the lower house of the legislature (Nitijela) is full of persons with chiefly titles.

28. On the role of traditional leaders in picking and approving candidates, see Pinsker 1997: 161, 171.

29. One of the first anthropologists to study political authority in Palau in the postwar years concluded that the "right to rule was circumscribed" (Useem 1950:144). Although other anthropologists made the same point in their study of other places, the limitations on chiefly authority is a point that remains poorly understood by Westerners.

30. On the intricacies of the Yapese political system, see Lingenfelter 1975.

31. Described in McKnight 1960.

32. Petersen writes that "most Micronesians feel that their chiefs can more effectively serve them by remaining outside the national government" (1997:183).

33. This interpretation is also consistent with the repeated failure of the periodic attempts to establish a special chamber in the FSM government for traditional leaders. See Petersen 1997.

34. The failure of the Marshalls to separate the two authority systems was not without its cost, however. The problems resulting from the consolidation of the two systems in the Marshalls have been felt intensely by its people and have been commented on frequently by outsiders.

35. Spoehr 1949:91–95. The new authority figures that Spoehr finds in the Majuro community were also to be found on other islands at that time.

36. For further discussion on the ways in which government offices throughout Micronesia differ from "pure" bureaucracies, see Hezel 1998.

37. Literally, the saying can be translated: "If you're a relative, you will be given a tent." This expression stems from the time, following a typhoon, that emergency tents were being distributed to the homeless in Chuuk. Those who distributed the tents allegedly gave them to their relatives first.

Chapter 9: Population and Migration

1. Some estimates put the precontact population of the islands much higher than this. Estimates for Palau and Yap, based on house foundations, can be as great as 40,000 or 50,000 per island group. If Freeman's figures were used, for instance, the precontact population of the Caroline and Marshalls would reach 160,000 (1951:248). As Norma McArthur (1967) has shown, early population estimates for the Pacific were often greatly exaggerated. For a breakdown of my estimate of 55,000, see Hezel 1983:317–318.

2. The population of the Federated States of Micronesia in 1994 was 105,000; Palau was 17,000; and the preliminary 1999 census count in the Marshalls was 51,000. See FSM 1996b; Republic of Palau 1997.

3. See Hezel 1983:271, 317–318.

4. It was this decline that was to blame for the loss of so many cultural features in Kosrae. By contrast, Pohnpei, which was missionized at the same time, showed a much slighter cultural impact. See Hezel 1983:59.

5. About 20,000 Japanese nationals were living in the islands by 1937, with most of them residing in Palau. That number increased enormously as the Japanese military entered the islands, so that by the end of the war there were 100,000 Japanese in the Caroline and Marshall Islands. See Hezel 1995:190, 248; Richard 1957, 2:17–21.

6. The total local population of the Japanese Mandate, including the Marianas, as recorded in the 1935 census was 50,573 (U.S. Department of State 1981: app. 1). In 1946 the population, based on field reports, was 48,221. Most of the net loss of 2,352 persons was probably in the Northern Marianas, where the combat was heaviest and the local population most exposed to shelling and bombing. It is known from other sources that the net loss in Palau during this period was only about 200. The Marshalls, although bombed and invaded by Allied forces, suffered a loss of life that was only a little larger. See Hezel 1995:241.

7. See Chapter 4.

8. The population for 1946 is found in U.S. Department of State 1948:76; the 1954 population appears in a table in U.S. Department of State 1981: app 1.

9. These figures are taken from the U.S. Department of State annual reports on the Trust Territory of the Pacific for the United Nations.

10. Micronesian Seminar 1984:8. The population figures used to compile the percentages are drawn from U.S. Department of State 1981: app 1.

11. Hezel 1995:324.

12. Between 1973 and 1989, the total number of children born to the average woman in the Federated States of Micronesia dropped from 8.3 to 5.6; and by 1994 it was down to 4.6 (FSM 1991:40; FSM 1996a:31). During approximately the same period (1973–1990), the average in Palau fell from 6.6 to 3.1 (Republic of Palau 1993a:86). In the Marshalls, however, the average showed only a slight decrease between 1973 and 1988: 8.4 to 7.2 (Republic of the Marshall Islands 1989:102).

13. FSM 1996a:10.

14. The low tally in the Marshalls seems to have surprised everyone. As of this writing, the Marshall Islands government has yet to publish even the preliminary census figures.

15. In 1995, the total resident population of Palau was 17,225. Over one-quarter of the total population, or 4,437, were non-Palauans (Republic of Palau 1997).

16. Solenberger 1953:7–8.

17. This figure is based on a gate-count but checked against an estimate of the natural growth rate less the recorded resident population in Palau. This estimate, made by Michael Johanek in an unpublished paper, is cited in Hezel and Levin 1990:43–45.

18. This figure, also derived from Johanek's work, is presented in Hezel and Levin 1990:45–46.

19. Hezel and Levin 1990:48–49.

20. Hezel and McGrath 1989:50–51.

21. Employment count is derived from social security records and compiled by the Micronesian Seminar in an unpublished database. Employment figures for the years before 1980 are listed in U.S. Department of State 1981: app. 51.
22. Hezel and Levin 1990:57–59.
23. U.S. Department of Interior 1998.
24. This estimate of the Marshallese emigrant community size is found in Hess et al. 1999:3. The estimate of Palau community size is given in Republic of Palau 1993b:142.
25. Hezel and Levin 1996:105–106. The percentage of those holding college degrees is three times higher in the resident FSM population than among FSM migrants on Guam, but high school diplomas are more common among the migrants.
26. Mike McCoy, personal communication, August 1997. Two studies of low island populations in the area, on Nukuoro and Eauripik, show that a population balance was sustained for a long period before the twentieth century; see Carroll 1975 and Levin 1976.
27. Hezel and McGrath 1989:59.
28. Guam newspapers throughout this period carried numerous stories of Micronesian mayhem on Guam. See also Hezel and McGrath 1989:54–55.
29. Rubinstein 1993.
30. The establishment of the church was followed by other community institutions for Palauans. In 1978, the Palau Association of Guam was chartered, and shortly after, with the aid of the Palau Women's Club, a *bai* (meeting house) was built to serve as a community center for all Palauans on Guam. Associations such as these provided assistance for Palauans in need and a center for cultural and political activities of Palauans on Guam. See Smith 1992:26–27.
31. Hess et al. 1999.
32. The average household size in Costa Mesa was seven members, nearly always including members of the extended family. The mean age of the migrant population had dropped to under twenty-one by that time. See Hess et al. 1999.
33. Interestingly, this parallels the sequence of events that occurred in Guam during Palauan migration there.
34. Hess et al. 1999:19.
35. Ibid.
36. Figure derived from FSM 1994 Census, cited in Hezel and Levin 1996:110–111.

Summing Up

1. Marshall provides a number of sources that confirm the fact that kinship can be created by nurturance (1999:116–117), although none of the authors affirms the opposite—that is, that relationships can be weakened or lost altogether by failure to provide nurturance.
2. The estimated cash equivalent for the entire island of Pohnpei during the height of the whaleship trade in the 1840s and 1850s was $8,000 (in 1850 dollars) per year, or about two dollars per person. For estimates of the magnitude of the other early trade in Micronesia, see Hezel 1984:12–14.
3. The per capita cash earnings from wage employment before the 1960s were not sufficient to provide the basics of life. During the vaunted Japanese "economic miracle" of the late 1930s, the per capita income to Micronesians from exports and wages brought in only an estimated $8 a year in postwar dollars. The per capita cash income during the early postwar years (1950–1962) ranged from $30 to $40 in constant dollars. By the late 1960s this figure had doubled to $82, and by 1977 it had tripled to $114. See Hezel 1989:63–66.

References

Aldridge, Bob, and Ched Myers
    1990   *Resisting the Serpent: Palau's Struggle for Self-Determination*. Baltimore, Md.: Fort-
          kamp Publishing Company.

Alkire, William H.
    1965   *Lamotrek Atoll and Inter-Island Socioeconomic Ties*. Urbana, Ill.: University of Illi-
          nois Press.
    1977   *Introduction to the Peoples and Cultures of Micronesia*. California: Cummings Pub-
          lishing Company.
    1982   "Traditional Classification and Treatment of Illness on Woleai and Lamotrek in the
          Caroline Islands, Micronesia." *Culture* 2 (1): 29–41.

Barnabas, Seberiano, and Francis X. Hezel
    1992   "The Changing Pohnpeian Family." Unpublished paper, Micronesian Seminar,
          Pohnpei.

Bollig, Laurentius
    1927   *Die Bewohner der Truk-Inseln: Religion, Leben und Kurze Grammatik Eines Mikro-
          nesien-Volkes*. Anthropos Ethnologische Bibliothek, Vol. 3. Münster: Anthropos.

Brady, Ivan
    1976   *Transactions in Kinship: Adoption and Fosterage in Oceania*. ASAO Monograph
          Series No. 4. Honolulu: University of Hawai'i Press.

Burrows, Edwin G., and Melford E. Spiro
    1953   *An Atoll Culture: Ethnography of Ifaluk in the Central Carolines*. New Haven:
          Human Relations Area Files.

Burton, Michael, et al.
    1996   "Regions Based on Social Structure." *Current Anthropology* 37 (1): 87–123.

Carroll, Vern
    1970a *Adoption in Eastern Oceania*. ASAO Monograph Series No. 1. Honolulu: Univer-
          sity of Hawai'i Press.
    1970b "Adoption on Nukuoro." In *Adoption in Eastern Oceania*, edited by Vern Car-
          roll, 121–157. ASAO Monograph Series No. 1. Honolulu: University of Hawai'i
          Press.
    1975   "The Population of Nukuoro in Historical Perspective." In *Pacific Atoll Popula-
          tions*, edited by Vern Carroll, 344–416. Honolulu: University of Hawai'i Press.

Carucci, Lawrence M.
    1997   "Irooj Ro Ad: Measures of Chiefly Ideology and Practice in the Marshall Islands."
          In *Chiefs Today: Traditional Pacific Leadership and the Postcolonial State*, edited

by Geoffrey M. White and Lamont Lindstrom, 197–210. Stanford, Calif.: Stanford University Press.

Damas, David
1994   *Bountiful Island: A Study of Land Tenure on a Micronesian Atoll.* Waterloo, Ontario: Wilfrid Laurier University Press.

DeBrum, Oscar, and Henry J. Rutz
1967   "Political Succession and Intra-Group Organization in Laura Village." In *The Laura Report*, edited by Leonard Mason. Honolulu: University of Hawai'i .

Dobbin, Jay, and Francis X. Hezel, S.J.
1996   "The Distribution of Spirit Possession and Trance in Micronesia." *Pacific Studies* 19 (2): 105–148.

Egan, James
1998   "Taro, Fish, and Funerals: Transformation in the Yapese Cultural Topography of Wealth." Ph.D. dissertation, University of California, Irvine.

Ehrlich, Paul
1978   "Henry Nanpei: Pre-eminently a Ponapean." In *More Pacific Islands Portraits*, edited by Deryck Scarr, 131–154. Canberra: Australian National University Press.

Endo, Hisashi
1997   "The Politics of Burial: From the Case Studies Inside and Outside of Palau." *Man and Culture in Oceania* 13:117–134.

Erdland, August P.
1914   *Die Marshall-Insulaner: Leben und Sitte, Sinn und Religion eines Südsee-Volkes.* Münster: Aschendorffsche Verlagsbuchhandlung.

Fischer, Ann
1950   *The Role of the Trukese Mother and Its Effect on Child Training.* A Report to the Pacific Science Board of the National Research Council. Cambridge, Mass.: Scientific Investigation of Micronesia, Radcliffe College.

Fischer, John L.
1958   "Contemporary Ponape Island Land Tenure." In *Land Tenure Patterns in the Trust Territory of the Pacific Islands*, edited by John E. DeYoung, 77–160. Guam: Trust Territory of the Pacific Islands.

Fischer, John, and Ann M. Fischer
1957   *The Eastern Carolines.* Behavior Science Monographs. New Haven: Human Relations Area Files.

Fischer, John L., Roger Ward, and Martha Ward
1976   "Ponapean Conceptions of Incest." *The Journal of the Polynesian Society* 85 (2): 199–207.

Flinn, Juliana
1992   *Diplomas and Thatch Houses: Asserting Tradition in a Changing Micronesia.* Ann Arbor: University of Michigan Press.

Force, Roland W., and Maryanne Force
1972   *Just One House: A Description and Analysis of Kinship in the Palau Islands.* Bishop Museum Publications 235. Honolulu: Bishop Museum.

Freeman, Otis W., ed.
1951   *Geography of the Pacific.* New York: John Wiley and Sons.

FSM (Federated States of Micronesia)
1991   *Second National Development Plan: 1992–1996.* Pohnpei: Office of Planning and Statistics.
1996a   *1994 FSM Census of Population and Housing: National Census Report.* Pohnpei: Office of Planning and Statistics.
1996b   *1994 FSM Census of Population and Housing: National Detailed Tables.* Pohnpei: Office of Planning and Statistics.

Futterman, Ann, and Annabel Lyman
    1998 *Palau Substance Abuse Needs Assessment (SANA)*. Koror, Palau: Palau Ministry of Health.
Gladwin, Thomas
    1953 "The Role of Man and Woman on Truk: A Problem in Personality and Culture." *Transactions of the New York Academy of Sciences* 15:305–309.
Gladwin, Thomas, and Seymour B. Sarason
    1953 *Truk: Man in Paradise*. Viking Fund Publications in Anthropology 20. New York: Wenner-Gren Foundation for Anthropological Research.
Goodenough, Ward
    1949 "Premarital Freedom on Truk: Theory and Practice." *American Anthropologist* 51 (4): 615–620.
    1956 "Residence Rules." *Southwestern Journal of Anthropology* 12:22–35.
    1961 *Property, Kin, and Community on Truk*. New Haven: Yale University Press.
    1974 "Changing Social Organization on Romónum, Truk, 1947–1965." In *Social Organization and the Applications of Anthropology: Essays in Honor of Lauriston Sharp*, edited by Robert J. Smith, 68–93. Ithaca, N.Y.: Cornell University Press.
Gorenflo, Larry J.
    1993 "Demographic Change in Kosrae State, Federated States of Micronesia." *Pacific Studies* 16 (2): 67–118.
    1995 "Regional Demographic Change in Chuuk State, Federated States of Micronesia." *Pacific Studies* 18 (3): 47–118.
    1996 "Demographic Change in the Republic of Palau." *Pacific Studies* 19 (3): 37–106.
Government of Guam
    1995 *Statistical Report*. Office of Vital Statistics, Department of Public Health and Social Services. Agana: Government of Guam.
    1997 *Statistical Report*. Office of Vital Statistics, Department of Public Health and Social Services. Agana: Government of Guam.
Hage, Per
    1998 "Was Proto-Oceanic Society Matrilineal?" *The Journal of the Polynesian Society* 107 (4): 365–379.
Hanlon, David.
    1988 *Upon a Stone Altar: A History of the Island of Pohnpei to 1890*. Pacific Islands Monograph Series No. 5. Honolulu: University of Hawai'i Press.
Hess, Jim, Karen L. Nero, and Michael L. Burton
    1999 "Creating Options: Forming a Marshallese Community in Orange County, California." Unpublished paper.
Hezel, Francis X.
    1979 "Education Explosion in Chuuk." *Micronesian Reporter* 16 (4): 24–33.
    1983 *The First Taint of Civilization: A History of the Caroline and Marshall Islands in Pre-Colonial Days, 1521–1885*. Pacific Islands Monograph Series No. 1. Honolulu: University of Hawai'i Press.
    1984 "A Brief Economic History of Micronesia" In *Past Achievements and Future Possibilities: A Conference on Economic Development in Micronesia*, edited by Francis X. Hezel. Chuuk: Micronesian Seminar.
    1985 *Sale of Land*. Justice Issues in Micronesia, No. 1. Chuuk: Micronesian Seminar.
    1987a "Dilemmas of Development: The Effects of Modernization on Three Areas of Island Life." In *The Ethics of Development: The Pacific in the Twenty-first Century*, edited by Susan Stratigos and Philip Hughes, 60–74. Port Moresby: University of Papua New Guinea Press.
    1987b "Truk Suicide Epidemic and Social Change." *Human Organization* 46 (4): 283–291.
    1989 "Suicide and the Micronesian Family." *Contemporary Pacific* 1 (1): 43–74.

1992 "The Unmaking of the Micronesian Family." Unpublished paper, Micronesian Seminar, Pohnpei.

1993 "Land Issues in Chuuk." Report on conference on land issues in Chuuk sponsored by the Catholic Conference on Justice and Development. Unpublished paper, Micronesian Seminar, Pohnpei.

1995 *Strangers in Their Own Land: A Century of Colonial Rule in the Caroline and Marshall Islands.* Pacific Islands Monograph Series No. 13. Honolulu: University of Hawai'i Press.

1997 "Hibiscus in the Wind: The Micronesian Chief and His People." *Micronesian Counselor,* series 2, no. 3.

1998 "Why Don't Our Government Offices Work?" *Micronesian Counselor,* series 2, no. 5.

Hezel, Francis X., and Michael J. Levin

1990 "Micronesian Emigration: Beyond the Brain Drain." In *Migration and Development in the South Pacific,* edited by John Connell, 42–60. National Centre for Development Studies, Pacific Research Monograph No. 24. Canberra: Australian National University Press.

1996 "New Trends in Micronesian Migration: FSM Migration to Guam and the Marianas, 1990–1993." *Pacific Studies* 19 (1): 91–114.

Hezel, Francis X., and Thomas B. McGrath

1989 "The Great Flight Northward: FSM Migration to Guam and the Northern Mariana Islands." *Pacific Studies* 13 (1): 47–64.

Hijikata, Hisakatsu

1941 "Notes on the Funeral Rites among the Satawal Islanders." *Japanese Journal of Technology* 7 (1): 249–264. In "Japanese Translations," (English Translations of Japanese Articles on Anthropology in Micronesia), vol. 2. Bishop Museum, Honolulu. Mimeographed.

Hunt, Edward, Nathaniel Kidder, and David Schneider

1954 "Depopulation of Yap." *Human Biology* 26:21–51.

Johnson, Giff

1998 "US Adoptions Becoming Major Industry in the Marshalls." *Pacific Islands Monthly* 68 (2): 9–10.

Kaneshiro, Shigeru

1958 "Land Tenure in the Palau Islands." In *Land Tenure Patterns in the Trust Territory of the Pacific Islands,* edited by John E. DeYoung, 289–339. Guam: Trust Territory of the Pacific Islands.

Kihleng, Kimberly

1992 "Kinswomen in Production and Exchange: Pohnpei Women in the Nineteenth Century." In *Pacific History: Papers from The Eighth Pacific History Association Conference,* edited by Donald Rubinstein, 169–176. Guam: University of Guam Press.

1996 "Women in Exchange: Negotiated Relations, Practice, and the Constitution of Female Power in Processes of Cultural Reproduction and Change in Pohnpei, Micronesia." Ph.D. dissertation, University of Hawai'i.

Kirkpatrick, John T., and Charles R. Broder

1976 "Adoption and Parenthood on Yap." In *Transactions in Kinship: Adoption and Fosterage in Oceania,* edited by Ivan Brady, 200–227. ASAO Monograph Series No. 4. Honolulu: University of Hawai'i Press.

Kiste, Robert C., and Michael A. Rynkiewich

1976 "Incest and Exogamy: A Comparative Study of Two Marshall Island Populations." *Journal of Polynesian Society* 85 (2): 209–226.

Labby, David

1976 *Demystification of Yap: Dialectics of Culture on a Micronesian Island.* Chicago: University of Chicago Press.

Larmour, Peter
    1997   "Chiefs and States Today." In *Chiefs Today: Traditional Pacific Leadership and the Postcolonial State,* edited by Geoffrey M. White and Lamont Lindstrom, 276–287. Stanford, Calif.: Stanford University Press.
LeBar, Frank M.
    1964   *The Material Culture of Truk.* Yale University Publications in Anthropology No. 68. New Haven: Yale University Press.
Lessa, William
    1966   *Ulithi: A Micronesian Design for Living.* New York: Holt, Rinehart and Winston.
Lieber, Michael D.
    1970   "Adoption on Kapingamarangi." In *Adoption in Eastern Oceania,* edited by Vern Carroll, 158–205. ASAO Monograph Series No. 1. Honolulu: University of Hawai'i Press.
Lingenfelter, Sherwood G.
    1975   *Yap: Political Leadership and Culture Change in an Island Society.* Honolulu: University of Hawai'i Press.
Levin, Michael J.
    1976   *Eauripik Population Structure.* Ph.D. dissertation, University of Michigan. Ann Arbor: University Microfilms International.
Marcus, Mariano
    1991   "Child Abuse and Neglect in Micronesia." Unpublished paper, Micronesian Seminar, Pohnpei.
Marksbury, Richard
    1979   *Land Tenure and Modernization in the Yap Islands.* Ph.D. dissertation, Tulane University. Ann Arbor: University Microfilms International.
    1993   *The Business of Marriage: Transformations in Oceanic Matrimony.* ASAO Monograph Series No. 14. Pittsburgh: University of Pittsburgh Press.
Marshall, Mac
    1975   "Changing Patterns of Marriage and Migration on Namoluk Atoll," In *Pacific Atoll Populations,* edited by Vern Carroll, 160–211. Honolulu: University of Hawai'i Press.
    1999   " 'Partial Connections'?: Kinship and Social Organization in Micronesia." In *American Anthropology in Micronesia: An Assessment,* edited by Robert C. Kiste and Mac Marshall, 107–143. Honolulu: University of Hawai'i Press.
Marshall, Mac, and Leslie B. Marshall
    1979   "Breasts, Bottles and Babies: Historical Changes in Infant Feeding Practices in a Micronesian Village." *Ecology of Food and Nutrition* 8:241–249.
    1980   "Infant Feeding and Infant Illness in a Micronesian Village." *Social Science and Medicine* 14B:33–38.
    1990   *Silent Voices Speak: Women and Prohibition in Truk.* California: Wadsworth Publishing Company.
Mason, Leonard
    1954   *Relocation of the Bikini Marshallese: A Study in Group Migration.* Ph.D. dissertation, Yale University. Ann Arbor: University Microfilms International.
McArthur, Norma
    1967   *Island Populations of the Pacific.* Canberra: Australian National University Press.
McCutcheon, Mary
    1985   "Landlessness in Palau." In *Modernization and the Emergence of a Landless Peasantry: Essays on the Integration of Peripheries to Socioeconomic Centres,* edited by G. N. Appell, 53–82. Studies in Third World Societies, Publication No. 33. Williamsburg, Va.: College of William and Mary, Anthropology Department.
    1990   "Individual Land Tenure in Palau." Unpublished paper.

McGrath, William, and W. Scott Wilson

    1971   "The Marshall, Caroline and Mariana Islands: Too Many Foreign Precedents." *In Land Tenure in the Pacific*, edited by Ron Crocombe, 172–191. Melbourne: Oxford University Press.

McKnight, Robert

    1960   "Competition in Palau." Ph.D. dissertation, Ohio State University, Columbus.

Micronesian Seminar

    1984   *Past Achievements and Future Possibilities: A Conference on Economic Development in Micronesia.* Edited by Francis X. Hezel. Chuuk: Micronesian Seminar.

    1997a *Alcohol and Drug Use in the Marshall Islands: An Assessment of the Problem and Treatment.* Pohnpei: Micronesian Seminar.

    1997b *Alcohol and Drug Use in the Federated States of Micronesia: An Assessment of the Problem with Implications for Prevention and Treatment.* Pohnpei: Micronesian Seminar.

Oneisom, Innocente

    1992   "The Changing Family in Chuuk: 1950–1990." Unpublished paper, Micronesian Seminar, Pohnpei.

Parker, Patricia

    1985   *Land Tenure in Trukese Society: 1850–1980.* Ph.D. dissertation, University of Pennsylvania. Ann Arbor: University Microfilms International.

Parmentier, Richard J.

    1984   "House Affiliation Systems in Belau." *American Ethnologist* 11 (4): 656–676.

    1988   "Transactional Symbolism in Belauan Mortuary Rites: A Diachronic Study." *Journal of the Polynesian Society* 97 (3): 281–312.

Peoples, James

    1985   *Island in Trust: Culture Change and Dependence in a Micronesian Economy.* Boulder: Westview Press.

Petersen, Glenn

    1982   "Ponapean Matriliny: Production, Exchange, and the Ties That Bind." *American Ethnologist* 91 (1): 129–144.

    1997   "A Micronesian Chamber of Chiefs?" In *Chiefs Today: Traditional Pacific Leadership and the Postcolonial State*, edited by Geoffrey M. White and Lamont Lindstrom, 183–196. Stanford, Calif.: Stanford University Press.

    1999   "Politics in Postwar Micronesia." In *American Anthropology in Micronesia: An Assessment*, edited by Robert C. Kiste and Mac Marshall, 145–195. Honolulu: University of Hawai'i Press.

Pinsker, Eve

    1997   "Traditional Leaders in FSM." In *Chiefs Today: Traditional Pacific Leadership and the Postcolonial State,* edited by Geoffrey M. White and Lamont Lindstrom, 150–182. Stanford, Calif.: Stanford University Press.

PNCPC (Palau National Committee on Population and Children)

    1998   *The International Convention on the Rights of the Child and the Children of Palau.* Koror, Palau: Palau National Committee on Population and Children.

Republic of the Marshall Islands

    1989   *Census of Population and Housing 1988: Final Report.* Majuro: Office of Planning and Statistics.

    1990   *Situation Analysis of the Marshallese Child.* Majuro: Office of Planning and Statistics.

Republic of Palau

    1993a *1990 Census Monograph: Population and Housing Characteristics.* Republic of Palau: Office of Planning and Statistics.

1993b *Palau 2020: National Master Development Plan Progress Report*. Republic of Palau: Office of the Task Force and NMDP Team.

1997　*1995 Census of the Republic of Palau*. Vol. 1. Republic of Palau: Office of Planning and Statistics.

Richard, Dorothy E.

1957　*United States Naval Administration of the Trust Territory of the Pacific Islands*. 3 vols. Washington, D.C.: U.S. Office of Naval Operations.

Riesenberg, Saul

1968　*Native Polity of Ponape*. Washington, D.C.: Smithsonian Press.

Riesenberg, Saul, and J. L. Fischer

1955　"Some Ponape Proverbs." *Journal of American Folklore* 68 (267): 9–18.

Roff, Sue Rabbitt

1991　*Overreaching in Paradise: United States Policy in Palau since 1945*. Alaska: Denali Press.

Rubinstein, Donald H.

1979　"An Ethnography of Micronesian Childhood: Contexts of Socialization on Fais Island." Ph.D. dissertation, Stanford University.

1993　"Movements in Micronesia: Post-Compact (1987) Micronesian Migrants to Guam and Saipan." In *A World Perspective on Pacific Islander Migration: Australia, New Zealand and the USA*, edited by Grant McCall and John Connell, 259–263. Pacific Studies Monograph No. 6. Sydney: University of New South Wales Printing Section.

1995　"Social Organization and Burial Practices of Fais Island." In *The Acceptance of the Outside World on Fais Island in Micronesia*, edited by Michiko Intoh, 16–33. Yap: Yap State Historic Preservation Office.

Rynkiewich, Michael A.

1972　"Land Tenure among Arno Marshallese." Ph.D. dissertation, University of Minnesota, Minneapolis.

1976　"Adoption and Land Tenure among Arno Marshallese." In *Transactions in Kinship: Adoption and Fosterage in Oceania*, edited by Ivan Brady, 93–119. ASAO Monograph Series No. 4. Honolulu: University of Hawai'i Press.

Schneider, David M.

1961　"The Distinctive Features of Matrilineal Descent Groups." In *Matrilineal Kinship*, edited by David Schneider and Kathleen Gough, 1–29. Berkeley: University of California Press.

Shineberg, Dorothy

1971　*The Trading Voyages of Andrew Cheyne, 1841–1844*. Pacific History Series No. 3. Canberra: Australian National University Press.

Smith, DeVerne Reed

1983　*Palauan Social Structure*. New Brunswick, N.J.: Rutgers University Press.

1992　"The Palauans on Guam." Unpublished paper.

Solenberger, R. R.

1953　*The Social and Cultural Position of Micronesian Minorities on Guam*. South Pacific Commission Technical Paper No. 49. Noumea: South Pacific Commission.

Spoehr, Alexander

1949　*Majuro: A Village in the Marshall Islands*. Fieldiana Anthropology 39. Chicago: Natural History Museum.

Stege, Kristina E.

1997　"Modernizing Moments in Marshallese Culture." B.A. thesis, Princeton University.

Steimle, Petra

1992　"The Status of Women in Palau." In *Pacific History: Papers From the Eighth Pacific History Association Conference*, edited by Donald Rubinstein, 163–181. Guam: University of Guam Press.

Tobin, Jack A.

    1958   "Land Tenure in the Marshall Islands." In *Land Tenure Patterns in the Trust Territory of the Pacific Islands*, edited by John E. DeYoung, 1–76. Guam: Trust Territory of the Pacific Islands.

U.S. Department of State

    1948   *Annual Report on the Administration of the Trust Territory of the Pacific Islands.* Washington, D.C.: U.S. Government Printing Office.

    1981   *Annual Report on the Administration of the Trust Territory of the Pacific Islands.* Washington, D.C.: U.S. Government Printing Office.

U.S. Department of the Interior

    1998   "The Impact of the Compacts of Free Association on the US Territories and Commonwealths and on the State of Hawaii." Washington, D.C.: Office of Insular Affairs.

Useem, John

    1946   *Report on Yap and Palau.* U.S. Commercial Company's Economic Survey of Micronesia, Report No. 6. Mimeographed. Honolulu: U.S. Commercial Company.

    1950   "Structure of Power in Palau." *Social Forces* 29 (2): 22–25.

Vidich, Arthur

    1949   *Political Factionalism in Palau: Its Rise and Development.* CIMA Report 23. Washington, D.C.: National Research Council, Pacific Science Board.

Ward, Martha C.

    1989   *Nest in the Wind: Adventures in Anthropology on a Tropical Island.* Prospect Heights, Ill.: Waveland Press.

Wilson, Lynn B.

    1993   *Speaking to Power: Gender, Politics, and Discourse in the Context of United States Military Priorities in Belau, Western Micronesia.* Ph.D. dissertation, University of Massachusetts. Ann Arbor: University Microfilms International.

Wilson, Walter Scott

    1968   *Land, Activity and Social Organization of Lelu, Kusaie.* Ph.D. dissertation, University of Pennsylvania. Ann Arbor: University Microfilms International.

    1976   "Household, Land, and Adoption on Kusaie." In *Transactions in Kinship: Adoption and Fosterage in Oceania*, edited by Ivan Brady, 81–92. ASAO Monograph Series No. 4. Honolulu: University of Hawai'i Press.

Index

"absent father" syndrome, 20, 156
adolescence, 17, 19, 21, 22, 79
adoption, 28–32, 34, 153, 156; frequency of, 28, 30; in Marshalls, 31–32; reasons for, 29–32
alab, 10
alcohol, 1, 18, 22–24, 59, 61, 112, 148
Alkire, William, 34, 35, 60, 88–89
alliances, political, 122, 132
anger, 24, 27; suppression of, 20; toward wife, 24–27
arranged marriage, 79–80
Austronesian, 10
authority, 5, 47–48, 121–133, 159–160; dual system today, 127, 129–133, 159–160; in family, 16, 21, 22, 23; rooted in land, 35, 38, 122; as shared, 126, 132; traditional political, 5–6, 106–107, 122, 126, 131–132; of women, 48, 57, 60, 156–157

Belau. *See* Palau
betrothal, 35, 79, 161
Bikini, 154
birth, 66–78, 84, 152; dangers of, 67–68; return to lineage land for, 66–69, 92, 157; sexual relations ban after, 70–73; survival feasts, 75–78
birthrate, 71, 74, 142–143
brain drain, 147
breadfruit, 6, 7, 9, 16, 17, 30, 52, 143; preparation of, 9, 16, 47, 53
breast-feeding, 70–73
bureaucracy, 135
burial, 27–28, 35, 92, 94, 96–97, 157
Burrows, Edwin, 111
business, 39, 40, 65, 130, 134, 145, 150; marriage as, 87–90

canoe house, 9
canoe making, 47, 52–53, 55
canoe voyages, 1, 7, 125
Carucci, Lawrence, 124, 125
cash economy, 4, 12–14, 36, 40, 55, 142, 145, 160–161; as cause of social change, 155, 157, 160–161; creation of, 4, 13–14, 40; effect on family, 12–13, 26–27, 155; effect on land, 36, 155, 157
Catholic Church, 68, 70, 92, 104, 149. *See also* church
cemeteries, 92
Central Carolines, 7, 11, 80, 139; adoption, 30; canoe houses, 9, 47; chiefly authority, 122, 124–126; demography, 139, 144; description, 7; division of labor, 59; funeral practices, 93, 96, 98, 100, 104; land, 35, 38, 40, 58; menstrual houses, 68; residence patterns, 11, 64; respect behavior of women, 49; selection of marriage partner, 80; sexual taboos, 114, 117; women's roles, 58–60
Cheyne, Andrew, 55
chiefs, 6, 35, 48, 106, 122–126, 154; authority today, 127–133, 159–160; gender of, 47; obligations of, 123–124, 126; paramount, 5, 6, 122, 126; powers of, 123, 126; relation to land, 35, 38, 40, 122, 125, 159
child abuse, 16, 31, 117
child-rearing, 13–14, 20–22, 156–157; by women, 46, 56–57, 64, 157; by men, 63
church, 6, 38, 50, 61, 89, 131, 153; church organizations, 61, 124; doctrine, 14, 68, 92; at funerals, 103–104; support for migrants, 149–150, 151–152; pastors,

193

134–135, 150; at weddings, 86–88. *See also* Catholic Church; Protestant Church

Chuuk, 1, 6–11; adoption, 28, 30; childbirth, 67–68, 70–71, 73–76; choice of marriage partner, 79–81, 83; death and burial, 92–94, 96–97, 100, 102, 104, 107; description, 1, 6; family relationships, 16–19, 22–23, 25–27; land, 33–35, 38, 43–45, 58; marriage, 84, 89–90; migration abroad, 148, 150, 152–153; nepotism, 136; political authority, 122, 124, 126, 132; population, 139–141; sexual practices, 109, 111–112, 119; sexual taboos, 114–116; traditional residence, 8–11, 64; women's roles, 47, 53, 57–59, 61, 65

clans, 38, 122

clothing, 7, 60, 85, 115; of deceased, 96–97

cohabitation, 84, 110

Compact of Free Association, 143, 144, 150

conflict resolution, 14, 22–23, 45, 59, 90, 131, 156

conflicts, 59, 88; between brothers, 20–23; over land, 44–45

Congress of Micronesia, 5, 128, 132

cookhouse, 9, 11–13, 17, 47, 114; and family identity, 12

copra, 1, 53, 125

council, village, 7, 122, 129; Palau, 7, 38, 60; Yap, 7

cross-cousin marriage, 80

dancing, modern, 111–112

dating, 108, 112, 113

death, 91–107; burial, 92, 94; funeral celebration, 95–98; funeral ceremony, 103–107; Marshallese *erak*, 99–102; preparation of corpse, 93–94. *See also* funeral

democracy, 4, 125–126

demography, 138–139. *See also* population

dirges, 93

discipline, 17, 21, 156

disease, 70, 73–74, 139–140, 142

display of affection, 90, 110, 112–113

division of labor, 51–52, 63–64, 134; female work, 51–53, 55–62, 156–159; at funerals, 103–104; by gender, 46–47, 50, 52, 55, 56, 63–64, 158; male work, 51–56, 63

divorce, 64, 88, 89; rates, 89

domestic violence, 15, 24. *See also* child abuse; wife beating

"dual-chief" system, 127, 129–133, 159–160; role of each, 131–132; separation of authorities, 129–130, 132–133

dual economy, 4, 161

earth oven, 9, 11–13, 17, 53, 106

Eastern Carolines, 80, 96

eating, 9, 12, 97; eating from land, 34; taboos on eating, 115, 116

Ebeye, 52, 77, 92, 112

economic development, 4, 13, 39; US policy, 4

education, 3, 4, 14, 31, 160; effects on marriage, 82; effects on sexual behavior, 111–112; and migration, 144–145, 147, 150, 153

elected officials, 65, 127, 129–132, 134, 159–160

elections, 128–130

elopement, 80

embalming, 104

embroidery, 60–61

emigrant communities, United States: Arizona, 151; Arkansas, 145, 151; California, 150–151, 153; Florida, 145; Oklahoma, 153; Oregon, 145, 151; South Carolina, 145; Texas, 150. *See also* Hawaii; United States

employment, 13, 50, 55; abroad, 143–145, 147–148, 150; increase in, 13, 55; for women, 50, 55, 65, 158–159

erak (in Marshalls), 98–102

erek (in Chuuk), 100

exchanges, 64, 76–77, 98, 119, 162; at birth, 76–77; at funeral, 104–105; at marriage, 84–86; between migrants and relatives, 153–154; on initiating sexual affair, 111

Fais, 11, 30, 55, 91, 93, 97

family, 8–15, 31, 43, 63–65, 80; adoptive and natural, 29–30; change in size, 141–142; extended, 22, 155–156, 162; nuclearization of, 12–14, 22, 26, 44, 61, 63–65, 89–90, 119–120, 155–156; reconstituted abroad, 148–150; sexuality in, 114–120; two-parent, 15

family planning, 71, 141–142

fanang, 9

father, 13–14, 22, 43; "absent father," 20, 156; contrast with mother, 19; land inheritance from, 43–44; redefinition of role, 14, 18–19, 22, 63, 156; relation to daughter, 115; traditional role, 16–18, 21

feast house, 11–12

feasts, 60, 125, 162; first birth of women, 76; first birthday, 75–78; funeral, 97, 104–107; wedding, 84–85

Federated States of Micronesia, 1, 5, 13, 135, 141–143, 145–146, 148, 153; alcohol use, 24; description of, 1, 5; employment, 55, 65; migration from, 143, 145–146, 148; population growth, 141–142

feminism, 46, 50–51, 57

first birthday, 75–78, 151; expense of, 76–78

first fruits, 38, 123. See also tribute

Fischer, John, 38, 81, 89, 111, 117

fishing, 6–7, 16, 18, 55, 134; by gender, 47, 52–53, 84

food, 1, 3, 6–7, 104, 125; for feasts, 76–77, 84, 103, 105–106, 123; preparation of, 9, 16–17, 52–53, 55, 57

foreign labor, 142, 160

fosterage, 29

funeral, 93–100, 103–107, 157; family reconciliation, 95, 99–102; feast, 93, 104–107; length of, 104; placating spirit, 95–96, 98; preparation of corpse, 93–94; wake, 103. See also death

gender, 46–65, 158; equality, 50, 55, 57, 64; gender role, 46–48, 50, 55–57, 60, 61–62, 65, 158; reciprocity, 49–50

Germany, 3, 39–40, 43, 123, 139

ghosts, 67–68, 98. See also spirits

Gladwin, Thomas, 81, 97

Goodenough, Ward, 115, 116

government, modern, 127–133

grave, 95, 99–100, 103

grave goods, 96–97

Guam, 27, 69, 77, 143–150, 152–153, 162; college students, 82, 144; health care, 66–67, 69; migrant households, 148–149; migration to, 27, 120, 143–150; return from, 152–153

Hawaii, 66–67, 86–87, 132, 144–146, 150–151, 153–154; destination for childbirth, 66–67; FSM migration to, 86–87, 144–146, 150; Marshallese migration to, 146, 150–151

health aide, 134–135, 139

health care, 123; in Guam and Hawaii, 67, 69, 147; under US administration, 71, 139–140

history, 1–5; colonial rule, 3–5, 38–39, 43, 127–129, 139–141, 160–161; early exploration, 1; nineteenth-century contact, 1, 38, 139, 160; post-independence, 5

homestead, 6, 12, 40, 42

house building, 47, 52–53, 55

household, 9, 11–16, 28, 35, 65, 155–156; growing independence of, 12–15, 18, 22, 89, 119, 155–156; of Micronesians abroad, 145–150

housing, 3, 8–9, 13

identity: of migrants, 154; rooted in land, 34, 36, 69; rooted in lineage, 17

Ifaluk, 111, 116, 118, 124

imports, 1, 3, 160

incest, 81, 115, 117

individualism, 120, 157–158

infant mortality, 67, 71, 74–75, 140

iron pots, 9, 53

Jaluit, 123

Jake Jobal Eo, 151

Japan, 3, 39–40, 129, 139

Kapingamarangi, 57

kava, 6, 55. See also sakau

kemem, 75–78, 151

kiis, 84

"kitchen cabinet," 60

Kolonia, Pohnpei, 61, 140

Koreans, 144

Koror, 140

Kosrae, 1, 5–6, 57, 140; first birthday party, 76, 78; description, 5–6, 122; disease, 74; funerals, 99–100, 104, 107; land, 38–39, 43; male work roles, 52–53; marriage exchange, 85; political authority, 122, 131–132; population, 139–140; residence patterns, 10–11, 16, 67; treatment of women, 112, 118

kousapw, 10

kuhlyuhk, 99–100

Kwajalein, 125, 140

Tonga, 60, 122, 144, 154
town growth, 140–141
tribute, 38, 122–125; in form of money, 125
Trust Territory, 3, 5, 144
Trust Territory headquarters, 69, 129
tuba, 59, 143
turtles, 124

uhmw, 11
Ulithi: death and burial, 95–97, 100; divorce, 89; marriage, 80, 84, 110; pregnancy and birth, 68, 71; residence, 11
umbilical cord, 67, 69, 92
United States, 3–5, 73, 125; acquisition of Micronesia, 3–4; administration, 4–5, 39, 125, 128–129, 161; migration to, 119, 144–146, 150, 152–154; school in, 82, 112, 144
U.S. Army, 154
U.S. Department of the Interior, 4
U.S. Navy, 4, 125, 129, 139
upaj, 11
urbanization, 52, 69, 140–141
uut, 9–10

valuables, 25, 36, 60–61, 84; women's role in producing, 60–61

village, 6–7, 31, 61, 127, 140–141; in Palau, 7, 60, 122; in Pohnpei, 6; in Yap, 7, 122
Vitamin A deficiency, 74

wages, 13
wake, 103–104
wato, 10
Ward, Martha, 110, 113, 115
warfare, traditional, 122
weaving, 46, 60–61, 85
Weno, 61
Western Carolines, 28, 49, 92, 97
wife beating, 15, 24–27, 50, 156
Wilson, Scott, 56
Woleai, 68
women's club, 60
work roles. *See* division of labor
World War I, 3
World War II, 3, 39, 139

yalu, 68
Yap, 1, 7; adoption, 28, 30–31; chiefly authority, 122, 124, 129–132, childbirth, 70–71, 76; death and burial, 95, 97–98, 104, 107; description, 7; family, 18, 25; land, 35–36, 43, 58; marriage, 84, 89; migration, 144; population, 139–140; residence, 11–12; women's roles, 47, 58, 119

Printed in the United States
77765LV00004B/79